Strategic Planning for Public and Nonprofit Organizations

John M. Bryson

Strategic Planning for Public and Nonprofit Organizations

A Guide to Strengthening and Sustaining Organizational Achievement

Jossey-Bass Publishers

San Francisco • Oxford • 1990

STRATEGIC PLANNING FOR PUBLIC AND NONPROFIT ORGANIZATIONS
A Guide to Strengthening and Sustaining Organizational Achievement
by John M. Bryson

Copyright © 1988 by: Jossey-Bass Inc., Publishers
350 Sansome Street
San Francisco, California 94104
&
Jossey-Bass Limited
Headington Hill Hall
Oxford OX3 0BW

Library of Congress Cataloging-in-Publication Data

Bryson, John M. (John Moore) (1947)
    Strategic planning for public and nonprofit
organizations.

    (The Jossey-Bass public administration series) (The
Jossey-Bass management series)
        Bibliography: p.
        Includes index.
        1. Strategic planning.   2. Corporations, Nonprofit—
Management.   3. Public administration.   I. Title.
II. Series.   III. Series: Jossey-Bass management series.
HD30.28.B79   1988   658.4'012   87-46341
ISBN 1-55542-087-7 (alk. paper)

Manufactured in the United States of America

The paper in this book meets the guidelines for
permanence and durability of the Committee on
Production Guidelines for Book Longevity of the
Council on Library Resources.

JACKET DESIGN BY WILLI BAUM

FIRST EDITION
        First printing: April 1988
        Second printing: November 1988
        Third printing: June 1989
        Fourth printing: August 1989
        Fifth printing: August 1990

        Code 8814

A Joint Publication in
The Jossey-Bass
Public Administration Series
and
The Jossey-Bass Management Series

Contents

Preface

How can leaders and managers of public and nonprofit organizations cope with the challenges that confront their organizations now and in the years ahead? How can these leaders and managers determine how their organizations should respond to the increasingly turbulent environments in which these organizations operate? In other words, how should leaders respond to dwindling or unpredictable resources; new public expectations; demographic changes; deregulation; upheavals in the national, state, and local economies; and new roles for public, nonprofit, and business organizations? What should their organizations' missions be? How can leaders build on organizational strengths and take advantage of opportunities while minimizing weaknesses and overcoming threats to their organizations? These are the questions this book addresses.

Scope

Strategic Planning for Public and Nonprofit Organizations is based on the premise that leaders and managers of public and nonprofit organizations must be effective strategists if their organizations are to fulfill their missions and satisfy their constituents in the years ahead. These leaders and managers will need to exercise as much discretion as possible in the areas under their control, they will need to develop effective strategies to cope with changed and changing circumstances, and they must develop a coherent and defensible basis for decision making.

Strategic planning is a set of concepts, procedures, and tools designed to assist leaders and managers with the aforementioned tasks. Indeed, strategic planning may be defined as a disciplined effort to produce fundamental decisions and actions that shape and guide what an *organization* (or other entity) is, what it does, and why it does it. In the past twenty-five years, strategic planning has become a standard part of managerial thinking and practice in the business world. Only recently, however, have leaders and managers in the public and nonprofit sectors become aware of how strategic planning can help their organizations. But, before strategic planning can become standard practice for the public and nonprofit sectors, several things are needed. First, a simple yet effective strategic planning process designed specifically for public and nonprofit organizations must be developed. Second, there must be clear guidance on how to apply this process. Third, examples of how the process has been applied must be provided. And finally, the process must be tied to relevant research and literature so that readers know how the process applies and where they can gain insight into the nature and requirements of the process. This book is designed to help fill these needs.

Specifically, this book

- reviews the reasons why public and nonprofit organizations (and communities) should embrace strategic planning as a way of improving their performance.
- reviews and critiques the various approaches to private-sector strategic planning and discusses their applicability to the public and nonprofit sectors.
- presents an effective new strategic planning process for public and nonprofit organizations that builds on the strengths of the private-sector approaches and that has been used successfully by a number of public and nonprofit organizations.
- offers detailed guidance on applying the process.
- provides guidance on overcoming the major obstacles to strategic planning.
- includes examples of successful and unsuccessful strategic planning practice.

Audience

This book is written for two main groups: The first group consists of leaders, policy makers, general managers, and planners in all levels of government, public agencies, and nonprofit organizations who are responsible for and who want to learn more about strategic planning. The book will help these leaders and managers understand what strategic planning is and how to apply it in their organizations and, to a lesser extent, their communities. Thus, the book speaks to city managers and administrators; county administrators and commissioners; cabinet secretaries; school superintendents and principals; sheriffs and police chiefs; unit directors, chief executive officers, chief administrative officers, executive directors, and vice-presidents; directors and deputy directors; elected and appointed officials of governments and public agencies; and boards of directors of nonprofit organizations.

The second major audience consists of academics and students of strategic planning. A small but growing number of courses on strategic planning are being offered in schools of public affairs, public administration, planning, and public policy. This book offers participants in these courses a helpful blend of theory and practice.

Others who will find this book useful are businesspeople and citizens interested in increasing their understanding of how to improve the operations of governments, public agencies, and nonprofit organizations. This book is also intended to help these individuals understand and improve their communities.

Overview of the Contents

Chapter One introduces the concept of strategic planning and why such planning is important for governments, public agencies, nonprofit organizations, and communities. Attention is focused on strategic planning for (1) public agencies, departments, or major organizational divisions; (2) general-purpose governments; (3) nonprofit organizations; (4) functions, such as transportation, health care, or education, that bridge organizational and governmental boundaries; and (5) entire communities, urban or metropolitan areas, regions, or states seen as economic, social, and political entities. Benefits of strategic planning are emphasized as are the conditions under which strategic planning should *not* be undertaken. In addition, readers are introduced to four organizations whose experience with strategic planning will be cited throughout the book to illustrate key points. Two of these organizations are general-purpose units of government, one is a public agency, and one is a nonprofit organization.

Chapter Two describes and critiques the major approaches to strategic planning developed in the private sector and the applicability of these approaches to public and nonprofit sectors. The discussion covers the Harvard model, strategic planning systems, stakeholder management, content models (portfolio models and competitive analysis), strategic issues management, and process strategies (strategic negotiations, "logical incrementalism," and innovation).

In Chapter Three, I present my preferred approach to strategic planning. This approach has been used effectively by a variety of governments, public agencies, and nonprofit organizations. Chapters Four through Nine describe in detail how to apply this approach. Sample strategic planning worksheets are included in Resource A at the end of the text to help guide strategic planning teams through the planning process.

Chapter Four covers the initial agreement, or the "plan for planning," phase of the strategic planning process. Chapter Five focuses on the identification of mandates and clarification of the organization's mission and values. Chapter Six addresses the assessment of an organization's external and internal environments. Chapter Seven discusses strategic issues—what they are, how they can be identified, and how to critique them. Chapter Eight is devoted to the development of effective strategies. Chapter Nine covers the development of the organization's "vision of success," that is, what the organization should look like as it fulfills its mission and achieves its full potential.

In the next to last chapter, Chapter Ten, I address the human, process, structural, and institutional barriers to effective strategic thought and action in public and nonprofit orgaizations, as well as ways those barriers might be overcome. The organization that overcomes these barriers will have joined strategic planning, management, and governance to produce successful strategic change. Finally, Chapter Eleven assesses the strategic planning experiences of the four organizations used as examples throughout the text. This chapter also provides guidance on how to begin strategic planning.

Six resource sections are included at the end of the text. Resource A consists of sample strategic planning worksheets designed to help strategic planning teams apply this process. Resource B presents a model external scanning process. Resource C provides a review of selected literature relevant to strategic issue identification, and in Resource D, I review selected literature related to potential strategies for public and nonprofit organizations. Resource E offers a detailed example of strategies developed in response to strategic issues. And Resource F presents some useful concepts related to developing a vision of success.

These chapters and resource materials should provide much of the guidance that leaders, managers, and planners need in using the strategic planning process to make their organizations or communities more effective and more responsive to their environments. Readers will discover in this book a simple yet effective strategic planning process designed specifically for public and nonprofit organizations and detailed advice on how to apply this process, along with examples of its application. The entire exposition is grounded in relevant research and literature, so readers will know where the process fits in with prior research and practice and can gain added insight about how to apply the process.

Minneapolis, Minnesota   John M. Bryson
March 1988

Acknowledgments

The completion of this book would not have been possible without the contributions of many people and organizations. Let me start by expressing my deepest thanks to some very special mentors, colleagues, and friends in the planning field: André Delbecq, University of Santa Clara; Robert Einsweiler, University of Minnesota–Twin Cities; Jerome Kaufman, University of Wisconsin–Madison; and Bernard Taylor, Henley–The Management College, England. Much of what I have to offer in the planning area I owe to the instruction, advice, support, friendship, and encouragement of these four people. I am especially grateful to Bernard Taylor for being a valued confidant and friend at an important turning point in my career. Taylor, a professor of business policy at Henley–The Management College in Henley-on-Thames, England, instructed and delighted us at the Hubert H. Humphrey Institute of Public Affairs during his three-week stay as a visiting professor in the spring of 1984. It was during his visit that I decided to devote the next major portion of my professional life to the study and practice of strategic planning. This book is a product of that decision.

I would also like to thank my colleagues and friends at the Strategic Management Research Center, University of Minnesota–Twin Cities. Andrew Van de Ven, the Center's first director; Mary Nichols, the present director; and Robert King, an associate director, have been wholeheartedly supportive of the Center's research program on strategic planning and decision making, which I direct. Without their help and encouragement, the various publications that have grown out of that program—including this book—would not have been possible. I must also single out for special praise and recognition William Roering, a doctoral student in strategic management at the University of Minnesota–Twin Cities, and a research associate at the Center. He has been far more than a valued research assistant in strategic planning over the years. He has been a colleague, coauthor, and friend, and I miss his frequent companionship now that he has become an assistant professor of management at the University of Florida. In addition, Stuart Albert; Harold Angle; Edward Freeman, who has now moved on to the Colgate Darden School of Business at the University of Virginia; Michele Govekar; Todd Hostager; Alfred Marcus; Ian Maitland; John Mauriel; Peter Ring; and Raymond Willis each made contributions to this book although they might not be aware of them. One of the great strengths of the Center is that one learns a great deal simply by being there, and I have learned and been helped by each person named above. Susan McGuire and Linda Neumann of the Center's staff have also been especially helpful.

Several colleagues at the Humphrey Institute also deserve special mention. Richard Bolan, one of the world's premier planning theorists and acting associate dean of the Institute, has long acted as my teacher, friend, and supporter. Royce Hanson, the outgoing associate dean (now dean of the School of Social Science at the University of Texas, Dallas), and Harlan Cleveland, the recently retired dean, have both strongly encouraged me to pursue my interests in strategic planning and management. Yvonne Cheek, director of the Humphrey Institute's public education office, and, especially, Richard Grefe of the University of Minnesota–Twin Cities' Division of Continuing Education and Extension have assisted me over the years in fashioning highly effective strategic planning training programs for public and nonprofit sector leaders and managers.

Acknowledgments

I must express my heartfelt thanks to Frank So and his staff of the American Planning Association's (APA) national office, who helped put together a highly successful one-day program on strategic planning at the APA's annual conference in Los Angeles in May 1986, cochaired by Robert Einsweiler and myself. The presenters brought to the APA audience some of the best thinking available on strategic planning for public and nonprofit organizations. And, while everyone in the audience learned a great deal from the presenters, no one learned more than I did. In effect, the presenters both educated me and at the same time completed the literature review for this book. I wish to thank each of the conference presenters: Robert Backoff, Barry Bozeman, Michael Crow, Timothy Delmont, Philip Eckhert, Harvey Jacobs, David Johnson, Jerome Kaufman, Joseph King, Kathleen Haines, Paul Nutt, Ann Pflaum, William Roering, Michael Rubin, and Bart Wechsler.

A number of practitioners have provided invaluable assistance in the formulation and critique of the ideas presented in this book. I have already mentioned Timothy Delmont, Philip Eckhert, Kathleen Korbelik, Ann Pflaum, and Michael Rubin, but I must also mention many others. Barbara Arney, James Brimeyer, James Brusseau, John Connelly, Peter Hames, Lonnie Helgeson, John Hinton, Sharon Klumpp, William McCutcheon, Barbara O'Grady, James Scheibel, and Linda Stein have been great sources of practical insight into effective strategic planning. Susan Laxdal and John Walley of the Minneapolis office of the Institute of Cultural Affairs introduced me to the five-part strategy development process outlined in Chapter Eight and showed me how the "snow card" technique (which I learned from Richard Duke of the University of Michigan) might be applied to strategy development. John Carver, head of Carver Governance Design, Inc., of Carmel, Indiana, helped introduce me to the characteristics and functioning of effective policy-making boards, a topic I discuss in Chapter Four. And, I must single out Bryan Barry for special thanks. We first met when Bryan, presently senior vice-president of the Amherst H. Wilder Foundation in St. Paul, Minnesota, was a student in my project planning class at the Humphrey Institute. Now we have switched places; I have become a student of his in the area of strategic planning.

Most of the actual writing of this book was completed in London, where I was a visiting professor at the Institute for Public Sector Management (IPSM) at the London Business School (LBS) during the 1986–87 academic year. Andrew Likierman, director of IPSM, and Norman Flynn, a lecturer at LBS, have been especially valued colleagues at various stages in the preparation of this book. Both are skilled academics, strategists, and critics, and I appreciate their help. In addition, I would like to thank Sue Richards, Ellie Scrivens, and Carol Vielba for advice, help, and encouragement over the course of the year. Thanks to the IPSM faculty and staff; the principal of LBS, Peter Moore; and the faculty dean, John Hunt, I enjoyed delightful and informative conversation, magnificent staff support, a fantastic dining room, and peace and quiet for an entire academic year. I believe that I have now become hopelessly addicted to sabbatical leaves.

Two of the chapters in this book, and part of a third, have appeared elsewhere, and I would like to thank the editors and publishers of these earlier publications for allowing slightly revised versions to be printed here. Part of Chapter One and an earlier version of Chapter Two appeared, respectively, as the "Editors' Introduction to the Strategic Planning Symposium" (coauthored with Robert Einsweiler) and "Applying Private-Sector Strategic Planning in the Public Sector" (coauthored with William Roering) in the *Journal of the American Planning Association* (Bryson and Einsweiler, 1987; Bryson and Roering, 1987). The journal is coedited by Raymond Burby and Edward Kaiser. Both provided excellent advice and support as those articles moved from idea to printed page. Parts of Chapters One and Ten also appeared as a book chapter, which I coauthored with Andrew Van de Ven and William Roering (Bryson, Van de Ven, and Roering, 1987).

I must express my deepest gratitude to my wife, Barbara Crosby, and our two young children, Kee and Jessica, for their warmth and emotional support, which are sustaining forces in my life. In addition, Barbara, who is a skilled writer and editor, went over every chapter to improve its style and content. Without her help, I am not sure this book would have seen the light of day. Our children are a miracle and a blessing, and I have valued the chance to spend more time with them during my sabbatical year. Of course, their presence in my life has delayed the completion of this manuscript for a variety of good, often delightful, reasons, but they have also made the project more worthwhile to me. I believe that public and nonprofit organizations can be a powerful force for good in the world, and I hope that this book—in however small a way—can help such organizations make the world more safe, healthy, happy, and just for my children and everyone else's.

Finally, I must offer heartfelt thanks to three reviewers who went over the manuscript in great detail and provided me with splendid advice on how to revise the first draft: Douglas Eadie, president of Strategic Development Consulting, Inc., Shaker Heights, Ohio; Theodore Gaebler, president of the Gaebler Group, consultants in public entrepreneurial management, San Rafael, California; and Theodore Poister, director of the Institute of Public Administration, Georgia State University, Atlanta.

J.M.B.

The Author

John M. Bryson is associate professor of planning and public affairs at the Hubert H. Humphrey Institute of Public Affairs and associate director of the Strategic Management Research Center, both at the University of Minnesota–Twin Cities. He received a B.A. degree (1969) in economics from Cornell University and three degrees from the University of Wisconsin: an M.A. degree (1972) in public policy and administration, an M.S. degree (1974) in urban and regional planning, and a Ph.D. degree (1978) in urban and regional planning.

Bryson's interests include strategic planning, project planning, implementation, evaluation, and organizational design. In his research he explores ways of improving planning and policy-related theory and practice, particularly through situational approaches. He received the 1978 General Electric Award for Outstanding Research in Strategic Planning. In 1982 he was named Emerging Scholar of the Year at the University of Minnesota by the Honor Society of Phi Kappa Phi. And in 1983 he and Kimberly B. Boal received the Best Paper Award from the Public Sector Division of the Academy of Management for their research in strategic management.

Bryson has published numerous articles and book chapters. Recent articles have appeared in the *Journal of the American*

Planning Association, Strategic Management Journal, Academy of Management Review, Evaluation and Program Planning, Policy Studies Journal, Project Management Quarterly, and *Planning and Administration.* Recently he was guest coeditor (with Robert C. Einsweiler) of a special strategic planning symposium published by the *Journal of the American Planning Association.*

PART I

Understanding the Dynamics of Strategic Planning

The environments of public and nonprofit organizations have become not only increasingly turbulent in recent years but also more tightly interconnected; thus, changes anywhere in the system reverberate unpredictably—and often dangerously. This increased turbulence and interconnectedness requires a threefold response from public and nonprofit organizations (and communities). First, these organizations must think strategically as never before. Second, they must translate their insights into effective strategies to cope with their changed circumstances. And third, they must develop the rationales necessary to lay the groundwork for the adoption and implementation of their strategies.

Strategic planning can help leaders and managers of public and nonprofit organizations think and act strategically. Chapter One introduces strategic planning and its potential benefits, including a discussion of when it is and probably is *not* appropriate. Four organizations that have used a strategic planning process are introduced. Their experiences will be used throughout the book to illustrate the dynamics of strategic plannning.

Most of the literature on strategic planning in this century has focused on private sector applications. The extensive private sector experience with strategic planning, particularly

1

over the past twenty-five years, provides a rich storehouse of advice on how to apply it to public and nonprofit purposes. Chapter Two reviews the approaches to strategic planning typically used in the private sector in order to draw out those important lessons.

Part One concludes with a presentation in Chapter Three of my preferred strategic planning process. The process draws on the private sector approaches discussed in Chapter Two, but was designed specifically to help public and nonprofit organizations (and communities) think and act strategically. The process in practice typically is very fluid, iterative, and dynamic, but nonetheless allows for a reasonably orderly, participative, and effective approach to determining how to achieve what is best for an organization.

A key point will be emphasized again and again: it is strategic *thinking and acting* that are important, not strategic planning. Indeed, if any particular approach to strategic planning gets in the way of strategic thought and action, the planning approach should be scrapped!

Chapter 1

The Role of Strategic Planning in Public and Nonprofit Organizations

The Public and Nonprofit Sectors in a Changing World

Leaders and managers of governments, public agencies of all sorts, nonprofit organizations, and communities face difficult challenges in the years ahead. Turbulence and upheaval surround them. Consider, for example, several trends and events of the past decade: demographic changes, value shifts, the privatization of public services, tax levy limits, tax indexing, reductions in federal mandates and the devolution of federal responsibilities, shifts in federal and state funding priorities, a volatile economy, and the increased importance of the nonprofit sector.

This turbulence is aggravated by the increased interconnectedness of the world, so that changes anywhere typically result in changes elsewhere (Luke, 1988). The increased interconnectedness is perhaps most apparent in the blurring of three important types of distinctions: between domestic and international; among policy areas; and between public, private, and nonprofit

3

sectors (Cleveland, 1973, 1985; Ring and Perry, 1985). These changes have become dramatically apparent since the end of the Nixon Administration. The obsolescence of the domestic-international distinction was dramatized by the 1973 and 1978 oil embargoes, when it became obvious that the U.S. economy is part of a world economy and that any disturbance abroad has domestic repercussions.

The distinctions among policy areas are also hard to maintain. For example, educational reform is being touted as a kind of industrial policy that will help U.S. firms cope more effectively with foreign competition. A strong economy is now seen as a key to limiting human service costs. And the connections between national industrial or full employment policies and local economic development have become obvious.

Finally, the boundaries between public, private, and nonprofit sectors have eroded. Sovereignty, for example, is increasingly "farmed out." Weapons systems are produced not in government arsenals but by private industry. Taxes are not collected by government tax collectors but are withheld by private and nonprofit organizations from their employees and turned over to the government. The nation's health, education, and welfare are a public responsibility, yet increasingly we rely on private and nonprofit organizations for the production of services in these areas.

The blurring of the three distinctions means we have moved to a world of interconnections and interdependencies, a world in which no one organization or institution is fully in charge, yet many are involved (Luke, 1988; Bryson and Einsweiler, 1988a). This increased environmental uncertainty and ambiguity requires public and nonprofit organizations (and communities) to think and act strategically as never before. Strategic planning is designed to help them do so. The extensive private sector experience with strategic planning over the past twenty-five years and the increasing experience in the public and nonprofit sectors yield a rich storehouse of advice on how to apply strategic planning. We will draw on this storehouse throughout the book.

Strategic Planning

What is strategic planning? Drawing on Olsen and Eadie (1982, p. 4) we define strategic planning as a disciplined effort to produce fundamental decisions and actions that shape and guide what an organization (or other entity) is, what it does, and why it does it. At its best, strategic planning requires broad-scale information gathering, an exploration of alternatives, and an emphasis on the future implications of present decisions. It can facilitate communication and participation, accommodate divergent interests and values, and foster orderly decision making and successful implementation.

In this century most of the work on strategic planning has focused on for-profit organizations. Strategic planning in the public sector has primarily been applied to military purposes and the practice of statecraft on a grand scale (Quinn, 1980; Bracker, 1980).

It can, however, be applied to a number of other public and nonprofit purposes as well, as we shall see in Chapter Two. Specifically, strategic planning can be applied to

1. Public agencies, departments, or major organizational divisions.
2. General-purpose governments, such as city, county, or state governments.
3. Nonprofit organizations providing basically public services.
4. Specific functions, such as transportation, health, or education, that bridge organizational and governmental boundaries.
5. Entire communities, urban or metropolitan areas, regions, or states.

This book will concentrate primarily on strategic planning in public or nonprofit organizations, and secondarily on its application to communities and functions that bridge organizational boundaries. (Please note that the term *community* will be used throughout the book to refer to communities, urban or metropolitan areas, and regions or states.) Proponents argue that precisely because of its emphasis on organizations, strategic planning can help governments, public agencies, and nonprofit organizations deal with the wrenching changes many have experienced in recent years. Further, unless these organizations increase their own capacity to think and act strategically, they are unlikely to be effective supporters of their communities' well-being.

While the process detailed in this book can be applied to all the entities listed above, we must keep in mind how the specifics of application might differ. When strategic planning is focused on an organization, it is likely that most of the key decision makers will be "insiders." Certainly this would be true if the focus of attention is a public agency or department, a general-purpose government, or a nonprofit organization delivering "public" services. When most of the key decision makers are insiders, one might hope that it would be easier to get people together to decide important matters, to bargain and negotiate differences, and to coordinate the activities of affected parties. (Of course, whether or not the organization's board of directors or governing body consists of insiders or outsiders may be an open question, particularly if they are publicly elected. For instance, are the members of a city council insiders, outsiders, or both? However, the general point remains true: a major proportion of the key decision makers will be insiders.)

In contrast, when strategic planning is focused on a function that crosses organizational or governmental boundaries, or on a community, almost all the key decision makers will be outsiders. In these situations, the focus of attention will be on how to organize collective thought and action within an interorganizational network where no one person or institution is in charge, but in which many are involved. We should expect that it might be more difficult to organize an effective strategic planning process in such a "shared power" context (Bryson and Einsweiler, 1988a). More time probably will need to be spent on organizing forums for discussion; involving various diverse constituencies; bargaining and negotiating agreements; and coordinating the activities of numerous relatively independent participants (King and Johnson, 1988).

At this point strategic planning should be distinguished from two other kinds of planning with which readers may be familiar: organizationally based long-range planning, and comprehensive planning for cities and regions (often referred to as long-range community or master planning). *Strategic planning* and *long-range planning* for organizations are often used synonymously. While there may be little difference in outcome, in practice they usually differ in four fundamental ways. First, while both focus on an *organization* and what it should do to improve its performance, strategic planning relies more on identifying and resolving *issues*, while long-range planning focuses more on specifying goals and objectives and translating them into current budgets and work programs. Strategic planning therefore is more suitable for politicized circumstances, as identifying and resolving issues does not presume an all-encompassing consensus on organizational purposes and actions, while establishing goals and objectives and related budgets and work programs does.

Second, strategic planning emphasizes assessment of the environment outside and inside the organization far more than long-range planning does. Long-range planners tend to assume that current trends will continue into the future, while strategic planners expect new trends, discontinuities, and a variety of surprises (Ansoff, 1980). Strategic plans, therefore, are more likely than long-range plans to embody qualitative shifts in direction and to include a broader range of contingency plans.

Third, strategic planners are more likely than long-range planners to summon forth an idealized version of the organization—the "vision of success" (Taylor, 1984)—and ask how it might be achieved. Because they often are guided by a vision of success, strategic plans again often represent qualitative shifts in direction, while long-range plans typically are linear extrapolations of the present, often embodied in goal statements that represent projections of existing trends.

Finally, strategic planning is much more action oriented than long-range planning. Strategic planners usually consider a *range* of possible futures and focus on the implications of present decisions and actions in relation to that range. As a result, strategic planners are likely to consider a variety of possible streams of decisions and actions to try to keep the organization's options open as much as possible so that it can respond promptly and effectively to unforeseen contingencies. Strategic planners may still be guided by a vision of success, but they also know that different strategies may need to be pursued to achieve this vision if the future does not turn out as planned. Long-range planners, on the other hand, tend to assume a *most likely* future, and then work backward to map out the sequence of decisions and actions necessary to reach the assumed future. Long-range planners and plans therefore tend to get locked into a single stream of decisions and actions that may not be desirable if the future does not turn out as they assume it will.

Similarly, there may be little difference in outcomes between strategic planning and the best comprehensive planning for communities *if* the agency doing the comprehensive planning is tied directly to key governmental decision makers. Generally, however, the two tend to be quite different. Strategic planning typically focuses on an organization and comprehensive planning on a community. But even when strategic planning is undertaken on behalf of a community, there is a marked difference between it and conventional comprehensive (or long-range community or master) planning. Kaufman and Jacobs (1987), for example, argue that strategic planning on behalf of a community is more action-oriented, more broadly participative, more emphatic about the need to understand the community's strengths and weaknesses as well as the opportunities and threats it faces, and more attentive to intercommunity competitive behavior.

Second, comprehensive plans often are prepared to meet legal requirements related to land use and growth management and often must be formulated according to a legally prescribed process with legally prescribed content. As a legal instrument, the comprehensive plan can be an important influence on the effectiveness of community planning (Black, 1968; Einsweiler, 1980). The binding nature of the policy statements and resulting implementation vehicles (such as capital budgets and zoning codes) can, according to Rider (1983, p. 74), ''demand the attention of government officials and fulfill the plan's role as a commitment to prior decisions.'' On the other hand, the plan's typical rigidity can conflict with the political process in which public officials must ''cope with complex decision problems involving a high degree of uncertainty; in this process decision makers seek to retain flexibility, and commitments emerge incrementally from a continuous process of exploration.'' Strategic plans, therefore, even though they rarely have a legal status, can often provide a bridge from legally required and relatively rigid policy statements to actual decisions and operations (Kraemer, 1973, p. 25; Rider, 1983).

Third, while comprehensive community planning often has a substantial ''vision'' component, an idealized description of the future state of the place, there is a big difference between such a vision and that which often guides strategic planning. The visions that guide strategic planning usually involve actors (typically, but not necessarily, organizations), actions, and locales or focuses for actions. The visions that guide comprehensive planning typically include actions and places but leave out the actors, and thereby become irrelevant (R. C. Einsweiler, personal communication, 1987). The detailed ''end-state'' plan that fails to specify who will get you to the end state will not be very helpful.

In addition, comprehensive planning usually confines its agenda to a few of government's existing roles. For that reason it is of less use to key decision makers than strategic planning, which embraces all of government's actual and potential roles before deciding where, how, and why to act. Strategic planning is being used by key governmental decision makers precisely because drastic changes in the public sector are forcing them to think strategically about what government *ought* to be doing. Decision makers, in other words, now are asking themselves what effective private sector executives always ask: What businesses *should* we be in?

The reasons for the divergence between strategic planning and comprehensive planning result partly from the fact that strategic planning is a set of concepts, procedures, and tools and partly from the typical nature of public sector planning practice at the local level (Bryson and Einsweiler, 1987). On the theoretical side, public planning theorists have been urging public planners to behave more "strategically" for some time. But strategic planning is not a unitary set of concepts and procedures. There are a variety of approaches to strategic planning, and they are not all equally applicable to public situations. Although strategic planning is important and likely to become part of the standard repertoire of public planners, they must be very careful to tailor strategic planning approaches to serve their purposes and situations.

On the practice side, comprehensive planners often have difficulty behaving strategically because the practice of comprehensive planning is often channeled by the legislation governing its use, by program guidelines, and by the structural location of planning agencies within government. As a result of legislative requirements and program guidelines, comprehensive planning typically is not "comprehensive" at all, but is tied to land use, public facilities, transportation, utilities, housing, and perhaps a few other functions. The functional plans often are not integrated with one another, and they typically ignore what government ought to be doing (as contrasted with what it already does). The comprehensiveness now seems to come from adding up the separate functional parts (what in the 1960s and early 1970s was called "hardening of the categories"), and not from thinking comprehensively and strategically about a community and what its government might do to improve it.

Comprehensive planning also can be limited by the structural location of the planning agency within government. If the planners are not linked directly to the government's key decision makers, they typically are given responsibility for less than the full agenda of government. Further, because planners may be limited—through no fault of their own—in the kind of comprehensive planning they can practice, key decision makers may reach the unwarranted conclusion that public planners *cannot* be strategic planners.

We might summarize this discussion by saying that strategic planning requires a more comprehensive vision than that which normally guides comprehensive planning. At the same time, strategic planning produces a more selective action focus.

Benefits of Strategic Planning

Organizations engage in strategic planning for many reasons. Proponents of strategic planning typically try to persuade their colleagues with statements like these (Barry, 1986):

> "We face so many conflicting demands we need a process for figuring out our priorities."
> "We can expect a severe budget deficit next year unless we drastically rethink the way we do business."
> "A number of private-sector competitors are going after our clients; we have to figure out a way to meet the competition."
> "Issue X is staring us in the face and we need some way to help us think about its resolution, or else we will be badly hurt."
> "Our funders (or board of directors) have asked us to prepare a strategic plan."
> "Our organization has an embarrassment of riches, but we still need to figure out how we can have the biggest impact; we owe it to our stakeholders."
> "Everyone is doing strategic planning these days; we'd better do it, too."

Regardless of why public and nonprofit organizations engage in strategic planning, however, similar benefits are likely to result. A number of authors (Steiner, 1979; Barry, 1986; Bryson, Freeman, and Roering, 1986; Bryson, Van de Ven, and Roering, 1987) argue that strategic planning can help an organization:

Think strategically and develop effective strategies.
Clarify future direction.
Establish priorities.
Make today's decisions in light of their future consequences.
Develop a coherent and defensible basis for decision making.
Exercise maximum discretion in the areas under organizational control.

Make decisions across levels and functions.
Solve major organizational problems.
Improve organizational performance.
Deal effectively with rapidly changing circumstances.
Build teamwork and expertise.

Although strategic planning *can* provide all these benefits, there is no guarantee it will. For one thing, strategic planning is simply a set of concepts, procedures, and tools. Planners need to be very careful about how they engage in strategic planning, since all approaches are not equally useful, and since a number of conditions govern successful use of each approach. This book will present a generic strategic planning process for governments, public agencies, and nonprofit organizations that incorporates the major approaches, and will offer advice on how to apply the process in different circumstances. But the process will work only if decision makers and planners use it with common sense and a sensitivity to the particulars of their situation.

Furthermore, strategic planning is not always advisable (Barry, 1986). There are two compelling reasons for holding off on a strategic planning effort. First, strategic planning may not be the best first step for an organization whose roof has fallen. For example, the organization may need to remedy a cash flow crunch or fill a key leadership position before undertaking strategic planning. Second, if the organization lacks the skills, resources, or commitment of key decision makers to produce a good plan, strategic planning will be a waste of time. If strategic planning is undertaken in such a situation, it probably should be a focused and limited effort aimed at developing the necessary skills, resources, and commitment.

A number of other reasons also can be offered for not engaging in strategic planning. Too often, however, these "reasons" are actually excuses used to avoid what should be done. For example, one might argue that strategic planning will be of little use if the costs of the process are likely to outweigh any benefits, or if the process takes time and money that might be better used elsewhere. True enough, but recall that the purpose of strategic planning is to produce fundamental decisions and actions that define what an organization (or other entity) is, what it does, and why it does it. In Chapter Four we will argue that strategic planning probably should take no more than 10 percent of any key decision maker's ordinary work time during a year. When is the cost of that 10 percent likely to outweigh the benefit of focusing that time on fundamental decisions and actions? In my experience, hardly ever.

Second, many organizations prefer to rely on the intuition of extremely gifted leaders instead of formal strategic planning processes. If these leaders are strategically minded and experienced, there may be no need for strategic planning. It is rare, however, for any leader to have all the information necessary to develop an effective strategy, and rarer still for any strategy developed by a single person to engender the kind of commitment necessary for effective implementation. A reasonably structured and formalized strategic planning process helps develop the information necessary for effective strategy formulation and the commitment necessary for effective implementation.

Third, many organizations—particularly those that have enormous difficulty reaching decisions that cut across levels, functions, or programs—find that "muddling" is the only process that will work. Muddling legitimizes the existing distribution of power and resources in the organization and allows the separate parts of the organization to pursue opportunities as they arise. Unfortunately, muddling of this sort usually results in a chronic suboptimization of organizational performance, and key external and internal constituencies therefore may be badly served.

Finally, strategic planning perhaps should not be undertaken if implementation is extremely unlikely. To engage in strategic planning when effective implementation will not follow is the organizational equivalent of the average New Year's resolution. On the other hand, when armed with the knowledge that implementation will be difficult, key decision makers and planners can focus extra attention to ensuring implementation success.

Four Examples of Strategic Planning

Throughout this book the experiences of four organizations (three public and one nonprofit) will be used to illustrate key points about strategic planning. All of these organizations explicitly or implicitly adapted for their own purposes the strategic planning process that is outlined in the chapters to come. I was a consultant in strategic planning for three of the organizations, and a colleague consulted with the fourth.

The four organizations are: a central city in a major metropolitan area (Central City), a suburban city in the same metropolitan area (Suburban City), the public-health nursing service of a county government (Nursing Service), and a nonprofit health clinic (Health Center). Their actual identities have been masked to preserve the anonymity of the participants. A number of other, less detailed, examples will be used to clarify the discussion. A particular effort will be made to offer examples of the applicability of strategic planning to communities.

Central City. Central City is a 135-year-old Midwestern city that provides a full range of municipal services to its 270,000 residents. In the city's "strong mayor" form of government, the mayor is elected at large and seven city council members are elected to represent districts within the city. The city is particularly well known for its innovative downtown development and citizen participation initiatives. The city's 2,900 employees are organized into six departments (community services, finance and management services, fire and safety services, planning and economic development, police, and public works) and several units attached to the mayor's office (city attorney, city clerk, mayor's administrative staff, human rights, and personnel). In addition, there are a number of quasi-autonomous city authorities: the board of water commissioners, port authority, public housing agency, and civic center authority.

There have been two related strategic planning efforts in Central City, one undertaken by the executive branch and another initiated by the city council. The first was initiated by the mayor's executive assistant and the chief of police, but later was embraced by all key executive-branch decision makers.

The initial focus for the effort was concern over the city's three incompatible electronic data processing hardware systems. The mayor's office and the chief of police expected tough questioning from the city council about the systems' cost and lack of compatibility, and wanted to deal with the issue strategically. Once the effort was under way, however, the key decision makers decided that the real issue was the need for a better process of raising and resolving issues across functions and levels within the executive branch. The decision makers agreed to form a cabinet consisting of the mayor's executive assistant; department heads: community services, finance and management services, fire and safety services, planning and economic development, police, and public works; and the general manager of the water utility. The cabinet was charged with overseeing an executive-branch strategic planning process concerning the full range of issues confronting Central City. The cabinet has been particularly effective in making annual executive-branchwide budget recommendations to the mayor.

After observing the executive branch's strategic planning effort, a small majority of city council members decided that the council should engage in strategic planning. The council is the city's chief legislative, policy-making, and budget approval body, but several members felt that unless they became more effective at policy making, they would be steamrollered by the executive branch. They feared that the new cabinet and strategic planning system would allow the executive branch to take the initiative on all important city issues. If that happened, the council would be reduced to simply saying "yes" or "no" to executive branch initiatives. The main focus of the council's strategic planning effort, therefore, was on how to become a more effective policy-making body. One council member, in particular, and the council's staff director combined to push the process ahead.

Suburban City. Suburban City is in the same metropolitan area as Central City, but has a very different set of circumstances. Suburban City is slightly over 100 years old, and has a current population of 45,000, down from 50,000 in 1970. It is a classic residential suburb; most workers are employed elsewhere during the day and return home at night. The city's population expanded dramatically after World War II, as returning veterans and more prosperous Central City residents pursued the American dream of children, cars, and a single-family detached house in the suburbs. Now, however, as the children have grown up and moved away, and their parents and childhood homes age, a new set of problems related to maintenance and enhancement, rather than growth, face the city.

Suburban City has a council-manager form of government. In 1987 the city had 227 employees and a budget of $25.6 million. The city has a reputation for being extremely well managed and highly responsive to citizens' needs and desires.

The assistant city manager initiated and headed the strategic planning effort with the support of the city manager, and at least the nominal support of the city council. A council member and the city manager were active participants on the strategic planning team. A number of strategic issues were identified through the process, including the need to resolve a groundwater pollution problem, develop a positive community image, maintain and renew the city's aging public infrastructure, revitalize various industrial and commercial areas, manage the city's solid wastes, and expand the city's management information capacity. Strategies were developed to deal with the most important issues and implementation efforts were begun.

Nursing Service. Nursing Service is one of the units within the county government of a populous urban county. It has roughly eighty staff members and a yearly budget of approximately $3.5 million. The service is required by statute only to provide communicable disease control and to make its programs available to all county residents regardless of ability to pay. In fact, however, Nursing Service provides a wide range of other services, including home health care, community education, and health services through a network of community clinics. It also advocates changes in public health policy on behalf of the county's residents. The service is recognized both nationally and internationally as one of the best in the field.

Unlike Central City and Suburban City, in Nursing Service the impetus for strategic planning came from outside. The county's executive director became interested in strategic planning and asked the county's three human service departments to undertake pilot efforts, so that the rest of the county government might learn from their experience. The three departments were public health (of which Nursing Service is the largest division), community services, and corrections. They were selected because they deal with the public most directly, because the greatest changes were occurring in the human services field, and because they had the staff necessary to carry out the process.

The director, deputy director, and staff of Nursing Service saw strategic planning as an opportunity to rethink the service's mission and strategies in light of the rapidly changing health care environment. Some members of the team were concerned, however, that they had been selected as one of the "guinea pigs" for the executive director's experiment. The concern was twofold. First, Nursing Service has lived with the fear that it would be taken over, put out of business, or otherwise circumvented by the county government's huge medical center, a famous hospital that entered the home health care field (one of Nursing Service's main "businesses") shortly before Nursing Service began its strategic planning process. Some staff members were afraid that any information or arguments they created as part of the service's strategic planning process might be used against the service by the executive director and the county board to benefit the medical center. Second, some staff members were concerned that the county board would not fully support the activities of the service that were perceived to compete with the private sector. They were fearful that strategic planning would call attention to these activities. A number of reassurances from the executive director were necessary before several staff members would believe the service was not being "set up." Further, Nursing Service sought additional information about exactly what the executive director expected as output from the process.

Ironically, partway through the process, the county board forced the county's executive director to resign. Nursing Service then saw the strategic planning process as a real opportunity to think through its position so that it could have the greatest possible impact on the new executive director.

As a result of the process, Nursing Service identified a number of strategic issues that needed to be addressed. The principal issue was exactly what the mission of Nursing Service should be, given the changing health care environment. After rethinking its mission, Nursing Service identified a new set of strategic issues about how the new mission could be pursued and developed a set of strategies to deal with them; by the end of 1987 the strategies were well on their way to full implementation.

Health Center. Health Center began in 1968 as a federally financed government clinic providing health services to the primarily low-income residents in a central city neighborhood. Since then, its services and client base have expanded dramatically, while its legal and political status and funding sources have changed considerably. The center is now a free-standing nonprofit organization.

By the mid 1980s, services included internal medicine, family practice, pediatrics, obstetrics and gynecology, podiatry, ophthalmology, minor surgery, laboratory and X-ray services, dental care, a pharmacy, health education, and transportation. The clinic's staff of nineteen (fifteen full-time equivalents) served approximately 5,000 community residents each year, with an annual budget of approximately $600,000.

The federal Model Cities program provided most of Health Center's initial funding. In 1972 the center became part of the city's department of public health. In 1975 Model Cities funding phased out, to be replaced by Community Development block grants and HEW grants as the major sources of the center's funding. By 1980 the clinic's advisory board began to discuss whether the center might function more effectively as a free-standing nonprofit health center. In 1983 the advisory board and city officials decided to convert the center to nonprofit status.

When a new center director was hired in 1984, the center began strategic planning to manage the transition from city program to nonprofit agency. The issues to be addressed included the center's mission, target population, services, financing, staffing, structure, governance, marketing, and facilities, along with the necessary steps to implement the proposed changes. Health Center now is a highly successful nonprofit agency and its strategic plan has been implemented almost in its entirety.

Comparisons and Contrasts. Central City, Suburban City, Nursing Service, and Health Center offer a number of comparisons and contrasts. They differ greatly in size, staff complements, budgets, and legal status. Two are general-purpose units of local government. One is a single-function government agency located well down the organizational hierarchy. And one has evolved over its history into its present status as a single-function, free-standing, nonprofit organization.

They differ in the extent to which the strategic planning effort focused directly on the organization and what it should do, or on what should happen in the general community. The two general-purpose governments focused on both organizational and community planning. Nursing Service, while it obviously was concerned about the health of the community, focused more directly on what the service itself should do. Health Center concentrated almost exclusively on organizational planning.

In addition, the four organizations engaged in strategic planning for different reasons. Central City's executive branch began strategic planning because it saw a need to promote cross-functional decision making about electronic data processing, but came to realize it needed to make decisions across a variety of functions. The legislative branch of Central City undertook strategic planning because it felt threatened by the executive branch and felt it needed to become a more effective policy-making body. Suburban City was a well-managed city that simply wanted to do better. Nursing Service was asked to engage in strategic planning by the executive director of the government of which it was a part. Health Center saw strategic planning as a way to manage the transition from government agency to nonprofit organization.

There are a number of similarities in the four cases as well. First, each organization succeeded because it had leaders willing to act as *process sponsors* to endorse and legitimate the effort. The sponsors were not always particularly active participants, but they did let it be known that they wanted important decision makers to give the effort a good try. Second, each organization had *process champions* committed to making the process work. The champions did not have preconceived ideas about what specific issues and answers would emerge from the process, although they may have had some good hunches. They simply believed that the process would result in good answers and pushed until those answers emerged (see Kotler, 1976; Maidique, 1980; Kanter, 1983).

Third, each organization began with fairly clear agreement among key decision makers about what strategic planning was and what they expected from the process. Fourth, each followed a reasonably structured strategic thinking and acting process. Fifth, each established a decision-making or advisory body to oversee the process. Sixth, each designated a strategic planning team to manage the process, collect information and prepare for meetings, and draft a strategic plan. Seventh, each identified critical issues that required effective action if the organization was to avoid being victimized by serious threats, missing important opportunities, or both. Eighth, each worked hard to develop strategies that were politically acceptable, technically workable, and ethically responsible. Ninth, each relied on outside assistance, often in the form of a consultant, to help with the process. Tenth, each made a point of not getting so bogged down in the process that it lost sight of what was truly important: strategic thought and action. And finally, each gained many of the potential benefits of strategic planning outlined earlier in this chapter.

Summary

This chapter has discussed what strategic planning is and why it is important. Strategic planning has been defined as a disciplined effort to produce fundamental decisions and actions that shape and guide what an organization (or other entity) is, what it does, and why it does it. Its importance stems from its ability to help public and nonprofit organizations and communities respond effectively to the dramatically changed circumstances that now confront them.

Not only have the environments of public and nonprofit organizations and communities changed dramatically in the recent past, more upheaval is likely in the future. Those of us who grew up in the 1950s and early 1960s came to think that continuous progress was the norm, that everything would continue to get better in a straight-line extrapolation. How wrong we all were! The norm is not continuous progress, but turbulence. The period prior to the 1950s encompassed world wars, big booms, big busts, and major new roles for government. The period after brought the civil rights movement, women's movement, major student disruptions, the disastrous war in Vietnam, the environmental movement, dramatic shifts in the dominant political ideology in the United States, plus all the other changes noted in the opening paragraphs of this chapter.

Strategic planning is one way to help organizations and communities deal with their changed circumstances. It can help them formulate and resolve the most important issues they face. It can help them build on strengths and take advantage of major opportunities, while they overcome or minimize weaknesses and serious threats. It can help them be much more effective in a much more hostile world.

The next chapter will review the variety of approaches to strategic planning, developed primarily for use in the private sector. The review will cover the nature, strengths, and weaknesses of each approach, and assess its applicability to the public and nonprofit sectors.

Chapter 2

Lessons Learned from Corporate Planning Experiences

Public sector strategic planning has a long history. Indeed, the word "strategy" comes from the Greek word *stratego,* a combination of *stratos,* or army, and *ego,* or leader (O'Toole, 1985). Strategic planning thus began as the art of the general and now has become the art of the general manager.

For the most part, however, strategic planning has developed in the private sector. This history has been amply documented (Ansoff, 1980; Bracker, 1980). Recent experience now indicates that strategic planning approaches developed in the private sector can help public and nonprofit organizations, as well as communities or other entities, deal with their dramatically changing environments, and thus can help them be more effective.

That does not mean that all approaches to what might be called corporate-style strategic planning are equally applicable to the public and nonprofit sectors. This chapter will compare and contrast six approaches to corporate strategic planning (actually nine approaches grouped into six categories), discuss their applicability to the public and nonprofit sectors, and identify the most important contingencies that govern the successful use of these approaches in the public and nonprofit sectors.

As you read, remember that corporate strategic planning typically focuses on an *organization* and what it should do to improve its performance, not on a *community* or a *function,* such as health care within a community or personnel within an organization (Tomazinis, 1985). Most of this chapter deals primarily with organizations, but applications to communities and functions will be discussed as well.

It should be noted that careful tests of corporate-style strategic planning in the public and nonprofit sectors are few in number. (The same can be said, of course, about comprehensive, functional, and project planning; see Bryson, 1983; Boal and Bryson, 1987a.) Nevertheless, there is enough experience with corporate strategic planning in the private sector, and increasingly in the public and nonprofit sectors, to reach some tentative conclusions about what works under what conditions.

The remainder of this chapter is divided into two sections. The first discusses the six approaches and compares them along several dimensions, including key features, assumptions, strengths, weaknesses, and contingencies governing their use in the public and nonprofit sectors.

The second section presents conclusions about the applicability of private sector strategic planning to public and nonprofit organizations and purposes. The principal conclusions are (1) that public and nonprofit strategic planning are important and probably will become part of the standard repertoire of public and nonprofit planners and (2) that, nevertheless, public and nonprofit planners must be very careful how they engage in strategic planning, since not all approaches are equally useful and since a number of conditions govern the successful use of each approach.

Approaches to Corporate Strategic Planning

This section briefly sets forth six schools of thought or models of strategic planning developed in the private sector. The strategic planning process includes general policy and direction

Table 1. Comparison of Private-Sector Approaches to Strategic Planning and Their Applicability to the Public and Nonprofit Sectors.

Approach	Key features	Assumptions	Strengths	Weaknesses	Applicability to the public and nonprofit sectors
Harvard policy model (Andrews, 1980; Christensen et al., 1983)	Primarily applicable at the strategic business unit level SWOT analysis Analysis of management's values and social obligations of the firm Attempts to develop the best "fit" between a firm and its environment; i.e., best strategy for the firm	Analysis of SWOTs, management values, and social obligations of firm will facilitate identification of the best strategy Agreement is possible within the top management team responsible for strategy formulation and implementation Team has the ability to implement its decisions Implementation of the best strategy will result in improved firm performance (an assumption held in common with all strategic planning approaches)	Systematic assessment of strengths and weaknesses of firm and opportunities and threats facing firm Attention to management values and social obligations of the firm Systematic attention to the "fit" between the firm and its environment Can be used in conjunction with other approaches	Does not offer specific advice on how to develop strategies Fails to consider many existing or potential stakeholder groups	Organizations: Yes, if a strategic planning unit can be identified and additional stakeholder interests are considered, and if a management team can agree on what should be done and has the ability to implement its decisions Functions: SWOT analysis is applicable Communities: SWOT analysis is applicable if what is "inside" and "outside" can be specified
Strategic planning systems (Lorange, 1980; Lorange et al., 1986)	Systems for formulating and implementing important decisions across levels and functions in an organization Allocation and	Strategy formulation and implementation should be rational and anticipatory An organization's strategies should form an integrated whole The organization can control centrally all or most of its internal	Coordination of strategy formulation and implementation across levels and functions Can be used in conjunction with other approaches	Excessive comprehensiveness, prescription, and control can drive out attention to mission, strategy, and organizational structure	Organizations: Less comprehensive and rigorous forms of private sector strategic planning systems are applicable to many public and nonprofit

	control of resources within a strategic framework and through rational decision making / Attempts to comprehensively cover all key decision areas	operations / Goals, objectives, and performance indicators can be specified clearly / Information on performance is available at reasonable cost		The information requirements of planning systems can exceed the participants' ability to comprehend the information	sector organizations Functions: Necessary conditions for strategic planning systems to succeed are seldom met Communities: Unlikely
Stakeholder management (Freeman, 1984)	Identification of key stakeholders and the criteria they use to judge an organization's performance / Development of strategies to deal with each stakeholder	An organization's survival and prosperity depend on the extent to which it satisfies its key stakeholders / An organization's strategy will be successful only if it meets the needs of key stakeholders	Recognition that many claims, both complementary and competing, are placed on an organization / Stakeholder analysis (i.e., a listing of key stakeholders and of the criteria they use to judge an organization's performance) / Can be used in conjunction with other approaches	Absence of criteria with which to judge different claims / Need for more advice on how to develop strategies to deal with divergent stakeholder claims	Organizations: Yes, as long as agreement is possible among key decision makers over who the stakeholders are and what the organization's responses to them should be / Functions: Yes, with the same caveats / Communities: Yes, with the same caveats
Content approaches Portfolio methods (Henderson, 1979; Wind and Mahajan,	A corporation's businesses are categorized into groups based on selected dimen-	Aggregate assessment of a corporation's various businesses is important to the corporation's success / Resources should be channeled	Provides a method for evaluating a set of businesses against dimensions that are deemed to be of	Difficult to know what the relevant strategic dimensions are, what the relevant entities to be	Organizations: Yes, if economic, social, and political dimensions of comparison can be specified, entities to be

Table 1. Comparison of Private-Sector Approaches to Strategic Planning and Their Applicability to the Public and Nonprofit Sectors, Cont'd.

Approach	Key features	Assumptions	Strengths	Weaknesses	Applicability to the public and nonprofit sectors
1981; Mac-Millan, 1983)	sions for comparison and development of corporate strategy in relation to each business Attempts to balance a corporation's business portfolio to meet corporate strategic objectives	into the different businesses to meet the corporation's cash flow and investment needs A few key dimensions of strategic importance can be identified against which to judge the performance of individual businesses A group exists that can make and implement decisions based on the portfolio analysis	strategic importance to the corporation Provides a useful way of understanding some of the key economic and financial aspects of corporate strategy Can be used as part of a larger strategic planning process	compared are, and how to classify entities against dimensions Unclear how to use the tool as part of a larger strategic planning process	be compared can be identified, and a group exists that can make and implement decisions based on the portfolio analysis Functions: Yes, with the same caveats Communities: Yes, with the same caveats
Competitive analysis (Porter, 1980, 1985; Harrigan, 1981)	Analysis of key forces that shape an industry, e.g., relative power of customers, relative power of suppliers, threat of substitute products, threat of new entrants, amount of rivalrous activity, exit barriers to firms in the industry	Predominance of competitive behavior on the part of firms within an industry The stronger the forces that shape an industry, the lower the general level of returns in the industry The stronger the forces affecting a firm, the lower the profits for the firm Analysis of the forces will allow one to identify the best strategy whereby an industry can raise its general level of returns and	Provides a systematic method of assessing the economic aspects of an industry and the strategic options facing the industry and specific firms within it Gives relatively clear prescriptions for strategic action Can be used as part of a larger strategic planning process	Sometimes difficult to identify what the relevant industry is Excludes consideration of potentially relevant noneconomic factors Tends to ignore the possibility that organizational success may turn on collaboration, not competition	Organizations: Yes, for organizations in identifiable industries (e.g., public hospitals, transit companies, recreation facilities) if a competitive analysis is coupled with a consideration of noneconomic factors and if the possibility of collaboration is also considered Functions: Yes, if the

		whereby a firm within an industry can maximize its profits		function equates to an industry Communities: No
Strategic issues management (Ansoff, 1980; King, 1982; Pflaum and Delmont, 1987)	Attention to the recognition and resolution of strategic issues	Strategic issues are issues that can have a major influence on the organization and must be managed if the organization is to meet its objectives Strategic issues can be identified by the use of a variety of tools (e.g., SWOT analyses and environmental scanning methods) Early identification of issues will result in more favorable resolution and greater likelihood of enhanced organizational performance A group exists that is able to engage in the process and manage the issue	Ability to identify and respond quickly to issues Has a "real time" orientation and is compatible with most organizations Can be used in conjunction with other approaches	No specific advice is offered on how to frame issues other than to precede their identification with a situational analysis	Organizations: Yes, as long as there is a group able to engage in the process and manage the issue Functions: Yes, with the same caveat Communities: Yes, with the same caveat
Process strategies Strategic negotiations (Pettigrew, 1977; Fisher and Ury, 1981; Allison, 1971)	Bargaining and negotiation among two or more players over the identification and resolution of strategic issues	Organizations are "shared power" settings in which groups must cooperate, bargain, and negotiate with each other in order to achieve their ends and assure organizational survival Strategy is created as part of a relatively constant struggle among competing groups in an	Recognizes that there are many actors in the strategy formulation and implementation process and that they often do not share common goals Recognizes the desirability of bargaining	Little advice on how to ensure technical workability and democratic responsibility—as opposed to political acceptability—of results No assurance that	Organizations: Yes Functions: Yes Communities: Yes

Table 1. Comparison of Private-Sector Approaches to Strategic Planning and Their Applicability to the Public and Nonprofit Sectors, Cont'd.

Approach	Key features	Assumptions	Strengths	Weaknesses	Applicability to the public and nonprofit sectors
		organization	and negotiation in order for groups to achieve their ends and to assure organizational survival	overall organizational goals can or will be achieved; there may not be a whole equal to, let alone greater than, the sum of the parts	
		Strategy is the emergent product of the partial resolution of organizational issues	Can be used in conjunction with other approaches		
Logical incrementalism (Quinn, 1980; Lindblom, 1959)	Emphasizes the importance of small changes as part of developing and implementing organizational strategies	Strategy is a loosely linked group of decisions that are handled incrementally	Ability to handle complexity and change	No guarantee that the loosely linked, incremental decisions will add up to fulfillment of overall organizational purposes	Organizations: Yes, as long as overall organizational purposes can be identified to provide a framework for incremental decisions
	Fuses strategy formulation and implementation	Decentralized decision making is both politically expedient and necessary	Attention to both formal and informal processes		Functions: Yes, with the same caveat
		Small, decentralized decisions can help identify and fulfill organizational purposes	Political realism		Communities: Yes, with the same caveat
			Emphasis on both minor and major decisions		
			Can be used in conjunction with other approaches		

| Framework for innovation (Taylor, 1984; Pinchot, 1985) | Emphasis on innovation as a strategy
Reliance on many other approaches and specific management practices | Change is unavoidable, and continuous innovation to deal with change is necessary if the organization is to survive and prosper
A "vision of success" is necessary to provide the organization with a common set of superordinate goals toward which to work
Innovation as a strategy will not work without an entrepreneurial company culture to support it | Allows innovation and entrepreneurship while maintaining central control on key outcomes
Fosters a commitment to innovation
Can be used in conjunction with other approaches | Costly mistakes usually are necessary as part of the process of innovation
Decentralization and local control result in some loss of accountability | Organizations: Yes, but the public is unwilling to allow public organizations to make the mistakes necessary as part of the process, and development of an overall framework within which to innovate and maintain central control over key outcomes is difficult
Functions: Yes, but with the same caveats
Communities: Yes, with same caveats |

Source: Adapted from Bryson and Roering, 1987, pp. 12-14.

setting, situation assessments, strategic issues identification, strategy development, decision making, action, and evaluation. The first models cover more of the process and emphasize policy and direction setting; the others focus more narrowly on later elements of the process.

The Harvard Policy Model. The Harvard policy model was developed as part of the business policy courses taught at the Harvard Business School since the 1920s (Christensen and others, 1983). It is the principal inspiration behind the most widely cited recent models of public and nonprofit sector strategic planning (Olsen and Eadie, 1982; Sorkin, Ferris, and Hudak, 1984; Barry, 1986).

The main purpose of the Harvard model is to help a firm develop the best fit between itself and its environment; that is, to develop the best strategy for the firm. As articulated by Andrews (1980), strategy is "a pattern of purposes and policies defining the company and its business." One discerns the best strategy by analyzing the internal strengths and weaknesses of the company and the values of senior management, and by identifying the external threats and opportunities in the environment and the social obligations of the firm.

Effective use of the model presumes that senior management can agree on the firm's situation and the appropriate strategic response, and has enough authority to enforce its decisions. A final important assumption, common to all approaches to strategic planning, is that if the appropriate strategy is identified and implemented, the organization will be more effective.

My preferred approach, which will be presented in the next chapter and elaborated in subsequent chapters, is strongly influenced by the Harvard model. In it, primary attention is given to the internal strengths and weaknesses of the organization, to the values of key stakeholders (not just senior managers), and to the external threats, opportunities, and mandates (not just social obligations) affecting the organization.

In the business world, the Harvard model appears to be best applied at the strategic business unit (SBU) level. A strategic business unit is a distinct business that has its own competitors and can be managed somewhat independently of other units within the organization (Rue and Holland, 1986). The SBU, in other words, provides an important yet bounded and manageable focus for the model. Montanari and Bracker (1986) argue that the public equivalent of the SBU is the strategic public planning unit (SPPU), which typically would be an agency or department that addresses issues fundamentally similar to one another (such as related health issues, related transportation issues, or related education issues). Following their line of argument, the nonprofit equivalent of the SBU is the strategic nonprofit planning unit (SNPPU), which usually would be a nonprofit organization, division, or department that addresses issues sharing common themes (such as related community development issues or related social services issues).

The Harvard model is also applicable at the higher and broader corporate level—in the private, public, and nonprofit worlds. Here it probably would have to be supplemented with other approaches, however, such as the portfolio approaches discussed below. A portfolio approach is needed because a principal strategic concern at the corporate level is oversight of a portfolio of businesses (in the private sector), of agencies or departments (in the public sector), or of departments or activities (in the nonprofit sector).

The systematic assessment of strengths, weaknesses, opportunities, and threats—known as SWOT analysis—is the primary strength of the Harvard model. This element appears to be applicable in the public and nonprofit sectors to organizations, functions, and communities, although in the case of communities the distinction between internal and external may be problematic. The main weakness of the Harvard model is that it does not offer specific advice on how to develop strategies, except to note that effective strategies will build on strengths, take advantage of opportunities, and overcome or minimize weaknesses and threats.

Strategic Planning Systems. Strategic planning is often viewed as a system in which managers go about making, implementing, and controlling important decisions across functions and levels in the firm. Lorange (1980), for example, has argued that any strategic planning system must address four fundamental questions:

1. Where are we going? (mission)
2. How do we get there? (strategies)
3. What is our blueprint for action? (budgets)
4. How do we know if we are on track? (control)

Strategic planning systems vary along several dimensions: the comprehensiveness of decision areas included, the formal rationality of the decision process, and the tightness of control exercised over implementation of the decisions (Armstrong, 1982). The strength of these systems is their attempt to coordinate the various elements of an organization's strategy across levels and functions. Their weakness is that excessive comprehensiveness, prescription, and control can drive out attention to mission, strategy, and organizational structure (Frederickson and Mitchell, 1984; Frederickson, 1984) and can exceed the ability of participants to comprehend the system and the information it produces (Bryson, Van de Ven, and Roering, 1987).

Strategic planning systems are applicable to public and nonprofit organizations, for regardless of the nature of the particular organization, it makes sense to coordinate decision making across levels and functions and to concentrate on whether the organization is implementing its strategies and accomplishing its mission. It is important to remember, however, that a strategic planning system characterized by substantial comprehensiveness, formal rationality in decision making, and tight control will work only in an organization that has a clear mission, clear goals and objectives, centralized authority, clear performance indicators, and information about actual performance available at reasonable cost (Stuart, 1969; Galloway, 1979). While some nonprofit organizations, such as some hospitals and health care organizations, operate under such conditions, few public organizations do. As a result, most public and many nonprofit sector strategic planning systems typically focus on a few areas of concern, rely on a decision process in which politics plays a major role, and control something other than program outcomes—budget expenditures, for example (Wildavsky, 1979a).

The next chapter will present two examples of how a relatively tightly controlled strategic planning system might be implemented across levels in a public or nonprofit organization. One example is based on the experience of the 3M Corporation, while the other is the system used by Hennepin County, Minnesota.

Stakeholder Management Approaches. Freeman (1984) states that corporate strategy can be understood as a corporation's mode of relating or building bridges to its stakeholders. A stakeholder is any group or individual who is affected by or who can affect the future of the corporation—customers, employees, suppliers, owners, governments, financial institutions, critics. Freeman argues that a corporate strategy will be effective only if it satisfies the needs of multiple groups. Traditional private sector models of strategy have focused only on economic actors, but Freeman believes that changes in the current business environment require that other political and social actors be considered as well.

Because it integrates economic, political, and social concerns, the stakeholder model is one of the approaches most applicable to the public and nonprofit worlds. Many interest groups have stakes in public and nonprofit organizations, functions, and communities. For example, local economic development planning typically involves government, developers, bankers, the chamber of commerce, actual or potential employers, neighborhood groups, environmentalists, and so on. Local economic development planners would be wise to identify key stakeholders, their interests, what they will support, and strategies and tactics that might work in dealing with them (Kaufman, 1979).

Bryson, Freeman, and Roering (1986) argue that an organization's mission and values should be formulated in stakeholder terms. That is, an organization should figure out what its mission ought to be in relation to each stakeholder group; otherwise, it will not be able to differentiate its responses well enough to satisfy its key stakeholders. This advice to public and nonprofit organizations is matched by private sector practice in several well-managed companies (O'Toole, 1985). For example, the Dayton Hudson Corporation, a large retailer, identifies four key stakeholders—customers, employees, stockholders, and the communities in which its stores operate—and specifies its mission in relation to each. Dayton Hudson assumes that if it performs well in the eyes of each of those stakeholders, its success is assured.

The strengths of the stakeholder model are its recognition of the many claims—both complementary and competing— placed on organizations by insiders and outsiders and its awareness of the need to satisfy at least the key stakeholders if the organization is to survive. The weaknesses of the model are the absence of criteria with which to judge competing claims and the need for more advice on developing strategies to deal with divergent stakeholder interests.

Freeman has applied the stakeholder concept primarily at the corporate and industry levels in the private sector, but it seems applicable to all levels in the private, public, and non-profit sectors, including the community. Researchers have not yet made rigorous tests of the model's usefulness in the private, public, or nonprofit sectors, but several public and nonprofit case studies indicate that stakeholder analyses are quite useful as part of the strategic planning effort (Allan, 1985; Klumpp, 1986; Bryson, Freeman, and Roering, 1986; Bryson and Einsweiler, 1988b). If the model is to be used successfully, key decision makers must achieve reasonable agreement about who the key stakeholders are and what the response to their claims should be.

The three approaches presented so far have more to do with process than with content. The process approaches do not prescribe answers, although good answers are presumed to emerge from appropriate application. In contrast, the tools to be discussed next—portfolio models and competitive analysis— primarily concern content and do yield answers. In fact, the models are antithetical to process when process concerns get in the way of developing the "right" answers.

Portfolio Models. The idea of strategic planning as managing a portfolio of businesses is based on an analogy to investment practice. Just as an investor assembles a portfolio of stocks to manage risk and realize optimum returns, a corporate manager can think of the corporation as a portfolio of businesses with diverse potentials that can be balanced to manage return and cash flow. The intellectual history of portfolio theory in corporate strategy is complex (Wind and Mahajan, 1981). For our purposes, it is adequate to use as an example the portfolio model developed by the Boston Consulting Group: the famous BCG matrix (Henderson, 1979).

Bruce Henderson, founder of the Boston Consulting Group, argued that all business costs followed a well-known pattern: unit costs dropped by one-third every time volume (or turnover) doubled. Hence, he postulated a relationship, known as the experience curve, between unit costs and volume. This relationship leads to some generic strategic advice: gain market share, for then unit costs will fall and profit potential will increase.

Henderson said that any business could be categorized into one of four types, depending on how its industry was growing and how large a share of the market it had:

1. High-growth/high-share businesses ("stars"), which generate substantial cash but also require large investments if their market share is to be maintained or increased.
2. Low-growth/high-share businesses ("cash cows"), which generate large cash flows but require low investment and therefore generate profits that can be used elsewhere.
3. Low-growth/low-share businesses ("dogs"), which produce little cash and offer little prospect of increased share.
4. High-growth/low-share businesses ("question marks"), which would require substantial investment to become stars or cash cows (the question is whether the investment is worth it).

Although the applications of portfolio theory to the public and nonprofit sectors may be less obvious than those described above, they are nonetheless just as powerful (MacMillan, 1983). Many public and nonprofit organizations consist of "multiple businesses" that are only marginally related. Often resources from various sources are committed to these unrelated businesses, which means that managers must make portfolio decisions, though usually without the help of portfolio models that frame those decisions strategically. The BCG approach, like most private sector portfolio models, uses only economic criteria, not political or social criteria that might be necessary for public and nonprofit applications. Private sector portfolio approaches, therefore, must be modified substantially for public and non-profit use.

The Philadelphia Investment Portfolio is an example of applying a portfolio approach to the community level (Center for Philadelphia Studies, 1982a, 1982b). The portfolio consists of fifty-six investment options arranged according to the degree to which they take advantage of ongoing trends (their "position") and the degree to which they facilitate the strategic objectives of the greater Philadelphia area (their "attractiveness"). (The judgments of position and attractiveness were formulated through the collaborative efforts of about 750 people in the public, private, and nonprofit sectors.) Each of the two dimensions consists of a set of economic, political, and social criteria. The creators of the portfolio view greater Philadelphia as a community of interests and stakeholders, in which the activities of disparate parties can be loosely coordinated through a focus on specific investment options that are attractive to specific organizations or coalitions. An organization or coalition would pursue an option because that option fit its needs or desires, but the area as a whole also would benefit.

The strength of the portfolio approaches is that they provide a method of measuring entities of some sort (businesses, investment options, proposals, or problems) against dimensions of strategic importance (such as share and growth, or position and attractiveness). Weaknesses include the difficulty of knowing what the appropriate strategic dimensions are, difficulties of classifying entities against dimensions, and the lack of clarity about how to use the tool as part of a larger strategic planning process.

If modified to include political and social factors, portfolio approaches can be used in the public and nonprofit sectors to make informed strategic decisions. They can be used in conjunction with process approaches, such as the one outlined in the next chapter, to provide useful information on an organization, function, or community in relation to its environment.

Unlike the process models, however, portfolio approaches provide an "answer"; that is, once the dimensions for comparison and the entities to be compared are specified, the portfolio models prescribe how the organization or community *should* relate to its environment. Such models will work only if a dominant coalition is convinced that the answers it produces are correct.

Competitive Analysis. Another important content approach that assists strategy selection has been developed by Michael Porter (1980, 1985) and his associates. Called competitive analysis, it assumes that by analyzing the forces that shape an industry, one can predict the general level of profits throughout the industry and the likely success of any particular strategy for a strategic business unit.

Porter (1980) hypothesizes that five key forces shape an industry: relative power of customers, relative power of suppliers, threat of substitute products, threat of new entrants, and the amount of rivalrous activity among the players in the industry. Harrigan (1981) has argued that "exit barriers"—the barriers that would prevent a company from leaving an industry—are a sixth force influencing success in some industries. There are two main propositions in the competitive analysis school: (1) the stronger the forces that shape an industry, the lower the general level of returns in the industry; and (2) the stronger the forces affecting a strategic business unit, the lower the profits for that unit.

For many public and nonprofit organizations, there are equivalents to the forces that affect private industry. Client or customer power is often important; suppliers of services (contractors and the organization's own labor supply) also can exercise power. There are fewer new entrants in the public sector, but recently private and nonprofit organizations have begun to compete more forcefully with public organizations. Governments and public agencies often compete with one another (public hospitals for patients; states and communities for industrial plants). Nonprofit organizations often compete intensely among themselves for limited resources.

An effective organization in the public or nonprofit world, therefore, must understand the forces at work in its "industry" in order to compete effectively. On another level, planning for a specific public function (health care, transportation, or recreation) can benefit from competitive analysis if the function can be considered an industry. In addition, economic development agencies must understand the forces at work in given industries and on specific firms if they are to understand whether and how to nurture those industries and firms. Finally, although communities often compete with one another, competitive analysis probably does not apply at this level because communities are not industries in any meaningful sense.

The strength of competitive analysis is that it provides a systematic way of assessing industries and the strategic options facing SBUs within those industries. For public and nonprofit applications, competitive analysis has two weaknesses: it is often difficult to know what the "industry" is and what forces affect it, and the key to organizational success in the public and nonprofit worlds is often collaboration instead of competition. Competitive analysis in the public and nonprofit sectors, therefore, must be coupled with a consideration of social and political forces and the possibilities for collaboration.

Strategic Issue Management. We now leave content approaches to focus again on process approaches. Strategic issues management approaches are process components, pieces of a larger strategic planning process, such as the one outlined in the next chapter. In the private sector, this approach is primarily associated with Ansoff (1980) and focuses attention on the recognition and resolution of strategic issues—"forthcoming developments, either inside or outside the organization, which are likely to have an important impact on the ability of the enterprise to meet its objectives" (p. 133). In the public sector, strategic issue management is primarily associated with Eadie (1986).

The concept of strategic issues first emerged when corporate strategic planners realized a step was missing between the SWOT analysis of the Harvard model and the development of strategies. That step was the identification of strategic issues. Many firms now include a strategic issue identification step as part of full-blown strategy revision exercises and also as part of less comprehensive annual strategic reviews (King, 1982).

Full-blown annual revision has proved impractical because strategy revision takes substantial management energy and attention, and in any case most strategies take several years to implement. Instead, most firms are undertaking comprehensive strategy revisions several years apart (typically five) and in the interim are focusing their annual strategic planning processes on identifying and resolving a few key strategic issues that emerge from SWOT analyses, environmental scans, and other analyses (Hambrick, 1982; Pflaum and Delmont, 1987).

In recent years, many firms also have developed strategic issue management processes actually separated from their annual strategic planning processes. Many important issues emerge too quickly, with too much urgency, to be handled as part of an annual process. When confronted with such issues, top managers typically appoint task forces to develop responses for immediate implementation.

Strategic issue management is clearly applicable to governments, public agencies, and nonprofit organizations, since the agendas of these organizations consist of issues that should be managed strategically (Ring and Perry, 1985; Eadie and Steinbacher, 1985). In other words, they should be managed based on a sense of mission and mandates and in the context of an environmental assessment. The strength of the approach is its ability to recognize and analyze key issues quickly. Its weakness is that it offers no specific advice on exactly how to frame the issues other than to precede their identification with a situational analysis of some sort. The approach also applies to functions or communities, as long as some group, organization, or coalition is able to engage in the process and to manage the issue.

Strategic Negotiations. Several writers view corporate strategy as the partial resolution of organizational issues through a highly political process (Pettigrew, 1977; Mintzberg and Waters, 1985). As envisioned by Pettigrew (1977), strategy is a flow of actions and values embedded in a context, and thus strategic negotiations are context-bound.

The applicability of this view to the public sector is clear when one realizes that Allison's study (1971) of the Cuban missile crisis provided much of the stimulus for this line of private sector work. The approach is equally applicable to the nonprofit sector, in which negotiation is increasingly a way of life for leaders and managers. Negotiation has become an important focus of planning research and practice generally (Susskind and Ozawa, 1984). An example of planning-related strategic negotiations is the Negotiated Investment Strategy project of the Charles F. Kettering Foundation (1982), in which federal, state, and local agencies in several cities worked out a coordinated investment strategy designed to meet the objectives of each agency.

The strength of a negotiation approach is that it recognizes that power is shared in most public and nonprofit situations; no one person, group, or organization is ''in charge,'' and cooperation and negotiation with others are often necessary for people, groups, and organizations to achieve their ends (Bryson and Einsweiler, 1988a). The main weakness of negotiation approaches, as expounded, for example, by Fisher and Ury (1981) in *Getting to Yes*, is that although they can show planners how to reach politically acceptable results, they are not very helpful in assuring technical workability or democratic responsibility of results.

Logical Incrementalism. In incremental approaches, strategy is a loosely linked group of decisions that are handled incrementally. Decisions are handled individually below the corporate level because such decentralization is politically expedient—corporate leaders should reserve their political clout for crucial decisions. Decentralization also is necessary since often only those closest to decisions have enough information to make good ones.

The incremental approach is identified principally with Quinn (1980), although the influence of Lindblom (1959) is apparent. Quinn developed the concept of logical incrementalism—incrementalism in the service of overall corporate purposes—and as a result transformed incrementalism into a strategic approach. Logical incrementalism is a process approach that, in effect, fuses strategy formulation and implementation. The strengths of this approach are its ability to handle complexity and change, its emphasis on minor as well as major decisions, its attention to informal as well as formal processes, and its political realism. The major weakness of the approach is that it does not guarantee that the various loosely linked decisions will add up to fulfillment of corporate purposes. Logical incrementalism appears to be very applicable to public organizations, functions, and communities—the situations in which, and for which, Lindblom first developed the incremental model— as long as it is possible to establish some overarching set of strategic objectives. It also is applicable to nonprofit sector organizations, with the same caveat.

Strategic Planning as a Framework for Innovation. The earlier discussion of strategic planning systems noted that excessive comprehensiveness, prescription, and control can drive out attention to mission, strategy, and organizational structure. The systems, in other words, can become ends in themselves and drive out creativity, innovation, and development of new products and new markets, without which most businesses would die. Many businesses, therefore, have found it necessary to emphasize innovative strategies as a counterbalance to the excessive control orientation of many strategic planning systems. In other words, while one important reason for installing a strategic planning system is the need to exercise control across functions and levels, an equally important need for organizations is to design systems that promote creativity and entrepreneurship at the local level and prevent centralization and bureaucracy from stifling the wellsprings of business growth and change (Taylor, 1984).

The framework for innovation approach to corporate strategic planning relies on many elements of the approaches discussed above, such as SWOT analyses and portfolio methods. It differs from earlier approaches in four emphases: (1) innovation as a strategy; (2) specific management practices to support the strategy (such as project teams; venture groups; diversification, acquisition, and divestment task forces; research and development operations; new product and market groups; and a variety of organizational development techniques); (3) development of a "vision of success" that provides the decentralized and entrepreneurial parts of the organization with a common set of superordinate goals toward which to work; and (4) nurture of an entrepreneurial company culture (Pinchot, 1985).

The strength of the approach is that it allows for innovation and entrepreneurship while maintaining central control. The weaknesses of the approach are that typically, and perhaps necessarily, a great many, often costly, mistakes are made as part of the innovation process, and that there is a certain loss of accountability in very decentralized systems (Peters and Waterman, 1982). Those weaknesses reduce the applicability to the public sector, in particular, where mistakes are less acceptable and the pressures to be accountable for details (as opposed to results) are often greater (Ring and Perry, 1985). Many nonprofit organizations also will have trouble pursuing this approach because a shortage of important resources will magnify the risks of failure.

Nonetheless, the innovation approach would appear to be applicable to public and nonprofit organizations when the management of innovation is necessary (Zaltman, Florio, and Sikorski, 1977), as in the redesign of a public service (Savas, 1982; Kolderie, 1986). Innovation as a strategy also can and should be pursued for functions and communities. Too often a distressing equation has operated in the public sector: more money equals more service, less money equals less service. As public budgets have become increasingly strapped, there has not been enough innovation in public service redesign.

The equation does not have to be destiny; it is possible that creative effort and innovation might actually result in *more* service for *less* money (Kolderie, 1982). It is particularly interesting to note that nonprofit sector innovations may be the answer to many public sector problems. For example, many governments rely on nonprofit organizations to produce essentially "public" services on a contract basis. The nonprofits may be able to provide the services more efficiently, effectively, and flexibly than would be possible if the government delivered the services directly.

Conclusions

Several conclusions emerge from this review and analysis of corporate-style strategic planning. First, it should be clear that corporate strategic planning is not a single concept, procedure, or tool. In fact, it embraces a range of approaches that vary in their applicability to the public and nonprofit sectors and in the conditions that govern their successful use. The approaches also vary in the extent to which they encompass broad policy and direction setting, internal and external assessments, attention to key stakeholders, the identification of key issues, development of strategies to deal with each issue, decision making, action, and continuous monitoring of results.

Second, a strategic planning process applicable to public and nonprofit organizations and communities will need to allow for the full range of strategic planning activities, from policy and direction setting through monitoring of results. Such a process will contrast, therefore, with the private sector approaches, which tend to emphasize different parts of such a complete procedure. A further contrast would be that private sector approaches are focused only on organizations, not on functions that cross governmental or organizational boundaries, not on communities or larger entities.

Third, while any generic strategic planning process may be a useful guide to thought and action, it will have to be applied with care in a given situation, as is true of any planning process (Bryson and Delbecq, 1979; Galloway, 1979; Christensen, 1985). Because every planning process should be tailored to fit specific situations, every process in practice will be a hybrid.

Fourth, I believe familiarity with strategic planning should be a standard part of the intellectual and skill repertoire of all public and nonprofit planners. Given the dramatic changes in the environments of their organizations in recent years, we can expect key decision makers and planners to seek effective strategies to deal with the changes. When applied appropriately in public and nonprofit circumstances, strategic planning provides a set of concepts, procedures, and tools for formulating and implementing such strategies. The most effective public and nonprofit planners no doubt are now, and will be increasingly in the future, the ones who are best at *strategic* planning.

Fifth, asserting the increased importance of strategic planning raises the question of the appropriate role of the strategic planner. In many ways, this is an old debate in the planning literature. Should the planner be a technician, politician, or hybrid—both technician and politician (Howe and Kaufman, 1979; Howe, 1980)? Should the planner be a process expert, or what Bolan (1971) calls an "expert on experts"? Or should the planner be not a planner at all, at least formally, but rather a policy maker or a line manager (Bryson, Van de Ven, and Roering, 1987)? Clearly, the strategic planner can be solely a technician only when content approaches are used. When all other approaches are used, the strategic planner (or planning team) should be a hybrid, so that there is some assurance that both political and technical concerns are addressed. (Obviously, the specific proportions of technical expertise and political or process expertise would vary depending on the situation.) Furthermore, since strategic planning tends to fuse planning and decision making, it is helpful to think of decision makers as strategic planners and to think of strategic planners as facilitators of strategic decision making across levels and functions. This issue of the role of the strategic planner, regardless of the formal job title, is important, and will be discussed later.

Finally, research must explore a number of theoretical and empirical issues in order to advance the knowledge and practice of strategic planning in the public and nonprofit worlds. In particular, strategic planning processes that are responsive to different situations in the public and nonprofit sectors must be developed and tested. These processes should specify key situational factors governing their use; provide specific advice on how to formulate and implement strategies in different situations; be explicitly political; indicate how to deal with plural, ambiguous, or conflicting goals or objectives; link content and process; indicate how collaboration as well as competition is to be handled; and specify roles for the strategic planner. Progress has been made on all these fronts (Checkoway, 1986; Bryson and Einsweiler, 1988b). Indeed, the process outlined in the next chapter addresses each of these concerns and, it is hoped, represents an advance over other approaches. But future research should greatly enhance what is offered here.

The next chapter will present my preferred approach to strategic planning for governments, public agencies, nonprofit organizations, functions, and communities. Subsequent chapters will discuss the process and how to apply it. This process is offered in the hope that it will help public and nonprofit organizations, functions, and communities fulfill their missions and serve their stakeholders effectively, efficiently, and responsibly.

Chapter 3

An Effective Strategic Planning Approach for Public and Nonprofit Organizations

I skate to where I think the puck will be.
Wayne Gretzky

Men, I want you to fight vigorously and then run. And
as I am a little bit lame, I'm going to start running now.
Gen. George Stedman
U.S. Army (Civil War)

This chapter will present my preferred approach to strategic
planning for public and nonprofit organizations, functions, and
communities. The process encompasses broad policy and direction setting, internal and external assessments, attention to key
stakeholders, identification of key issues, development of strategies to deal with each issue, decision making, action, and continuous monitoring of results. The process draws on the private
sector approaches outlined in the previous chapter and applies
them to public and nonprofit purposes. Subsequent chapters will
provide detailed guidance on moving through the steps.

First, however, let me emphasize that *any* strategic planning process is worthwhile only if it helps key decision makers
think and *act* strategically. Strategic planning is not an end in
itself, but merely a set of concepts to help leaders make important decisions and take important actions. Indeed, if any strategic planning process gets in the way of strategic thinking and
acting, the process should be scrapped—not the thinking and
acting!

The two quotes that begin this chapter help make the point
that strategic thinking and acting are more important than any

46

particular approach to strategic planning. Wayne Gretzky, one of the world's greatest ice hockey players, is talking about strategic thinking and acting when he says, "I skate to where I think the puck will be." He does not skate around with a thick strategic plan in his back pocket; hockey uniforms may not always *have* back pockets. What he does is think and act strategically every minute of the game, in keeping with a typically simple game plan worked out with his coaches in advance.

But let us explore Gretzky's statement further. Think about what one must know and be able to do in order to make, and deliver on, such a comment. One obviously would need to know the purposes and rules of the game, the strengths and weaknesses of one's own team, the opportunities and threats posed by the other team, the game plan, the arena, the officials, and so on. One would also have to be a well-equipped, well-conditioned, strong, and able hockey player. And it doesn't hurt to play for a very good team. In other words, those who can express confidently that they "skate to where they think the puck will be" know basically everything there is to know about strategic thinking and acting in hockey games.

Let us also consider the humorous statement of General George Stedman of the U.S. Army in the Civil War. At one point he and his men were badly outnumbered by Confederate soldiers. A hasty retreat was in order, but it made sense to give the lame and wounded, including the general, a chance to put some distance between themselves and the enemy before a full-scale retreat was called. They would then be in a position to fight another day. Stedman had no thick strategic plan in his back pocket, either, although we can assume he did *have* a back pocket. At most he probably had a fairly general battle plan worked out with his fellow officers and recorded in pencil on a map. Again, strategic thinking and acting were what mattered, not any particular planning process.

An Eight-Step Strategic Planning Process

Now, with that caution in mind, let us proceed to a more detailed exploration of the eight-step process. The process, presented in Figure 1, is more orderly, deliberative, and participative than the process followed by Gretzky or Stedman while they are on the move. The steps are:

1. Initiating and agreeing on a strategic planning process.
2. Identifying organizational mandates.
3. Clarifying organizational mission and values.
4. Assessing the external environment: opportunities and threats.
5. Assessing the internal environment: strengths and weaknesses.
6. Identifying the strategic issues facing an organization.
7. Formulating strategies to manage the issues.
8. Establishing an effective organizational vision for the future.

These eight steps should lead to actions, results, and evaluation. I also emphasize that action, results, and evaluative judgments should emerge at each step in the process. In other words, implementation and evaluation should not wait until the end, but should be an integral and ongoing part of the process.

Step 1. Initiating and Agreeing on a Strategic Planning Process. The purpose of the first step is to negotiate agreement with key internal (and perhaps external) decision makers or opinion leaders about the overall strategic planning effort and the key planning steps. Their support and commitment are vital if strategic planning is to succeed (Olsen and Eadie, 1982). Also, involving key decision makers outside the organization usually is crucial to the success of public programs if implementation will involve multiple parties and organizations (McGowan and Stevens, 1983).

Obviously, some person or group must initiate the process. One of the initiators' first tasks is to identify exactly who the key decision makers are. The next task is to identify which persons, groups, units, or organizations should be involved in the effort. The initial agreement will be negotiated with at least some of these decision makers, groups, units, or organizations.

The agreement itself should cover the purpose of the effort; preferred steps in the process; the form and timing of reports; the role, functions, and membership of any group or committee empowered to oversee the effort; the role, functions, and membership of the strategic planning team; and commitments of necessary resources to proceed with the effort.

Step 2. Clarifying Organizational Mandates. The formal and informal mandates placed on the organization are "the *musts*" it confronts. Actually, it is surprising how few organizations know precisely what they are mandated to do and not do. Typically, few members of any organization, for example, have ever read the relevant legislation, ordinances, charters, articles, and contracts that outline the organization's formal mandates. It may not be surprising, then, that many organizations make one or both of two fundamental mistakes. Either they believe they are more tightly constrained in their actions than they are; or they assume that if they are not explicitly told to do something, they are not allowed to do it.

Step 3. Clarifying Organizational Mission and Values. An organization's mission, in tandem with its mandates, provide its *raison d'être*, the social justification for its existence. For a government corporation or agency, or for a nonprofit organization, this means there must be identifiable social or political needs that the organization seeks to fill. Viewed in this light, organizations must always be considered a means to an end, not an end in and of themselves. Communities also should not be seen as an end in themselves, but must justify their existence based on how well they meet the social and political needs of their various stakeholders, including those stakeholders' needs for a "sense of community."

Identifying the mission, however, does more than merely justify the organization's existence. Clarifying purpose can eliminate a great deal of unnecessary conflict in an organization and can help channel discussion and activity productively. Agreement on purposes defines the arenas within which the organization will compete and, at least in broad outline, charts the future course. Moreover, an important and socially justifiable mission is a source of inspiration to key stakeholders, particularly employees. Indeed, it is doubtful that any organization ever achieved greatness or excellence without a basic consensus among its key stakeholders on an inspiring mission.

Figure 1. Strategic Planning Process.

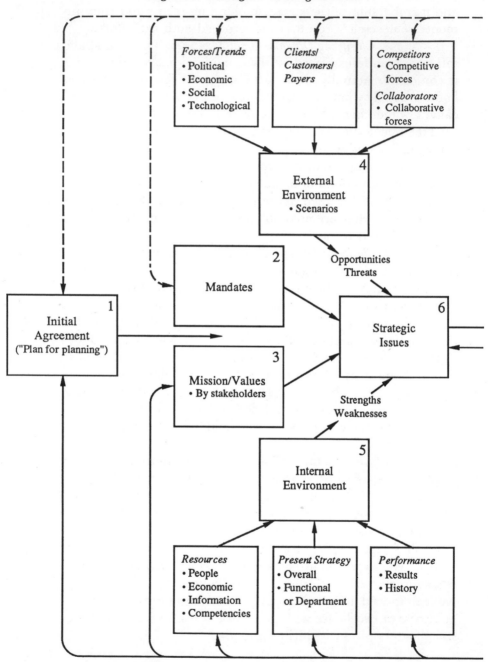

Source: Bryson and Roering, 1987, p. 10.

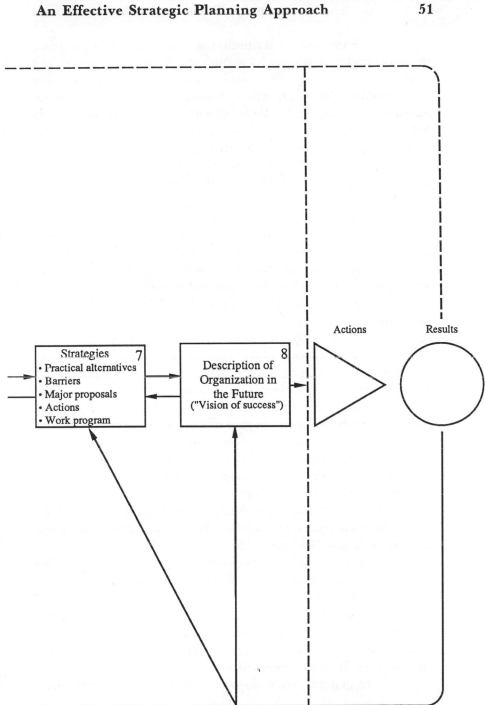

Strategies 7
• Practical alternatives
• Barriers
• Major proposals
• Actions
• Work program

Description of
Organization in
the Future
("Vision of success") 8

Actions

Results

◄— Strategy formulation | Implementation —►

Before developing a mission statement, an organization should complete a stakeholder analysis. A *stakeholder* is defined as any person, group, or organization that can place a claim on an organization's attention, resources, or output, or is affected by that output. Examples of a government's stakeholders are citizens, taxpayers, service recipients, the governing body, employees, unions, interest groups, political parties, the financial community, and other governments. Examples of a nonprofit organization's stakeholders include clients or customers, third-party payers or funders, employees, the board of directors, other nonprofit organizations providing complementary services or involved as coventurers in projects, banks holding mortgages or notes, and suppliers. Attention to stakeholder concerns is crucial because *the key to success in public and nonprofit organizations is the satisfaction of key stakeholders.*

A complete stakeholder analysis will require the strategic planning team to identify the organization's stakeholders, their stake in the organization or its output, their criteria for judging the performance of the organization, how well the organization performs against those criteria, how the stakeholders influence the organization, and in general how important the various stakeholders are. A complete stakeholder analysis also should identify what the organization needs from its various stakeholders—for example, money, staff, or political support. A stakeholder analysis will help clarify whether the organization should have different missions and perhaps different strategies for different stakeholders.

After completing the stakeholder analysis, a strategic planning team can proceed to development of a mission statement by responding to six questions.

1. Who are we as an organization (or community)? This question can be surprisingly difficult for a strategic planning team to answer succinctly.

2. In general, what are the basic social or political needs we exist to fill, or the basic social or political problems we exist to address? Again, the answer to this question provides the justification for the organization's existence.

3. In general, what do we do to recognize or anticipate

and respond to these needs or problems? This query should reveal whether the organization is active or passive, what it does to stay in touch with the needs it is supposed to fill, and in general what it does to make sure it does not become an end in itself. The answer to this question will also tell organizational members whether they will be praised or punished for bringing bad news to the organization about troubling events in the environment or critical evaluations by key stakeholders. Too many organizations shoot the messenger instead of attending to the message. Organizational members need to know they will not be punished for bringing back important but troubling information; otherwise, they will simply keep quiet and the organization will not have the benefit of useful feedback.

4. How should we respond to our key stakeholders?

5. What is our philosophy and what are our core values? Clarity about philosophy and core values will help an organization maintain its integrity. Furthermore, since only those strategies consistent with an organization's philosophy and values are likely to work, the response to this question also helps the organization choose effective strategies (Pfeiffer, Goodstein, and Nolan, 1986).

6. What makes us distinctive or unique? If there is nothing unique or distinctive about the organization, perhaps it should not exist. If it is a government corporation or agency, perhaps the private or nonprofit sectors should take over the organization's functions. If the private or nonprofit sectors fail to meet an important social or political need, perhaps a government corporation or agency should enter the field.

The mission statement itself might be very short, perhaps not more than a paragraph or a slogan. But development of the statement should grow out of lengthy discussions in response to these six questions. Complete answers to these questions actually may serve as a basic outline for a description of the organization in the future, its "vision of success," the last step in the process. But considerable intermediate work is necessary before a complete vision of success can be articulated.

Step 4. Assessing the External Environment. The planning team should explore the environment outside the organization to identify the opportunities and threats the organization faces. Basically, "inside" factors are those controlled by the organization and "outside" factors are those the organization does not control (Pfeffer and Salancik, 1978). Opportunities and threats can be discovered by monitoring a variety of political, economic, social, and technological forces and trends. PESTs is an appropriate acronym for these forces and trends, because organizations typically must change in response to them and the change can be quite painful. Unfortunately, organizations all too often focus only on the negative or threatening aspects of these changes, and not on the opportunities they present.

Besides monitoring PESTs, the strategic planning team also should monitor various stakeholder groups, including clients, customers, payers, competitors, or collaborators. The organization might construct various scenarios to explore alternative futures in the external environment, a practice typical of private sector strategic planning (Linneman and Klein, 1983).

Members of an organization's governing body, particularly if they are elected, often are better at identifying and assessing external threats and opportunities than the organization's employees. This is partly because a governing board is responsible for relating an organization to its external environment and vice versa (Thompson, 1967). Unfortunately, neither governing boards nor employees usually do a systematic or effective job of external scanning. As a result, most organizations are like ships trying to navigate treacherous waters without benefit of human lookouts or radar and sonar equipment.

Because of this, both employees and governing board members should rely on a relatively formal external assessment process. The technology of external assessment is fairly simple, and allows organizations—cheaply, pragmatically, and effectively—to keep tabs on what is happening in the larger world that is likely to have an effect on the organization and the pursuit of its mission.

Step 5. Assessing the Internal Environment. To identify internal strengths and weaknesses, the organization might monitor resources (inputs), present strategy (process), and performance (outputs). Most organizations, in my experience, have volumes of information on their inputs, such as salaries, supplies, physical plant, and full-time equivalent (FTE) personnel. They tend to have a less clear idea of their present strategy, either overall or by function. And typically they can say little, if anything, about outputs, let alone the effects those outputs have on clients, customers, or payers. For example, while schools may be able to say how many students they graduate—an output—most cannot say how "educated" those students are. The recent movement toward standardized testing of school graduates is an attempt to measure outcomes in order to remedy this shortcoming (Flynn, 1986).

The relative absence of performance information presents problems both for the organization and for its stakeholders. Stakeholders will judge the worth of an organization according to how well it does against the criteria the stakeholders—not necessarily the organization—wish to use. For external stakeholders in particular, these criteria typically relate to performance. If the organization cannot demonstrate its effectiveness against the stakeholders' criteria, then regardless of any inherent worth of the organization, stakeholders are likely to withdraw their support.

The absence of performance information may also create, and harden, major organizational conflicts. This is because without performance criteria and information, there is no way to evaluate the relative effectiveness of alternative strategies, resource allocations, organizational designs, and distributions of power. As a result, organizational conflicts are likely to occur more often than they should, serve narrow partisan interests, and be resolved in ways that do not further the organization's mission.

The difficulties of measuring performance are well known (Flynn, 1986). But regardless of the difficulties, the organization will be continually challenged to demonstrate effective performance to its stakeholders. Government leaders and staff, for example, might interpret the recent willingness of the public to limit or even decrease taxation (as seen in Proposition 13 in California, Proposition 2½ in Massachusetts, and the 1981 and 1986 federal tax cuts) as pure selfishness on the public's part.

One might also interpret these limitations on public expenditure as an unwillingness to support organizations that cannot demonstrate unequivocally effective performance.

Step 6. Identifying the Strategic Issues Facing an Organization. Together the first five elements of the process lead to the sixth, the identification of strategic issues—the fundamental policy questions affecting the organization's mandates, mission and values, product or service level and mix, clients, users or payers, cost, financing, or management.

Strategic planning focuses on achievement of the best "fit" between an organization and its environment. Attention to mandates and the external environment, therefore, can be thought of as planning from the outside in. Attention to mission and values and the internal environment can be considered planning from the inside out. Usually, it is vital that strategic issues be dealt with expeditiously and effectively if the organization is to survive and prosper. An organization that does not respond to a strategic issue can expect undesirable results from a threat, a missed opportunity, or both.

The iterative nature of the strategic planning process often becomes apparent in this step when participants find that information created or discussed in earlier steps presents itself again as strategic issues. For example, many strategic planning teams begin their task with the belief that they know what their organization's mission is. They often find out in this step, however, that a key issue is lack of clarity on exactly what the mission should be. In other words, the organization's present mission is found to be inappropriate, given the team members' new understanding of the situation the organization faces, and a new mission must be created.

Strategic issues, virtually by definition, involve conflicts of one sort or another. The conflicts may involve ends (what); means (how); philosophy (why); location (where); timing (when); and the groups that might be advantaged or disadvantaged by different ways of resolving the issue (who). In order for the issues to be raised and resolved effectively, the organization must be prepared to deal with the almost inevitable conflicts that will occur.

A statement of a strategic issue should contain three elements. First, the issue should be described succinctly, preferably in a single paragraph. The issue itself should be framed as a question that the organization can do something about. If the organization cannot do anything about it, it is not an issue—at least for the organization (Wildavsky, 1979b). An organization's attention is limited enough without wasting it on issues it cannot resolve.

Second, the factors that make the issue a fundamental policy question should be listed. In particular, what is it about mandates, mission, values, or internal strengths and weaknesses and external opportunities and threats that make this a strategic issue? Listing these factors will become useful in the next step, strategy development. Every effective strategy will build on strengths and take advantage of opportunities while it minimizes or overcomes weaknesses and threats. The framing of strategic issues therefore is very important because the framing will contain the basis for the issues' resolution.

Finally, the planning team should define the consequences of failure to address the issue. A review of the consequences will inform judgments of just how strategic, or important, various issues are. For instance, if no consequences will ensue from failure to address an issue, it is not an issue, at least not a strategic issue. At the other extreme, if the organization will be destroyed by failure to address an issue, or will miss a highly significant and valuable opportunity, the issue clearly is *very* strategic and should be dealt with immediately. The strategic issue identification step therefore is aimed at focusing organizational attention on what is truly important for the survival, prosperity, and effectiveness of the organization.

There are three basic approaches to identifying strategic issues: the direct approach, the goals approach, and the "vision of success" approach (Barry, 1986). The *direct approach* probably is the one that will work best for most governments and public agencies. It involves going straight from a review of mandates, mission, and SWOTs (strengths, weaknesses, opportunities, and threats) to the identification of strategic issues. The direct approach is best when there is no agreement on goals, or if the goals on which there is agreement are too abstract to be useful. In other words, it works best when there is no value congruence. It is best if there is no preexisting vision of success and developing a consensually based vision would be too difficult. This approach also works best when no hierarchical authority can impose goals on other actors. Finally, it is best when the environment is so turbulent that limited actions in response to issues seem preferable to development of goals and objectives or visions that may be rendered obsolete quickly. The direct approach, in other words, can work in the pluralistic, partisan, politicized, and relatively fragmented worlds of most public sector organizations (and communities), as long as there is a dominant coalition strong enough and interested enough to make it work.

The *goals approach* is more in line with conventional planning theory, which stipulates that an organization should establish goals and objectives for itself and then develop strategies to achieve them. This approach can work if there is fairly broad and deep agreement on the organization's goals and objectives, and if they are detailed and specific enough to guide the development of strategies. The approach also can be expected to work when there is a hierarchical authority structure with leaders at the top who can impose goals on the rest of the system. The strategic issues then will involve how best to translate goals and objectives into actions. This approach is more likely to work in a single-function public or nonprofit organization than in multi-organizational, multi-functional situations.

Finally, there is the *vision of success* approach, where the organization develops a "best" or "ideal" picture of itself in the future as it successfully fulfills its mission. The strategic issues then concern how the organization should move from the way it is now to how it would look and behave according to its vision. The vision of success approach is most useful if it will be difficult to identify strategic issues directly; if no detailed and specific agreed-upon goals and objectives exist and will be difficult to develop; and if drastic change is likely to be necessary. As conception precedes perception (May, 1969), development of a vision can provide the concepts to enable organizational

members to see necessary changes. This approach also is more
likely to work in a nonprofit organization than in a public sector
organization.

The statement that there are three different approaches to
the identification of strategic issues may raise the hackles of some
planning theorists and practitioners who believe one should *always*
start with either issues, or goals, or an idealized scenario for the
organization. I argue that what will work best depends on the
situation, and that the wise planner should assess the situational
factors discussed above and choose an approach accordingly.

Step 7. Formulating Strategies to Manage the Issues. A strategy
is defined as a pattern of purposes, policies, programs, actions,
decisions, or resource allocations that define what an organization is, what it does, and why it does it. Strategies can vary by
level, function, and time frame.

This definition is purposely broad, in order to focus attention on the creation of consistency across *rhetoric* (what people say), *choices* (what people decide and are willing to pay for),
and *actions* (what people do). Effective strategy formulation and
implementation processes will link rhetoric, choices, and actions
into a coherent and consistent pattern across levels, functions,
and time (Philip Bromiley, personal communication, 1986).

I favor a five-part strategy development process (to which
I was first introduced by staff of the Institute of Cultural Affairs in Minneapolis). Strategy development begins with identification of practical alternatives, and dreams or visions for
resolving the strategic issues. It is of course important to be practical, but if the organization is unwilling to entertain at least
some dreams or visions for resolving its strategic issues, it probably should not be engaged in strategic planning. In other words,
if the organization is willing to consider only minor variations
on existing strategic themes, then it probably is wasting its time
on strategic planning. After completing a strategic planning process, an organization may decide that minor variations are the
best choice, but if it *begins* the process with that assumption,
it is wasting its time with strategic planning.

Next, the planning team should enumerate the barriers
to achieving those alternatives, dreams, or visions, and not focus

directly on their achievement. A focus on barriers at this point is not typical of most strategic planning processes. But doing so is one way of assuring that any strategies developed deal with implementation difficulties directly rather than haphazardly.

Once alternatives, dreams, and visions, along with barriers to their realization, are listed, the team develops major proposals for achieving the alternatives, dreams, or visions either directly or indirectly, through overcoming the barriers. (Alternatively, the team might solicit proposals from key organizational units, various stakeholder groups, task forces, or selected individuals.) For example, a major Midwestern city government did not begin to work on strategies to achieve its major ambitions until it had overhauled its archaic civil service system. That system clearly was a barrier that had to be changed before the city government could have any hope of achieving its more important objectives.

After major proposals are submitted, two final tasks remain. Actions needed over the next two to three years to implement the major proposals must be identified. And finally, a detailed work program for the next six to twelve months must be spelled out to implement the actions.

An effective strategy must meet several criteria. It must be technically workable, politically acceptable to key stakeholders, and must accord with the organization's philosophy and core values. It should be ethical, moral, and legal. It must also deal with the strategic issue it was supposed to address. All too often I have seen strategies that were technically, politically, morally, ethically, and legally impeccable, but failed to deal with the issues they were developed to address. The strategies therefore were virtually useless.

Step 8. Establishing an Effective Organizational Vision for the Future. In the final step in the process, the organization develops a description of what it should look like as it successfully implements its strategies and achieves its full potential. This description is the organization's "vision of success" (Taylor, 1984). Few organizations have such a description or vision, yet the importance of such descriptions has long been recognized by well-managed companies (Ouchi, 1981; Peters and Waterman, 1982) and organizational psychologists (Locke, Shaw, Saari, and Latham, 1981). Typically included in such descriptions are the organization's mission, its basic strategies, its performance criteria, some important decision rules, and the ethical standards expected of all employees.

Such descriptions, to the extent that they are widely known and agreed to in the organization, allow organizational members to know what is expected of them without constant direct managerial oversight. Members are free to act on their own initiative on the organization's behalf to an extent not otherwise possible. The result should be a mobilization and direction of members' energy toward pursuit of the organization's purposes, and a reduced need for direct supervision.

Visions of success should be short—not more than several pages—and inspiring. People are inspired by a clear and forceful vision delivered with heartfelt conviction. Inspirational visions, such as Dr. Martin Luther King, Jr.'s "I Have a Dream" speech, have the following attributes: They focus on a better future, encourage hopes and dreams, appeal to common values, state positive outcomes, emphasize the strength of a unified group, use word pictures, images and metaphors, and communicate enthusiasm and excitement (Kouzes and Posner, 1987).

Some might question why development of a "vision of success" comes last in the process rather than much earlier. There are two basic answers. First, development of a vision does not have to come last. Some organizations are able to develop a fairly clearly articulated vision of success much earlier in the process.

However, most organizations will not be able to develop a vision of success until they have gone through several iterations of strategic planning—if they are able to develop a vision at all. A challenging yet achievable vision embodies the tension between what an organization *wants* and what it *can have*. Often several cycles of strategic planning are necessary before organizational members know what they want, what they can have, and how the two differ. A vision that motivates people will be challenging enough to spur action, yet not so impossible to achieve that it demotivates and demoralizes people. Most organizations, in other words, will find that their visions of success are likely to serve more as a guide for strategy implementation and less as a guide for strategy formulation.

Further, for most organizations, development of a vision of success is not *necessary* to produce marked improvements in performance. In my experience, most organizations could demonstrate a substantial improvement in effectiveness if they simply identified and resolved satisfactorily a few strategic issues. Most organizations most of the time simply do not address what is truly important; just gathering key decision makers to deal with a few important matters in a timely way would enhance organizational performance substantially.

Application Across Levels and Functions. To return to Wayne Gretzky and George Stedman, one can easily imagine them zooming almost intuitively through the eight steps, while already on the move, in a rapid series of discussions, decisions, and actions. The eight steps merely make the process of strategic thinking and acting more orderly and allow more people to participate.

The process might be applied across levels and functions in an organization as outlined in Figure 2. The application is based on the system used by the 3M Corporation (Tita and Allio, 1984). The system's first cycle consists of "bottom up" development of strategic plans within a framework established at the top, followed by reviews and reconciliations at each succeeding level. In the second cycle, operating plans are developed to implement the strategic plans. Depending on the situation, decisions at the top of the organizational hierarchy may or may not require policy board approval, which explains why the line depicting the process flow diverges at the top.

A similar cyclic system is used by Hennepin County, Minnesota (the county that contains Minneapolis), to address fourteen areas of strategic concern (for example, finance, employment and economic development, transportation, program fragmentation and coordination). The system includes three cycles: strategic issue identification, strategy development, and strategy implementation (Eckhert, Haines, Delmont, and Pflaum, 1988).

Figure 2. Annual Strategic Planning Process.

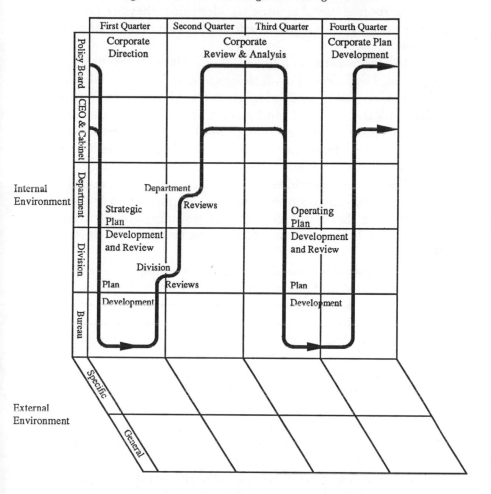

Source: Adapted from Bryson and Roering, 1987, p. 16.

Caveats. Although the steps are laid out in a linear, sequential manner, it must be emphasized that the process in practice is iterative. Participants typically rethink what they have done several times before they reach final decisions. Moreover, the process does not always begin at the beginning. Organizations typically find themselves confronted with a strategic issue that leads them to engage in strategic planning, but then they are likely to go back and begin at the beginning. In addition, implementation usually begins before all the planning is complete. As soon as useful actions are identified, they are taken—as long as they do not jeopardize future actions that might prove valuable.

In other words, in a linear, sequential process, the eight steps would be followed by decisions and actions to implement the strategies, and by evaluation of results. However, implementation typically does not, and should not, wait until the eight steps have been completed. For example, if the organization's mission needs to be redrafted, then it should be. If the SWOT analysis turns up weaknesses or threats that need to be addressed immediately, they should be. If aspects of a strategy can be implemented without awaiting further developments, they should be. And so on. Both strategic thinking *and* acting are important, and all the thinking does not have to occur before any actions are taken.

The process is applicable to public and nonprofit organizations, functions, and communities. The only general requirements are a "dominant coalition" (Thompson, 1967) willing to sponsor and follow the process, and a process champion willing to push it. Specific contingencies applicable at each step of the process will be noted in the chapters that follow.

Many organizational strategic planning teams that are familiar with and believe in the process should be able to complete it in a two- or three-day retreat, with an additional half-day meeting three to four weeks later to review the resulting strategic plan. Responsibility for preparing the plan can be delegated to a planner assigned to work with the team, or the organization's chief executive may choose to draft the plan personally. Additional time might be needed for further reviews and signoffs by key decision makers. Additional time also might be necessary to secure information or advice for specific parts of the plan, especially recommended strategies.

If the organization is fairly large, then specific linkages will be necessary to join the process to different functions and levels so that the process can proceed in an orderly and integrated manner. One effective way to achieve such a linkage is to appoint the heads of all functional departments to the strategic planning team—indeed, to make *them* the strategic planning team. All department heads then can be sure that their departments' information and interests are represented in strategy formulation, and can oversee strategy implementation in their departments.

Indeed, the key decision makers might wish to form themselves into a permanent strategic planning committee or cabinet. I certainly would recommend this approach if it appears workable for the organization, for it emphasizes the role of policy makers and line managers as strategic planners and the role of strategic planners as facilitators of decision making by the policy makers and line managers. Pragmatic and effective strategies and plans are likely to result. Temporary task forces, strategic planning committees, or a cabinet can work, but whatever the arrangement, there is no substitute for the direct involvement of key decision makers in the process.

When applied to a function that crosses organizational boundaries or to a community, the process probably will need to be sponsored by a committee or task force of key decision makers, opinion leaders, "influentials," or "notables" representing important stakeholder groups. Additional working groups or task forces probably will need to be organized at various times to deal with specific strategic issues or to oversee the implementation of specific strategies. Because so many more groups will need to be involved, and because implementation will have to rely more on consent than authority, the process is likely to be much more time-consuming than strategic planning applied to an organization.

In addition, special efforts will be necessary to make sure that important connections are made, and incompatibilities resolved, between strategic plans and the community's comprehensive plan and the various devices used to implement it, such as the government's capital improvements program, subdivision controls, zoning ordinances, and the official map. The fact that these connections must be made, however, should not unduly hamper the process. Strategic planning and comprehensive planning can be complementary, and efforts should be made to assure they are, if the community's best interests and those of its various stakeholders are to be advanced (Rider, 1983; King and Johnson, 1988).

As we noted earlier, strategic planning is likely to embrace a far more comprehensive potential agenda than comprehensive planning, to be more broadly participative, to be more emphatic about the need to understand the community's strengths and weaknesses as well as the opportunities and threats it faces, to attend to other communities' competitive behavior, to be much more flexible in its design and output, to be less legalistic in its design and execution, and to be much more action-oriented. Strategic planning thus can infuse comprehensive planning with more strategic thought and action than ordinarily would occur. In addition, strategic planning can be used to develop practical strategies to implement the vision and policies likely to be found in comprehensive plans.

Why Strategic Planning Is Here to Stay

Many managers are likely to groan at the prospect of having yet another new management technique foisted upon them. They have seen cost-benefit analysis, planning-programming-budgeting systems, zero-based budgeting, management by objectives, and a host of other techniques trumpeted by their inventors, various authors, and cadres of management consultants. They have also seen the techniques all too often fall by the wayside after a burst of initial enthusiasm by their adoptors. The managers frequently, and justifiably, feel as if they are the victims of some sort of perverse management hazing (Philip Eckhert, personal communication, 1985).

Strategic planning, however, is not just a passing fad, at least strategic planning of the sort proposed in this book. That is because the strategic planning process presented in this chapter builds on the nature of *political* decision making. So many of the other management techniques have failed because they have ignored, or tried to circumvent, or even tried to contradict the political nature of life in private, public, and nonprofit organizations. Too many planners and managers, at least in my experience, just do not understand that such a quest is almost guaranteed to be quixotic.

Most of these new management innovations have attempted to improve government decision making and operations by trying to impose a formal rationality on systems that are not rational, at least in the conventional meaning of that word. Political organizations are *politically rational,* and any technique that is likely to work well in such organizations must accept and build on the nature of political rationality (Wildavsky, 1979b).

Let us pursue this point further by contrasting two different kinds of decision making: the "rational" planning model and political decision making (R. C. Einsweiler, personal communication, 1985). The rational planning model is presented in Figure 3. It is a rational-deductive approach to decision making that begins with goals, from which are deduced policies, programs, and actions to achieve the goals. If there is traditional planning theology, this model is one of its icons. Indeed, if there were a planning Moses, Figure 3 would have been etched on his tablets when he came down from the Mount.

Figure 3. "Rational" Planning.

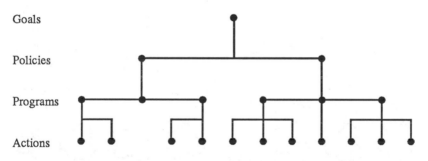

But now let us examine a fundamental assumption of the rational planning model—that in the fragmented, shared-power settings that characterize many public and nonprofit organizations and communities, there will be a *consensus* on goals, policies, programs, and actions necessary to achieve organizational aims. The assumption just does not hold. Only in fairly centralized, authoritarian, and quasi-military bureaucracies will the assumption hold—maybe.

Now let us examine a model that contrasts sharply with the rational planning model, the political decision-making model presented in Figure 4. This model is inductive, not rational-deductive. It begins with issues, which by definition involve conflict, not consensus. The conflicts may be over ends, means, timing, location, political advantage, and philosophy or reasons—and the conflicts may be severe. As efforts proceed to resolve the issues, policies and programs emerge that address the issues and that are politically rational, that is, they are politically acceptable to involved or affected parties. Over time, more general policies may be formulated to capture, frame, shape, guide, or interpret the policies and programs developed to deal with the issues. The various policies and programs are in effect treaties among the various stakeholder groups and, while they may not exactly record a consensus, at least they represent a reasonable level of agreement among stakeholders (Pfeffer and Salancik, 1978).

Figure 4. Political Decision Making.

Most general policies

More general policies

Policies and programs

Issue area

Now, recall that the heart of the strategic planning process discussed in this chapter is the identification and resolution of strategic—which is to say important—issues. The process, in other words, accepts political decision making's emphasis on issues and seeks to inform the formulation and resolution of those issues. Effective strategic planning therefore should make political decision makers more effective, and, if practiced consistently, might even make their professional lives easier. Since every key decision maker in a large public or nonprofit organization is, in effect, a political decision maker, strategic planning can help them and their organizations. Strategic planning therefore is an innovation that will last in government and nonprofit organizations. It will last because it accepts and builds on the nature of political decision making, and if done well actually improves political decisions, programs, and policies.

Now, having drawn a sharp distinction between the rational planning model and political decision making, I must emphasize that the two models are not inherently antithetical. They may simply need to be sequenced properly. The political decision-making model is necessary to work out a consensus on what programs and policies will best resolve key issues. The rational planning model can then be used to recast that consensus in the form of goals, policies, programs, and actions. While the planning and decision making that go into the formulation of a strategic plan may look fairly sloppy to an outsider, once a consensus is reached on what to do, the resulting strategic plan can be rewritten in a form that looks perfectly rational. The advantage of the strategic planning process outlined in this chapter is that it does not presume consensus where consensus does not exist.

Summary

This chapter has outlined an eight-step process for promoting strategic thinking and acting in governments, public agencies, nonprofit organizations, communities, or other entities. The steps are:

1. Initiating and agreeing on a strategic planning process.
2. Identifying organizational mandates.
3. Clarifying organizational mission and values.
4. Assessing the external environment: opportunities and threats.
5. Assessing the internal environment: strengths and weaknesses.
6. Identifying the strategic issues facing an organization.

7. Formulating strategies to manage the issues.
8. Establishing an effective organizational vision for the future, the "vision of success."

    Following these eight steps come actions, results, and evaluation—all three of which should also emerge in each step of the process. Furthermore, while the process was presented in a linear, sequential fashion, typically it proceeds iteratively as groups continuously rethink connections among the various elements in the process on their way to formulating effective strategies. A set of sample strategic planning worksheets designed to help strategic planning teams work through the process is presented in Resource A.

    Strategic planning is a management innovation that is likely to persist because, unlike many other recent innovations, it accepts and builds on the nature of *political* decision making. Raising and resolving important issues is the heart of political decision making, just as it is the heart of strategic planning. Strategic planning seeks to improve on the rawest forms of political decision making, however, by assuring that issues are raised and resolved in ways that benefit the organization and its key stakeholders.

    In the next chapter we will discuss how to negotiate an initial agreement on the purpose and process of a strategic planning effort among key internal, and perhaps external, decision makers or opinion leaders. The agreement will shape the nature and direction of discussions, decisions, and actions designed to deal with what is truly important to the organization or community.

PART II

Key Steps in Thinking and Acting Strategically

The eight-step strategic planning process is presented in detail in Part Two. It is a reasonably orderly, deliberative, and participative approach to facilitating strategic thought and action by key decision makers.

Chapter Four will cover the initial agreement phase, the "plan for planning." Chapter Five will focus on clarifying organizational mandates and mission. Chapter Six will describe the assessment of an organization's strengths and weaknesses, as well as the opportunities and threats it faces. Chapter Seven will discuss strategic issues—what they are, how they can be identified, and how to critique them. Chapter Eight will be devoted to formulating effective strategies. And Chapter Nine will cover development of the organization's "vision of success," a description of what the organization should look like as it fulfills its mission and achieves its full potential.

An organization that completes the eight steps should be well on its way toward improving and maintaining effectiveness. It should be clearly focused on satisfying its key stakeholders in ways that are politically acceptable, technically workable, and legally, morally, and ethically defensible.

Chapter 4

Initiating and Agreeing on a Strategic Planning Process

The purpose of the first step in the process is to develop among key internal decision makers or opinion leaders (and, if their support is necessary for the success of the effort, key external leaders as well) an initial agreement about the overall strategic planning effort and main planning steps.

The support and commitment of key decision makers are vital (Olsen and Eadie, 1982). But the importance of their early involvement goes beyond the need for their support and commitment. They supply information vital to the planning effort: who should be involved, when key decision points will occur, and what arguments are likely to be persuasive at various points in the process. They can provide critical resources: legitimacy, staff assignments, a budget, and meeting space.

Every strategic planning effort is in effect a story. The story must have all the ingredients: the correct setting; themes; plots and subplots; actors; scenes; a beginning, middle, and conclusion; and interpretation (Hostager and Bryson, 1986). Only key decision makers will have enough information and resources to allow for the effective development and direction of such a story.

Planning Focus and Desired Outcomes

Ideally, this step will produce agreement on four issues:

1. The worth of the strategic planning effort.
2. Organizations, units, groups, or persons who should be involved or informed.
3. Specific steps to be followed.
4. The form and timing of reports.

A strategic planning coordinating committee and a strategic planning team probably should be formed. Finally, the necessary resources to begin the endeavor must be committed.

As a general rule, the strategic planning effort should focus on that part of the organization (or function, or community) controlled or overseen by the key decision makers interested in strategic planning. In other words, only under unusual circumstances would it make sense to develop strategic plans for organizations over which the key decision makers involved have no control, or for which they have no responsibility.

Benefits of the Process

The process of reaching an initial agreement is straightforward in concept, but often rather circuitous in practice. It usually proceeds through the following stages:

1. Introducing the concept of strategic planning.
2. Developing an understanding of what it can mean in practice.
3. Thinking through some of its more important implications.
4. Developing a commitment to strategic planning.
5. Reaching an actual agreement.

The more numerous the decision makers and the less they know about strategic planning, the more time-consuming the process will be and the more indirect the route to agreement. Indeed, typically a series of agreements must be reached before the strategic planning process can begin in earnest.

A number of significant benefits flow from a good initial agreement (Delbecq, 1977). The first is simply that the worth of the strategic planning effort is likely to be widely recognized by the affected parties, leading to broad sponsorship and legitimacy. Broad sponsorship dispels any suspicion that the effort is a power play by one advocate group and ensures that the results of the effort are likely to be seen as objective, not manipulated to serve narrow partisan interests.

Legitimacy justifies the occasions, content, and timing of the discussions in the next stages of the process. Such discussions—particularly when they involve key decision makers across functions, levels, and organizational boundaries—will not occur without prompting. And they will not be prompted unless they are authorized.

This authorization is an enormous resource to the planners who organize the discussions, because they gain considerable control over the forums in which they occur, the agenda, the information provided, and the framing of the issues discussed. Typically the discussions will be cross-functional, rather than under the control of any unit or department. As facilitators of such cross-functional discussions and decisions, planners gain leverage. Control of this sort, rather than being manipulative in a partisan sense, can assure that the organization as a whole is looked at and discussed, rather than only the separate parts.

In Central City, for example, a group composed of the top nineteen executive-branch decision makers began the administration's strategic planning process. It was the first time in the memory of those present that the key decision makers of the city's executive branch had sat down together to discuss what was important for the city as a whole. Previously each had been concerned with his or her own department, and the task of looking out for the city as a whole had been left to the mayor and the city council. Adopting a citywide perspective required a change in thinking so profound that several department heads became convinced that their job descriptions should be changed.

It was precisely this kind of changed thinking that the mayor's executive assistant and the chief of police (the "planners" who had initiated the process) had hoped would emerge.

A well-articulated initial agreement also provides a clear definition of the network to be involved and the process by which it is to be maintained. The National Aeronautics and Space Administration, for example, explicitly follows a "doctrine of no surprises" as it develops its networks and moves toward major decisions. The doctrine means that major stakeholders are kept informed of progress, events, and impending decisions; nothing is dropped on them "out of the blue." When the need for cooperation and the risks of failure are high, such a doctrine appears to be quite valuable (Delbecq and Filley, 1974). The NASA approach may be the best in other situations as well, even when there seem to be good reasons for keeping certain stakeholders in the dark. In an era when a basic characteristic of information seems to be that it "leaks" (Cleveland, 1985), full and prompt disclosure may be advisable. As Ben Franklin used to say, "Three people can keep a secret if two of them are dead."

A good initial agreement will include an outline of the general sequence of steps in the strategic planning effort. The outline must ensure that the process is tied to key organizational decision points, such as budget decisions, elections, and the rhythm of the legislative cycle. Time in organizations is not linear; it is "junctural" (Leo Jakobson, personal communication, 1987). And the most important junctions are decision points.

To revert to our story metaphor, a good initial agreement will name the actors, outline the plot that is about to unfold, specify the way it will be broken into acts and scenes, designate the stage on which it will be played, and describe the general character of the story and themes to be followed.

Moreover—and this will dramatically affect the story that develops—the agreement should specify exactly what in the organization's history is to be taken as given, at least at the start. Examples of such "givens" might be existing legal commitments, mandates, personnel complements, organizational designs, mission statements, resource allocations, or job descriptions. It is very important to be clear from the start what is off

limits for the exercise; otherwise, several key decision makers
are unlikely to participate. With too much "up for grabs" the
process will be too threatening or dangerous, will result in un-
constructive or downright damaging conflict, or will produce
a strategic plan that is useless because it lacks adequate support. Of course, the more history that is taken as given, the less
useful strategic planning is likely to be. Indeed, if *everything* must
be taken as given, there is no point in engaging in strategic planning at all.

A good agreement also provides mechanisms, such as a
strategic planning task force or coordinating committee, for buffering, consultation, negotiation, or problem solving among
units, groups, or persons involved in or affected by the effort.
Without these mechanisms, conflicts are likely to stymie or even
destroy the effort (Filley, 1975; Fisher and Ury, 1981).

These mechanisms also will allow errors to be detected
and corrected as the process proceeds; a strategic planning task
force or coordinating committee can make needed midcourse
corrections. A task force also will be a valuable sounding board
for ideas.

A good initial agreement guarantees the necessary resources. Money typically is not the most needed resource for
strategic planning; the time and attention of key decision makers
are needed more. In addition, staff time will be needed to gather
information and provide logistical and clerical support, probably
one staff person part time in a small organization, several people in a larger organization.

Finally, a good initial agreement signifies the beginnings of
extensive and intensive political support from key decision makers
or opinion leaders at several levels in the organization and at
different points in the process. For strategic planning to work,
a coalition must develop that is large enough and strong enough
to formulate and implement strategies that deal effectively with
key issues. Such coalitions do not develop quickly. Instead, they
coalesce around the important strategic ideas that emerge from
the sequence of discussions, consultations, mutual education,
and reconceptualization that are at the heart of any strategic planning effort (Bryson, Van de Ven, and Roering, 1987).

Developing an Initial Agreement

So far we have covered the purpose, desired outcomes, and benefits of this first step in strategic planning. Now we can go into more depth on specific aspects of the process of developing an initial agreement.

Who Should Be Involved? Obviously someone or some group must initiate and champion the process. This person will need to decide whom to involve in the process. If the object of strategic planning is an entire organization, then the key decision makers for the organization, and perhaps some representatives of external stakeholders, should be involved. For example, the executive branch of Central City chose a two-tiered system of involvement. The first tier included nine people: the mayor, his executive assistant, and the heads of the seven major city departments. The second tier included ten people: deputies of the seven department heads and the heads of three minor city departments. Those in the first tier obviously were *the* key decision makers, but they chose to involve their deputies and other department heads in a consultative role in order to get the necessary information, support, commitment, and resources to make the strategic planning effort work for the executive branch as a whole. The group decided not to involve external stakeholder groups the first time through; they felt they needed to learn how strategic planning worked before adding the potential complications of outsiders' involvement.

If the strategic planning focus is on an organizational subunit, or on a function, or on a community, then the key decision makers for those entities, possibly with representatives of important external stakeholder groups, should be involved. For example, the initial agreement for Nursing Service's strategic planning effort was negotiated among the director of the service, the director of the department of public health (DPH), of which Nursing Service is a part, the office of the executive director of the county government of which DPH and Nursing Service are a part, all the unit and station heads within Nursing Service, the health planner assigned by DPH to assist with the effort, and the strategic planning consultant hired to provide additional support.

For strategic planning efforts focused on an organization, it may be advisable to involve (in addition to key outsiders) people from three levels of the organization: top policy and decision makers, middle management, and technical core or front line personnel (Thompson, 1967). Top policy and decision makers should be involved for several reasons. First, they are formally charged with relating the organization to its domain. Second, because of their responsibilities they are often highly effective "boundary spanners," with links to many people and organizations both inside and outside the organization (Leifer and Delbecq, 1978). Third, they often are most responsive to external threats and opportunities affecting the organization. Finally, they control the resources necessary to carry out the strategic planning effort and implement the recommendations that grow out of it. It is simply very difficult to plan around these people, so they should be included from the start, if at all possible.

In governments and public agencies, this group is likely to include members of an elected or appointed board as well as high-level executives. In council-manager cities, for example, the initial agreement typically is negotiated among council members, the city manager, and key department heads. In nonprofit organizations, the key decision-making group is likely to include the top managers and board of directors.

Middle management personnel should be included because of their vital role in translating policies and decisions into operations. Also, they are likely to bear the brunt of any managerial changes that result, and therefore should be involved to reduce unnecessary resistance and make transitions smoother (Kahn and others, 1964; Kanter, 1983).

Technical core or front line personnel also may need to help fashion an initial agreement. Again, there are several reasons to involve them. First, they are in charge of the day-to-day use of the core technologies contributing to, or affected by, strategic change, and so they are likely to be either hurt or helped by change. Early involvement may be necessary to assure that strategic changes can be made operational, or at least to minimize resistance. Second, technical or front line personnel will probably be asked for their opinions by key decision makers in any event, so anything that can make them receptive to strategic change is a plus. Finally, because of their technical knowledge or daily contact with customers, clients, or users, these people can be very severe and effective challengers of strategic changes adopted without their support. In extreme cases they might undermine or even sabotage change efforts. Getting their cooperation early can be an important key to strategic planning success.

An important caveat is in order. If it is clear from the start that strategic planning will result in the elimination of certain positions, work groups, or departments, then it may be both unnecessary and counterproductive to involve those positions. The effective and humane approach may be to involve these people in planning for their transition to new jobs, including retraining, placement, and severance arrangements.

How to Get Started. If an organization is the focus of attention, often the best way to reach initial agreement is to hold a retreat that begins with an introduction to the nature, purpose, and process of strategic planning. Often key decision makers need such an introduction before they are willing fully to endorse a strategic planning effort. Orientation and training methods might include lecture-discussions; case presentations by representatives of organizations that use strategic planning, followed by group discussion; analysis by key decision makers of written case studies followed by group discussion; circulation of reading materials; or strategy films.

A possible format for the first day of a strategic planning retreat is:

Morning: lecture-discussion about the nature, purpose, and process of strategic planning.

Lunch: presentation from a representative of a similar organization that engages in strategic planning, highlighting the benefits and liabilities of the process.

Afternoon: analysis and discussion of a written strategic planning case study, plus instruction in any special techniques necessary for successful strategic planning, such as brainstorming, the nominal group technique (Delbecq, Van de Ven, and Gustafson, 1975), or the snow card technique (Greenblat and Duke, 1981).

By the end of the first day it should be clear whether or not the key decision makers wish to proceed. If so, the second day might be organized as follows:

Morning: stakeholder analysis, followed by development of a draft mission statement.
Lunch: a speaker presenting another case example.
Afternoon: SWOT analysis and discussion.

The retreat might end at this point, after next steps have been mapped out consensually, or it might continue for a third day. The morning of the third day can be devoted to identifying and discussing strategic issues, and the afternoon to establishing priorities among them and specifying how they will be addressed. The retreat should not end until agreement is reached on what the next steps in the process will be and who will be responsible for what in each step.

If a group can reach quick agreement at each point, less than three days might be sufficient. If quick agreement is not possible, more time may be necessary, and sessions may have to be spread out over several weeks.

If a community is the focus of attention, a retreat also might help key decision makers reach agreement about the nature of the strategic planning effort. Such a retreat, however, might be very difficult to organize. More groundwork probably would be necessary to reach agreement on the purposes, timing, and length of the retreat. The retreat itself probably would have to be shorter than three days, and post-retreat logistics, coordination, and followthrough would probably take more time and effort. Nonetheless, a retreat can provide an important signal and symbol that the community is about to address its most important issues and concerns; can provoke desirable media attention and pressure to continue; and can prompt other stakeholders, who might have been more lukewarm about the process, to participate.

How Many "Initial" Agreements? Sometimes sequential agreements among successively larger groups of key decision makers may be necessary before everyone is on board. Central City's executive branch actually had two "initial" agreements.

The first agreement involved the mayor's executive assistant, the chief of police, and a strategic planning consultant. Both the executive assistant and the chief of police had attended seminars led by the consultant and had concluded that the executive branch would benefit from strategic planning; they convinced the first tier of key decision makers to attend a three-day strategic planning retreat. The first day of the retreat was a training and orientation session, after which the group would decide whether to proceed with strategic planning. They did decide to proceed; they completed the three-day retreat and a followup half-day retreat, adopted the consultant's recommendations for a strategic planning system, and formed themselves into a cabinet that now meets regularly to oversee strategic and operational issues for the executive branch as a whole.

What Should the Agreement Contain? The initial agreement should cover the desired outcomes listed at the beginning of this chapter: agreement that the strategic planning effort is worth trying; agreement on the organizations, units, groups, or persons who should be involved; a shared understanding about the nature and sequence of the steps in the process; and agreement on the form and timing of reports.

Next, a committee probably should be established to oversee the strategic planning effort, headed by someone with enough standing and credibility to assure that the effort is given visibility and legitimacy. Ideally, this person should be trusted by all or most factions in the organization so the effort is not seen as a narrow partisan affair. The committee can be an existing group, such as a board of directors or city council, that adds strategic planning oversight to its responsibilities, or it can be a committee or task force established for the specific purpose. (Central City's executive branch combined these approaches. The executive branch's key decision makers first formed themselves into a task force to explore strategic planning, and then, when they decided to go ahead with it, formed themselves into a permanent cabinet to oversee the effort.) The oversight committee probably will be the body with whom the initial agreement is formulated, although it may be necessary to work out agreements first with various groups and factions who then send representatives to sit on the oversight body.

Next, a team to carry out the staff work probably will be necessary. The team should include planners and change advocates but also helpful critics, to make sure that difficulties that arise are recognized and constructively addressed. For example, Central City's team at first comprised the mayor's executive assistant and a consultant. Later, specific tasks were assigned to individuals or task forces supervised by the mayor's executive assistant.

Finally, the necessary resources to begin the endeavor must be committed. Obtaining needed financial resources may not be difficult, since they will be relatively minor in comparison with an organization's overall budget. The more important—and typically scarce—resources are the attention and involvement of key decision makers. Depending on the scale of the effort, strategic planning may demand from five to twenty-five days of attention from each key decision maker over the course of a year—in other words, up to 10 percent of ordinary work time. Is it too much? Not for what is truly important for the organization. If there is not enough time for everything, then something else—not strategic planning—should go.

The end of this first step typically is the first major decision point in the process, if the organization (or community) is large, if the situation is complex, and if many people need to be involved. (If the organization is small, few people are involved, and the situation is simple, the first major decision point will come later, although precisely when will depend on the situation.) If agreement is reached on the various content items, then it makes sense to go ahead with the process. If agreement is not reached, then either the effort can go on anyway—with little likelihood of success—or else this step should be repeated until an effective agreement can be worked out.

It usually makes sense to repeat the step, or else to scale down the effort to focus on a smaller area where agreement is possible. Part of the scaled-down effort might be to develop effective strategies to involve the other parts later.

Process Guidelines

The following process guidelines may be helpful in development of the initial agreement for a strategic planning effort.

1. Some person or group must initiate and champion the process. Strategic planning doesn't just happen; involved, courageous, and committed people make it happen. In each of our cases the process worked in large part because there were people, usually key decision makers and leaders, who championed the process (also see Kotler, 1976, p. 200; Maidique, 1980; Kanter, 1983, p. 296). They believed in the process, and were committed to it, not to any preconceived answers. They may have had good hunches about what might emerge, but their main belief was that following the process would produce good answers. Indeed, they were willing to be surprised by the answers that emerged. The champions were not necessarily the initiators, but they often were. For example, the initiators of Nursing Service's strategic planning process included the county's executive director, but he was not a champion; Nursing Service's director and the health planner were the champions.

2. Some person or group must sponsor the process to give it legitimacy. Sponsoring a strategic planning process is different from championing it, although sponsors and champions may be the same people. Sponsorship provides legitimacy; championship provides the energy and commitment to follow through. Early sponsors may be very different from later sponsors. In the case of Nursing Service, for example, the county board became a sponsor long after the process was initiated and after the executive director had been forced to resign. The strategic planning coordinating committee or task force discussed below often serves as the legitimizing, sponsoring body.

3. Decide whether a detailed, jointly negotiated initial agreement is needed. An informal understanding may suffice when the organization is small, few people need to be involved, and the situation faced is relatively straightforward. Conversely, a detailed, jointly negotiated initial agreement is likely to be needed if the organization is large, many people need to be involved, and the situation is complex, or if a strategic plan for a community is to be developed.

A formal contract is probably unnecessary (except, of course, for contracts with outside consultants), but someone should prepare a written memorandum that outlines the content of the agreement, including statements on the following items: the worth of the effort; organizations, units, groups, or persons who should be involved; steps to be followed; form and timing of reports; role, functions, and membership of a strategic planning coordinating committee; role, functions, and membership of the strategic planning team; and commitment of necessary resources to begin the effort. The agreement might be summarized in a chart and distributed to all planning team members. An example is Table 2, which outlines the basics of Health Center's initial agreement.

4. Form a strategic planning task force or coordinating committee, if one is needed. If the organization is small, few people need to be involved, and the situation is easy to comprehend, then such a task force or committee probably will not be needed. But if the organization is large, many people need to be involved, and the situation is complex, then a task force or committee probably should be appointed.

Such a group, however, should not be formed too early. It is easier to include someone later, after the committee is formed, than it is to drop a troublesome participant who is already a member. Consult with trusted advisers before inviting people to participate.

Also keep in mind that there is a big difference between giving people a seat on a committee and consulting with them as part of the process. People can supply a great deal of information and advice—and legitimacy for the process—without actually having a vote on a committee. Unless membership in the committee is limited, it may balloon in size and become unmanageable and unproductive.

If an organization is the focus of attention, the coordinating committee might include: top-level decision makers, mid-level managers, technical and professional opinion leaders, outside resource persons, representatives of key stakeholder groups, process experts, and critics. Remember, however, there is a tradeoff between a broadly representative committee—which may be large—and an effective body—which probably should number no more than nine. Two groups may in fact be necessary: a large representative and legitimizing body, and a smaller

Table 2. Strategic Planning Process: Health Center.

Steps	Responsible
1. Get agreement on planning steps.	Executive director Board chair Consultant

Meeting 1 *(5-hour meeting with board and key staff)*:

Steps	Responsible
2. Orient board and staff to strategic planning.	Consultant
3. Do situation analysis: History and present situation Mission Opportunities and threats Strengths and weaknesses Critical issues for the future	Participants Consultant
4. Form board/staff team to complete the plan.	Board chair Executive director
5. Summarize situation analysis (between meetings).	Executive director Consultant

Meeting 2 *(2 hours)*:

Steps	Responsible
6. Develop scenarios for the future (scenario approach). Develop scenarios. Note areas of agreement and choices.	Planning team Consultant
7. Summarize scenarios and choices (between meetings).	Executive director Consultant
8. Gather information to test feasibility of scenarios (between meetings).	Executive director

Meeting 3 *(2 hours)*:

Steps	Responsible
9. Evaluate scenarios (e.g., fit with mission, fit with needs, financial feasibility). Select the best scenario.	Planning team Consultant
10. Develop first draft of strategic plan. Include sections on mission, services, staffing, finances, facilities, and implementation (between meetings).	Executive director Consultant

Meeting 4 *(2 hours)*:

Steps	Responsible
11. Review first draft. Note suggested improvements.	Planning team Consultant
12. Revise first draft (between meetings).	Executive director Consultant

Table 2. Strategic Planning Process: Health Center, Cont'd.

Steps	Responsible
Review, adopt, and implement plan:	
13. Review second draft with	
Board	Board chair
Staff	Executive director
2–3 outsiders	Executive director
Note reactions and suggestions for improvement.	
14. Review reactions and make needed revisions; prepare final draft.	Planning team Consultant
15. Adopt plan.	Board
16. Implement plan. Review progress every 6 months. Update plan yearly.	Executive director Board
Total meeting time, including review sessions: 18–20 hours. Time to develop plan: 3 months.	

Source: Barry, 1986, p. 26.

executive committee that engages in the most extensive discussions and makes recommendations to the larger group. If a community is the focus of attention, a large, representative, and legitimizing body could coordinate the process and smaller representative bodies could attend to specific issue areas.

5. If a coordinating committee is formed, use it as a mechanism for consultation, negotiation, problem solving, or buffering among organizations, units, groups, or people involved. The committee is likely to be the body that officially legitimizes the initial agreement and makes subsequent decisions, although it also may serve as an advisory body to the "official" decision makers. For example, Nursing Service's strategic planning committee acted as an advisory body to the director of the service, who in turn made recommendations to the director of the public health department and the county's executive director.

Committee decisions should be recorded in writing and probably should be circulated to key stakeholder groups. It is possible that the committee should include more than one representative from each key stakeholder group, so that a clearer picture of stakeholder preferences, interests, and concerns emerges. Also, if the group is to be a standing committee that oversees annual strategic planning efforts, it probably is wise to rotate membership to keep new ideas flowing and widen involvement in the process.

You will not necessarily be asking for a major commitment of time from committee members, but they should expect to spend from five to twenty-five days on strategic planning over the course of a year. And that time must be "quality" time, typically away from the office, and concentrated in one- to three-day blocks.

6. The process is likely to flow more smoothly and effectively if the coordinating committee and any other policy board that is involved are effective policy-making bodies. Recall that strategic planning has been defined as a disciplined effort to produce fundamental decisions and actions that shape and guide what an organization is, what it does, and why it does it. It is hard to produce those decisions unless the process is overseen by effective policy-making bodies.

Effective policy-making bodies (Carver, 1986):

- Focus most of their attention on their policy-making role.
- Have a mission statement that clearly states their purposes as a policy-making body.
- Discipline themselves to focus on policy making.
- Establish a set of policy objectives for the organization, function, or community they oversee.
- Control managers primarily through the questions they ask; the general form of these questions is "How does this recommendation (proposal, strategy, budget) serve these purposes, values, or policies?"
- Concentrate their resources to be more effective as policy makers.
- Have staff help them become better policy makers.
- Rely on various media (newsletters, press announcements, videos) to transmit information to the media, employees, and other key stakeholders.

- Hold periodic retreats to develop strategic plans and work programs for subsequent years.

Not many public or nonprofit organizations, functions, or communities are governed by effective policy-making bodies. A strategic issue that often arises therefore is how to make the governing bodies more effective policy-making bodies. An influential group of members on Central City's city council decided that the most important strategic issue faced by the council was how to become a more effective policy-making body. We will see later that Suburban City's city council came to virtually the same conclusion. Thus for both city councils, a major focus of strategic planning was on how to increase the capacity of the organization (or function, or community) to produce fundamental decisions.

7. Form a strategic planning team if one is needed. In theory, a team would be assigned the task of facilitating decision making by the strategic planning coordinating committee. The team would gather information, advise, and produce recommendations for committee action. The committee would legitimize the process, provide guidance to the team, and make decisions on team-produced recommendations. In practice, a team may or may not be formed and may or may not serve as facilitators of decision making by a coordinating committee.

A team may not be needed if the organization (or community) is small, few people need to be involved in the effort, and the situation is relatively easy to handle. In these cases, a single planner, perhaps with the assistance of an outside consultant, probably will suffice.

On the other hand, if the organization is large, many people need to be involved, and the situation is complex, a team probably will be necessary. Most of the team members probably will not need to work full time on the effort, except for brief periods. But formation of a team brings many different skills to bear at important times. The team should be headed by an organizational statesperson and should include members skilled in boundary spanning, process facilitation, technical analysis, advocacy, and self-criticism. A team almost certainly will be needed if a large community is the focus of attention.

Whether the team actually does much of the strategic planning itself or facilitates strategic planning by key decision makers
will depend on several factors. If team members actually possess
most of the information needed to prepare the plan, and if they
hold positions of substantial power, then they may go ahead
and prepare the plan themselves. In this situation the planners
are themselves the key decision makers. On the other hand, if
a number of key decision makers already possess much of the
necessary information, and if the planners are not themselves
powerful by virtue of their position or person, then the planners will need to serve primarily as facilitators of the process.

In my experience, planners typically can be of greatest
service as facilitators of cross-functional and cross-level planning, policy making, and decision making by key decision
makers. On the other hand, planners must have at least some
substantive knowledge of the topic areas under discussion to be
good facilitators. A blend of process skill and content knowledge
thus is typically required of strategic planners and strategic planning teams; the specific proportions of process and content vary
by situation.

The government of Hennepin County, Minnesota, is a
large and complex organization, with 8,000 employees and annual revenues of almost $700 million. The county's strategic
planning effort is staffed by planners from the county's office
of planning and development. Two planners work full time on
the process, twenty others part time. The part-time team members primarily provide facilitation and staff support to task forces
charged with developing and implementing strategies for specific
issues (Eckhert, Haines, Delmont, and Pflaum, 1988).

Once you have decided that a strategic planning team is
needed, you can turn your attention to procedures that will make
the team more effective. First, to recruit skilled, committed team
members, you may need to use special hiring, transferring, or
compensating procedures. If people cannot see how their careers
can be helped by participating on the team, they are not likely
to join voluntarily. If the assignment is temporary, people must
be assured that they can return to their old job—or an even better
one—when the effort is completed. Second, clear and good work-

ing relationships must be negotiated among team members and supervisors. Third, the team should meet frequently and communicate effectively.

In the case of strategic planning for a community, the team or teams may have many volunteer members. Personnel hiring, transfer, and compensation procedures may not be an issue for volunteers, but clear and good working relationships and effective communication are likely to be very important.

8. Key decision makers may need orientation and training about the nature, purpose, and process of strategic planning before they can negotiate an initial agreement.

9. A sequence of "initial" agreements may be necessary, involving a successively expanding group of key decision makers, before a full-scale strategic planning effort can proceed.

10. In complex situations, the initial agreement will be the first big decision point. If an effective agreement cannot be reached among key decision makers, then the effort should not proceed. The initiators may want to try again or focus on areas in which key decision makers can reach agreement. In relatively simple situations, the first major decision points are likely to be reached later in the process, although precisely when will depend on the particular situation.

Summary

The initial agreement essentially is an understanding among key internal (and perhaps external) decision makers or opinion leaders about the overall strategic planning effort. The agreement should cover: the worth of the effort; persons, units, groups, or organizations to be involved; steps to be followed; form and timing of reports; role, functions, and membership of strategic planning committee members, if such a committee is formed; role, functions, and membership of strategic planning team members, if one is formed; and commitment of necessary resources to begin the effort.

The importance of an initial agreement is highlighted by viewing every strategic planning effort as a story that raises and resolves the most important questions an organization faces. For such a story to have a successful ending, the agreement needs to sketch out the setting, themes, plots and subplots, actors, scenes, beginning, climax, conclusion, and final interpretation. As the tale itself unfolds, content and detail will be added to this sketch, making it a rich and instructive drama, lived by the actors. In the absence of such an agreement, the story may never reach a climax or conclusion, and interpretation will be impossible.

An effective initial agreement helps planners raise and resolve key issues through discussions and decisions around which effective political coalitions can coalesce. Otherwise, issues and answers are likely to flow randomly through the organization, disconnected from the resources and decisions necessary for effective action (Cohen, March, and Olsen, 1972). Organizational survival, let alone effectiveness, will itself become random, and key decision makers will have abdicated their responsibility to focus on organizational purposes (Selznick, 1957).

In the next chapter we will move to Steps 2 and 3 in the process: the identification of mandates, and the clarification of mission and values. The two together stipulate the organizational purposes to be strategically pursued.

Chapter 5

Clarifying Organizational Mandates and Mission

If you don't know where you're going, any plan will do.
Peter Drucker

Three outstanding attitudes—obliviousness to the
growing disaffection of constituents, primacy of self
aggrandizement, and the illusion of invulnerable
status—are persistent aspects of folly.
Barbara Tuchman, March of Folly

For your information, let me ask you a few questions.
Sam Goldwyn

Mandates

This chapter will cover Steps 2 and 3, the identification of mandates and the clarification of mission and values. Together they provide the social justification for an organization's existence.

Although Step 3 is usually the more time-consuming of the two, it is not more important. Before an organization can define its mission and values, it must know exactly what it is *required* to do and not do by external authorities. These requirements are likely to be codified in laws, ordinances, articles of incorporation, or charters, and so may be easier to uncover and clarify than the organization's mission. Organizations often also face informal mandates, typically embodied in norms, that are no less binding.

Purpose and Outcomes. The purpose of Step 2 is to identify and clarify the nature and meaning of the externally imposed mandates, both formal and informal, affecting the organization. Three outcomes should be sought from this step:

1. Compilation of the formal and informal mandates faced by the organization.
2. Interpretation of what is required as a result of the mandates.
3. Clarification of what is not ruled out by the mandates, that is, the rough boundaries of the unconstrained field of action.

Clarification of what is not ruled out is particularly important. Alerting organizational members to what they *might* do can lead to valuable discussions about what the organization's mission ought to be. Too many organizations think they are more constrained than they actually are and, indeed, make the fundamental error of assuming that their mandates and mission are the same. They may be, but planners should not start out with that assumption.

Two units from the same county government prove instructive in this regard—Nursing Service and the county's department of corrections. Nursing Service is statutorily required only to prevent and control communicable diseases and to make its services available to all regardless of ability to pay. It does both. But it also does much more—providing, for example, the most cost-effective home health care service in the county, a variety of public health education services, a set of decentralized health clinics, and advocacy on behalf of the public health needs of the county's citizens. If Nursing Service staff had limited themselves only to communicable disease control, the people of the county might be worse off.

Corrections, on the other hand, is required statutorily to provide detention, probation, parole, and rehabilitation services for people who have run afoul of the law. They have chosen to interpret this mandate as meaning that is all they *can* do. They therefore will engage in no preventive services to keep individuals from needing detention, probation, parole, and rehabilitation. Given the department's resource constraints, and perhaps a desire not to infringe on the county's department of community services, perhaps such a choice is wise. On the other hand, Corrections has deliberately decided, for whatever reasons, that it will do no analyses to determine whether it might provide cost-effective preventive services to reduce the need for corrections services. In other words, Corrections has decided that corrections and prevention are two sharply different tasks, and that prevention is someone else's job. As a result, the people of the county may be worse off.

Benefits and Guidelines. There are two potential benefits of Step 2. First, clarity about what is mandated will increase the likelihood that mandates actually will be met. Research indicates that one of the most important determinants of goal achievement is the clarity of the goals themselves. The more specific the goal, the more likely it is to be achieved (Locke and others, 1981; Mazmanian and Sabatier, 1983; Boal and Bryson, 1987a). Second, the possibility of developing a mission that is not limited to mandates is enhanced. People are helped to examine the *potential* purposes of organizational action by knowing what is not explicitly forbidden.

The process guidelines for this step are straightforward:

1. Have someone compile the formal and informal mandates faced by the organization.
2. Review the mandates in order to clarify what is required and what is allowed.
3. Regularly remind organizational members what the organization is required to do, as a way of assuring conformity with the mandates.

In other words, institutionalize attention to the mandates. Certainly annual reports, staff retreats, and orientation sessions for new employees should include a section (perhaps a very brief one) on mandates. Other methods might prove useful as well.

Mission

The first two quotes that open this chapter highlight in different ways the importance of mission to organizational success. Peter Drucker emphasizes that without a sense of purpose we are quite literally lost. Mission provides that sense of purpose. In addition, it can be very helpful (although not always necessary or possible) to expand that mission into a "vision of success." Without a vision of success, organizational members may not know enough about how to fulfill the mission. Mission, in other words, clarifies an organization's *purpose,* or *why* it should be doing what it does; vision clarifies *what* it should look like and *how* it should behave as it fulfills its mission. This chapter concentrates on mission; Chapter Ten will discuss constructing a vision of success. For now it is enough to note simply that the foundation of any good vision is an organization's mission statement.

The quote from Barbara Tuchman makes a different point: any organization that becomes an end in itself is doomed to failure. One need only recall the fall in 1986 of the government of Ferdinand Marcos in the Philippines or, on a less grand scale, the announcement of Lyndon B. Johnson in 1968 that he would not run for reelection, to see how disregard for constituents' desires, self-aggrandizement, and illusions of invulnerability can lead to disaster.

Purpose and Outcomes. Ultimately strategic planning is about purpose, meaning, values, and virtue, and nowhere is this more apparent than in the clarification of mission and the subsequent development of a vision of success. The aim of mission clarification is to specify the purposes of the organization and the philosophy and values that guide it. Unless these purposes focus on socially useful and justifiable ends, and unless the philosophy and values are themselves virtuous, the organization cannot hope to command indefinitely the resources needed to survive, including high-quality, loyal, and committed employees (Selznick, 1957).

Step 3 has two main desired outcomes: a stakeholder analysis and a mission statement. A stakeholder analysis provides useful information and valuable preparation for a mission statement. Agreement on the stakeholder analysis and mission statement by key decision makers should clarify the organization's arena of action and many of the basic rules of the game within that arena. In addition, the agreement on mission, particularly if it is consensual, will of itself be a source of power for the organization (Pfeffer, 1981). Finally, agreement on an organizational mission that embraces socially desirable and justified purposes should produce enthusiasm, even excitement, among organizational members.

Benefits. A number of benefits flow from clarifying and agreeing on the organization's mission. Perhaps the most important benefit is simply that developing the statement begins a habit of focusing discussion on what is truly important. Too often key decision makers in a public or nonprofit organization never come together to discuss cross-functional issues or, more important, the organization as a whole. You may recall that Central City's strategic planning retreat was the first time in anyone's memory when all the key executive-branch decision makers had gotten together to discuss anything important affecting the city as a whole. And Central City certainly is not unique in this regard.

Often, if key decision makers do gather—for example, at a staff meeting—most of their time is taken up with announcements or relatively trivial matters, such as allocating parking spaces or scheduling floating holidays. Such discussions may serve to introduce key decision makers to one another, and may provide some of the social glue necessary to hold any organization together, but they are relatively useless and may in fact be a colossal waste of everyone's time.

The second important benefit, of course, is the clarification of organizational purpose. Since definition of mission may be thought of as the central function of leadership, more effective leadership is another benefit (Selznick, 1957). Clarity of purpose helps leaders in other ways too. In particular, a basis for embodying purpose into structures and systems, including the resource allocation system, will be established. In addition, leaders will be helped to order internal conflict, so that conflict furthers organizational ends. Leaders are required to guide the play of the game within the structure of the rules, but they also need to change the rules on occasion. Clarity of purpose provides a valuable basis for guiding conflict productively and for understanding which rules help with that task and which need to be changed.

A key point here is that organizational conflicts typically are about something other than what is nominally in dispute;

for resolution, the conflict must be reframed at a higher level of abstraction (Watzlawick, Weakland, and Fisch, 1974). Terry (1981), for example, describes a hierarchy with organizational purposes at the top, then power, structures and systems, and finally resources. He argues that disputes at any level in this hierarchy typically are really about what is at the next level up. Power struggles thus are usually ultimately about the purposes the power is to serve. Arguments about organizational structures and systems really are about who is empowered or disempowered by different designs. Disputes over resources typically are about how the use of those resources should be regulated in structures and systems. A focus on purpose—to the extent that there is agreement on it—therefore can frame most of these conflicts in such a way that they facilitate pursuit of organizational ends.

Agreement on purpose can also help parties in a conflict disconnect ends from means and thus be clear about what problems are to be addressed before solutions can be explored. This is advantageous because most conflicts typically are about solutions; that is, there usually is no agreement about what the problems are that the solutions are meant to solve (Filley, 1975). Further, the organization cannot really know what problems it ought to address without some sense of the purpose it serves. Once an organization understands its purpose, it can define the problems it is meant to solve and can better understand how to choose among competing solutions.

Agreement on purpose therefore gets the organization to approach conflict resolution in an effective sequence: agree on purposes, identify problems, and then explore and agree on solutions. The likelihood that successful solutions will be found is increased because the sequence narrows the focus to fulfillment of the mission, but broadens the search for acceptable solutions to include all that would further the mission.

Agreement on purpose provides a very powerful means of social control. To the extent that the purposes are socially justified and virtuous, agreement will invest organizational discussions and actions with a moral quality that can constrain self-serving and organizationally destructive behavior by organizational members. Said differently, agreement on purpose can lead to a mobilization of organizational energies based on pursuit of a morally justifiable mission beyond self-interest.

Another benefit of this step is the explicit attention given to philosophy and values. Organizations rarely discuss these matters directly. As a result they are likely to misread their strengths and weaknesses and therefore will make mistakes in the internal assessment step to come. Also, without understanding their philosophy and values, organizations are likely to make serious errors in the strategy formulation step. They may choose strategies that are not consonant with their philosophy and values and that therefore are doomed to failure.

Finally, by answering the six questions outlined below, the organization will be well on its way to developing a clear vision of success. Indeed, answers to the six questions may provide organizational members with the conception that must precede any actual perceptions of success (Mitroff, 1978; May, 1969).

Stakeholder Analyses. A stakeholder analysis is a valuable prelude to a mission statement, a SWOT analysis, and effective strategies. It is important because the key to success in the public and nonprofit sectors—and the private sector, too, for that matter—is the satisfaction of key stakeholders. If an organization does not know who its stakeholders are, what criteria they use to judge the organization, and how the organization is performing against those criteria, there is little likelihood that the organization (or community) will know what it should do to satisfy its key stakeholders.

Two examples may prove instructive at this point. The first comes from the division of fisheries and wildlife of the department of natural resources in a Midwestern state. The department (as the state's agent) is one of the major landowners in the United States and manages a vast array of water, forest, mineral, and land resources, in addition to huge populations of fish and wildlife. The fish and wildlife resources are important to in-state and out-of-state anglers and hunters and to the large recreational and tourist industry that depends on them. Something like a quarter of the state's people identify themselves

as anglers and hunters, and an almost equal number enter the
state each year to fish and hunt.

You would think that the division of fisheries and wildlife
would be one of the most protected and supported units of state
government, that legions of interest groups—from the National
Rifle Association, to resort industry groups, to recreational
equipment dealer associations—would be continually lobbying
state legislators and the governor to maintain, if not increase,
public financial support for the division. Until recently such was
most emphatically not the case. Indeed, quite the opposite. The
division has been under frequent attack from its stakeholders.
They argued that the division saw itself primarily as a regulator
of (or naysayer to) stakeholders, and was completely uninterested
in stakeholder satisfaction.

The division decided to engage in strategic planning to
turn around an increasingly bad situation. One of the first steps
was a stakeholder analysis. The most important piece of information to emerge from that analysis was that the professionals
in the division operated under the mistaken assumption that
their prime stakeholders were fish and deer! They felt their job
was to regulate anglers and hunters, so that the state's fish and
wildlife resources could be protected and managed for the long
term.

There would have been little problem with this view—if
the fish and deer could vote, spend money, and pay taxes. But
they do not. Anglers, hunters, and their families do, along with
the owners of resorts and sporting goods establishments. While
maintenance of fish and wildlife resources obviously is one criterion anglers and hunters use to judge the performance of the
division, there are many more, and the division was failing to
meet them. The result was hostility on the part of stakeholders
and attempts in the legislature to cut the division's budget and
curtail its powers. As a result of insights gained from their stakeholder analysis, the division is pursuing several strategies to increase stakeholder satisfaction.

The second example is from a primarily government-
funded nonprofit arts organization that also faced substantial
budget cuts. A stakeholder analysis uncovered a similar mistaken

assumption: that artwork—paintings, music, sculpture, dance, and so on—were the agency's key stakeholders. The agency did not think of artists, audiences, taxpayers, or other people, groups, and organizations as its key stakeholders. No wonder it faced hostility from its stakeholders and attempts by the government funders to cut its budget!

The first step in a stakeholder analysis is to identify exactly who the organization's stakeholders are. Figure 5 presents a typical stakeholder map for a government. The stakeholders are numerous; indeed, many organizations would have even more than are listed there, though others might identify fewer. For example, Central City Council listed twenty-seven, Nursing Service identified fifteen, and Suburban City listed seven.

Three additional points should be made about this figure. First, the diagram makes clear that any organization, but especially a government, is an arena in which individuals and groups contest for control of its attention, resources, and output (Pfeffer and Salancik, 1978). A major purpose of a stakeholder analysis is to get a more precise picture of the players in the arena. Second, special note should be made of future generations. Governments have an obligation to leave the world in as good shape as they found it—if not better. It is important in this era of special interest groups to keep this public trust in mind. As Theodore Roosevelt said, "We don't inherit the earth from our ancestors, we borrow it from our children."

Third, it is very important for key employee groups to be explicitly identified. Not all employees are the same. Different groups with different roles to play will use different criteria to judge organizational performance. Clarity about these groups is necessary to assure organizational responses sufficiently differentiated to satisfy each group.

Nursing Service presents an interesting example in this regard. It was very difficult to get the nurses of Nursing Service to name themselves as key stakeholders. Their self-effacing and altruistic view of themselves as public servants was admirable, but misplaced. By definition they are key stakeholders of Nursing Service and their own satisfaction is important to the success of the service. Furthermore, several of the key criteria

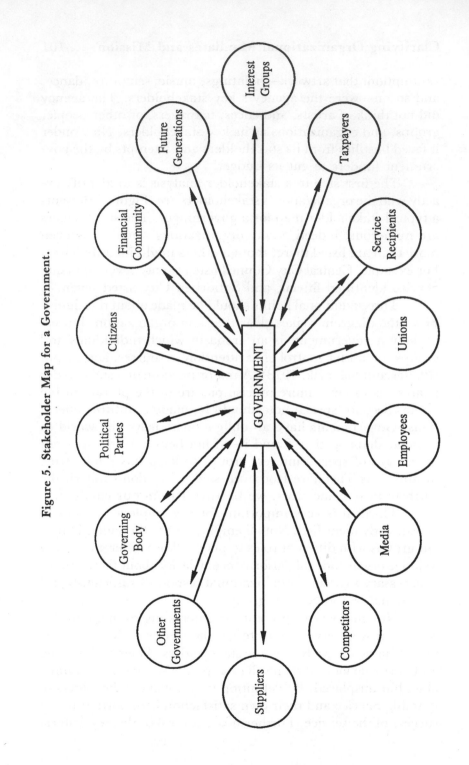

Figure 5. Stakeholder Map for a Government.

they use to judge organizational performance relate to the professional standards the service does or does not meet. In other words, it is the professional nurses themselves, not other stakeholders, who hold the organization to exacting professional standards of service.

The second step in the analysis is to specify the criteria the stakeholders use to assess the organization's performance. There are two approaches to this task. One is to guess what the criteria are; the second is ask the stakeholders themselves. The strategic planning team should always make its own guesses, but at some point it may prove instructive and politically useful to ask stakeholders (for example, through surveys, interviews, or group discussions) what their professed criteria are.

Why should the team always make its own guesses? For one thing, it is faster. Second, the stakeholders may not be completely honest. In the case of city council members, for example, city employees usually will say that one of the key criteria this important stakeholder group uses is whether the performance of city departments enhances their reelection prospects. Council members are unlikely to declare this criterion in public, even though it is important to them. On the other hand, asking stakeholders what their criteria are can be instructive, because the team's own guesses can be wrong.

The third step in the process is to make a judgment about how well the organization performs against the stakeholders' criteria. The judgments need not be very sophisticated. Simply noting whether the organization does poorly, okay, or very well against the criteria is enough to prompt a very useful discussion. Topics of discussion should include areas of organizational strength and weakness; overlaps, gaps, conflicts, and contradictions among the criteria; and opportunities and threats posed by the stakeholders as a result of the organization's current performance.

These three steps should help set the stage for a discussion of the organization's mission. In particular, a stakeholder analysis forces team members to place themselves in the shoes of others, especially outsiders, and to make a rather dispassionate assessment of the organization's performance from the outsiders' points of view. Such activity is one of the best possible ways to avoid the attributes of folly that Tuchman describes. In addition, the stakeholder analysis provides a valuable prelude to the SWOT analysis that will come in Steps 4 and 5, and to strategy development in Step 7. Sample stakeholder analysis worksheets are included in Resource A.

If time permits, or circumstances demand it, three additional steps may be advisable. The strategic planning team may wish to discuss exactly how the various stakeholders influence the organization. Many members of the team may not know precisely how the organization is influenced, and the discussion may also highlight the really important stakeholders.

Second, the strategic planning team may wish to discuss what the organization needs from each stakeholder group. I have emphasized the need for the organization to satisfy key stakeholder groups, but it may also be important to focus attention directly on what the organization needs to survive and prosper. The usual assumption is that if the organization satisfies key stakeholders, the organization can survive and prosper. But that may not be the case. A direct focus on what the organization needs to survive may reveal an important strategic issue: how can the organization secure the resources necessary to continue its mission when it does not already receive those resources from its key stakeholders?

Finally, the team may wish to establish a rough ordering among the stakeholders according to their importance to the organization. The order, of course, might vary with different issues, but it will give the team an idea of which stakeholders demand the most attention.

The team will have to decide whether to circulate the stakeholder analysis outside the strategic planning team. It is primarily just an input to other steps in the process, especially mission statement and strategy development, so there may be no good reason for more public discussion of it.

The Mission Statement. A mission statement is a declaration of organizational purpose. They are usually short, no more than a page, and often not more than a punchy slogan. They also should be inspiring.

The actual statement should grow out of discussions aimed at answering six questions (hence, the Sam Goldwyn quote that opens this chapter). The statement should at least touch on the answers, though for some purposes it may be distilled into a slogan. Answers to the six questions will also provide the basis for developing a vision of success later in the process.

The six questions are:

1. Who are we?
2. In general, what are the basic social and political needs we exist to fill or the social and political problems we exist to address?
3. In general, what do we want to do to recognize or anticipate and respond to these needs or problems?
4. How should we respond to our key stakeholders?
5. What is our philosophy and what are our core values?
6. What makes us distinctive or unique?

Developing answers to these questions is a valuable but very demanding process. The strategic planning team may need several hours of discussion to reach consensus on the answers, and perhaps additional time for reflection. Sometimes, as in the case of Nursing Service, the organization may need to come back and revise its mission statement in light of later discoveries.

At times the discussions may seem too philosophical or academic to be of much use. If discussions seem to get bogged down in minutiae, by all means move ahead. Assign someone the task of writing up what has been discussed so far, including points of agreement and disagreement, and come back for further discussions when the time seems right or when decisions are necessary. Strategic planning should not be allowed to get in the way of useful action.

However, it is important to remember that strategic planning *is* ultimately about purpose, meaning, value, and virtue, and therefore *is* philosophical in a very practical sense. As management guru Peter Drucker has said, "Strategic planning is basically a Socratic process." The six questions structure one of the most important parts of that Socratic dialogue. Let us briefly examine each of the questions.

1. Who are we? If your organization were walking down the street and someone asked it who it was, what would the answer be? The question is one of identity, and the answer may need to be more than just what appears on the organization's letterhead, since the name there may not mean much. Clarity about identity is crucial because, as the eminent psychiatrist R. D. Laing argues, the most effective way to influence people is not to tell them what to *do*, but to communicate who they *are* (quoted in Dalton and Thompson, 1986, p. 147). So, too, with organizations. To say that we are the Internal Revenue Service, or the U.S. Marine Corps, or Public Health Nursing Service, or the executive branch of Central City, or the government of Suburban City carries an enormous amount of meaning, and implies a great deal about what the organization can and ultimately will do.

It is also important to ask a question about identity to help the organization draw a distinction between what it is and what it does. Too many organizations make a fundamental mistake when they assume they are what they do. As a result, important avenues of strategic response to environmental conditions are unwittingly sealed off. An example of this sort of error is often cited in business texts. Earlier in this century companies that ran railroads thought of themselves as railroad companies—what they did at the time—rather than as transportation companies that happened to be in the railroad business. They were caught completely unaware by the emerging automobile and trucking industries. If they had defined themselves as transportation companies, they might have avoided the serious declines most of them experienced this century (Levitt, 1960).

2. In general, what are the basic social or political needs we exist to fill or the basic social or political problems we exist to address? The answer to this question, along with the organization's mandates, provides the basic social justification for the organization's existence. The purpose of the organization is to fill the needs or address the problems. Organizations can then

be seen as a means to an end, and not as an end in themselves.

3. In general, what do we do to recognize or anticipate and respond to these needs or problems? This question prompts the organization to actively stay in touch with the needs it is supposed to fill, or problems it is supposed to address. Left to their own devices, organizations generally will talk primarily to themselves, not to the outside (Wilensky, 1967; March and Simon, 1958). When we see individuals talk mainly to themselves, we often suspect mental illness. When we see organizations talking primarily to themselves, we should suspect some sort of pathology as well. To remain "healthy," organizations must be encouraged to stay in touch with the outside world that justifies their existence.

Furthermore, constant attention to external needs or problems is likely to prompt the innovations in mission, mandates, product or service mix, cost, financing, or management organizations need to remain effective. Successful innovations typically are a response to real needs or problems; mere technological feasibility is not enough (Zaltman, Duncan, and Holbek, 1973). Furthermore, most of the information critical to innovation usually comes from outside the organization (Kanter, 1983). The more people in the organization as a whole attend to external needs and problems, the more likely a climate conducive to innovation will prevail and the easier it will be to justify desirable innovations to internal audiences (Wilson, 1967).

Finally, people often need to be reassured that they will not be punished for returning from the outside world with bad news. We all have seen messengers shot down because key decision makers did not like the message. An explicit endorsement of contact with the outside world is likely to make the organization a safer haven for messengers who carry bad news that should be heard.

4. How should we respond to our key stakeholders? This question asks the organization to decide what relations it wishes to establish with its key stakeholders and what values it seeks to promote through those relations. If the key to success in the public and nonprofit sectors is the satisfaction of key stakeholders, what will the organization do to satisfy those stakeholders?

5. What is our philosophy and what are our core values? The importance of reflecting upon and clarifying an organization's philosophy and core values becomes most apparent in strategy development. Only strategies that are consonant with that philosophy and core values are likely to succeed; strategies that are not are likely to fail. Unfortunately, because organizations rarely discuss their philosophies and values, they often adopt strategies that are doomed to failure. Clarity about philosophy and values in advance of strategy development is one way to avoid this error.

Perhaps even more important, however, clarity about philosophy and core values will help an organization maintain its integrity. If an organization can be clear about its philosophy and core values, it will be able to say *no* more easily to any proposals or actions that are likely to damage its integrity and *yes* to those that maintain or enhance its integrity. In a time when public confidence in most institutions is low, it is vital to maintain organizational integrity. Once this integrity is damaged, it is very difficult to reestablish public confidence in the organization.

Consider, for example, the Johnson & Johnson (J&J) Corporation's response to the Tylenol scare. Recall that in 1982 seven people died as a result of swallowing Tylenol capsules laced with cyanide. Even though the poisonings did not occur on J&J premises, and all had happened in the Chicago area, the company promptly withdrew *all* Tylenol capsules from throughout the United States at an estimated cost of $100 million. At the same time, the company began a massive communication campaign, involving 2,500 employees, to alert providers and consumers to the potential dangers. The *Washington Post* commented at the time that "Johnson & Johnson has succeeded in portraying itself to the public as a company willing to do what's right, regardless of cost" (quoted in Bhambri, 1985, p. 6).

According to all accounts, there never was any question among insiders about what J&J would do. The reason is the company's credo, a statement of beliefs first formulated in the 1940s and used to guide the company ever since. The first line of the credo is, "We believe our first responsibility is to the doctors, nurses, and patients, to mothers and all others who use our products and services.'' The company's first responsibility, therefore, was to get the potentially harmful Tylenol capsules off the shelves of pharmacies, hospitals, doctors' offices, and home medicine chests as quickly as possible.

And what were the effects of J&J's response? Not unexpectedly, operating profits fell 50 percent from 1981 to 1983 (from $112.5 million to $75 million), but rose dramatically to $160 million in 1985. Tylenol regained its lost market share, and the company is now leading an industry switch from capsules to caplets. (The company quit making capsules after a Yonkers, New York, woman died from taking cyanide-laced Tylenol.) In effect, the company's integrity was never questioned. They got people to question *capsules,* not the company or Tylenol (Steinbreder, 1986). Employee morale and loyalty were enhanced because employees knew the company could be counted on to do what was right, even if its short-run profits suffered (Bhambri, 1985).

A caution is in order at this point, however. It might be argued that relatively open discussion of philosophy and values actually might damage an organization's effectiveness. Because only publicly acceptable philosophies and values are likely to be discussed in public, an organization whose success depends on pursuit of publicly unacceptable values could suffer. For example, a local economic development agency might in effect further the ends of wealthy land developers as part of its strategy of reliance on private markets, developers, and investors. No matter how beneficial such a strategy is to the community, it is simply unacceptable in most parts of the country for a public agency to say publicly that, in effect, it seeks to make the rich richer. Public discussion of the agency's philosophy and values therefore might require the agency to change its strategy and, as a result, become less effective. At the very least, the agency may need to engage in some public education about the virtues of private markets and the fact that there is no guarantee private developers and investors will survive in those markets.

Key decision makers will have to decide whether to go public with a discussion of the organization's philosophy and values. Those persons interested in "reform" are likely to favor public discussion; those against are not. The point to be made, of course, is that *any* discussion of philosophy and values, whether public or not, will have political consequences (R. C. Einsweiler, personal communication, 1986).

6. What makes us distinctive or unique? There was a time in the not too distant past when it seemed public organizations were, in Herbert Kaufman's (1976) term, "immortal." Not any more. "Cutback management" is now a term familiar to most public managers (Levine, 1979; Behn, 1983). The number of public organizations that have completely disappeared may be small, but the number of public functions being carried out privately has increased. Privatization is here to stay and its domain may be expected to increase (Savas, 1982; Kolderie, 1986). Public organizations must be quite clear about what makes them or the functions they perform distinctive or unique, or they will be likely candidates for privatization. Indeed if there is nothing distinctive or unique about a public organization or function, then perhaps it *ought* to be privatized.

Nonprofit organizations also need to be clear about what makes them distinctive or unique, or they too may find themselves at a competitive disadvantage. The world has become increasingly competitive, and organizations that cannot point to a distinct contribution may lose out.

Three Examples. Some examples can help illustrate how these mission questions might be answered, or at least touched upon. Two come from Central City, the third from a nonprofit organization. Central City's council and executive branch have complementary mission statements; they are presented in Exhibits 1 and 2. The two statements are on the long side, but they do address the six questions. The council's statement emphasizes that it is the chief legislative, policy-making, and budget approval body for the city. The executive branch's statement points out that it is the administrative arm of Central City's government. In all other respects the statements are quite similar and provide a clear basis for cooperation and collaboration in pursuit of the "health, welfare, safety, economic opportunity, quality of life, and common good of the people of Central City."

Exhibit 1. Mission Statement for Central City City Council.

The City Council is the chief legislative, policy-making, and budget approval body for the city, and consists of seven members elected to represent their districts and to govern the city as a whole in cooperation with the mayor. The council exists to provide for the health, welfare, safety, economic opportunity, quality of life, and common good of the people.

The council anticipates or recognizes and responds to needs, opportunities and concerns in these areas through:

- Effective collective and individual leadership.
- Provision for effective dialogue, cooperation and coordination among citizens, neighborhoods, the not-for-profit sector, educational and charitable institutions, businesses, city government and other units of government.
- Development of policy objectives, priorities, strategies, resources, legislation, and recommendations for the city and the city administration.
- Provision for and oversight of overall planning, programming, funding, and evaluation of city programs.
- Fulfillment of policies and mandates as required by other governments.

In its dealings with all persons, groups or organizations, the council will always, to the maximum extent possible:

- Be accessible.
- Listen and learn.
- Ask thoughtful questions.
- Provide timely answers and information to involved or affected parties.
- Respond effectively, fairly, and creatively to real needs, opportunities, and concerns.
- Speak, act, initiate, advocate, and lead on behalf of the city's districts and the city as a whole.
- Give people and organizations tools to be self-reliant.
- Follow through on its policy, legislative, and budgetary commitments.
- Make decisions in light of their future consequences and in light of the city's history, heritage, and environment.
- Observe the highest moral, ethical, and legal standards.

The council believes that government exists to meet people's needs and to provide for the common good. The council believes in democracy and representative government. It believes that the rights and dignity of all people must be respected. It is committed to openness, fairness, sensitivity, responsiveness, innovativeness, accountability, efficiency, and excellence. The council's aim is to make the city the best governed city it can be.

Council members are assisted in the pursuit of their mission by the following unique or distinctive features of the council:

- The council is legally charged with legislative, policy-making, and budget-approval responsibility for the city.

Exhibit 1. Mission Statement for Central City City Council, Cont'd.

- Each member comes from a different background and geographic area.
- The council is the elected legislative body closest to the people.
- The council is a workable size, has high visibility, and its members serve at the pleasure of the voters.
- The council is open and accessible, and its deliberations are informed by extensive dialogue with persons having information that should be considered.
- The council observes the highest moral, ethical, and legal standards.
- Council members individually and as a group exercise leadership on behalf of their districts and the city as a whole.

**Exhibit 2. Mission Statement for
the Central City Executive Branch.**

The executive branch of the government of Central City exists to enhance the health, welfare, safety, economic opportunity, quality of life, and common good of the people.

We anticipate or recognize and respond to needs and opportunities in these areas through:

- Effective leadership.
- The collection of information related to needs and opportunities.
- The development of policy recommendations.
- Advice and information to the city council and other involved or affected parties.
- Effective fulfillment of legislative mandates and policies.
- Cooperation and coordination with other units of government, businesses, the not-for-profit sector, educational and charitable institutions, the citizens of Central City, and the public in general.
- The provision of quality services in a timely and fiscally responsible manner.
- Constructive and timely evaluation of administrative, programmatic, and employee performance.
- Effective and generous support and recognition of employees, along with fair compensation.
- Job security for employees, to the extent possible.

In our dealings with those persons, groups, or organizations that have a legitimate claim on our attention, resources, and outputs, or that are affected by those outputs, we will always, to the maximum extent possible:

- Listen.
- Ask thoughtful questions.

Exhibit 2. Mission Statement for
the Central City Executive Branch, Cont'd.

- Respond effectively and creatively to real needs and opportunities.
- Follow through on our commitments.
- Act cooperatively and in a coordinated way.
- Deliver quality products, including advice, policy recommendations, programs and services.
- Observe the highest moral and ethical standards.

Our core values include a commitment to openness, honesty, fairness, sensitivity, responsiveness, innovativeness, accountability, efficiency, professional management, quality, and excellence. Our aim is to be the best city administration that we can be.

We are assisted in the pursuit of our mission by the following unique or distinctive features of our government:

- The quality of our leaders, managers, and work force.
- The high moral and ethical standards observed by and expected of all city employees.
- Our extensive reliance on lateral relations in addition to vertical ones within city government, and with persons, groups, and organizations outside city government.
- The freedom given our managers.
- Our extensive use of citizen participation.

Another example is provided by the Amherst H. Wilder Foundation, a large, nonprofit operating foundation located in St. Paul, Minnesota, that provides a wide range of effective, and often quite innovative, social services and programs. Its mission statement is presented in Exhibit 3. The statement clearly authorizes and prompts the foundation to seek the biggest impact it can in its chosen domain (Bryson, King, Roering, and Van de Ven, 1986).

Process Guidelines. Several process guidelines should be kept in mind as a strategic planning group works at clarification of mission and mandates:

1. Someone should be put in charge of compiling the formal and informal mandates the organization faces. The group should then review this list and make any modifications to it that seem appropriate.

Exhibit 3. The Amherst H. Wilder
Foundation's Mission Statement.

The foundation's purpose is to promote the social welfare of persons resident or located in the greater Saint Paul metropolitan area by all appropriate means, including relief of the poor, care of the sick and aged, care and nurture of children, aid to the disadvantaged and otherwise needy, promotion of physical and mental health, support of rehabilitation and corrections, provision of needed housing and social services, operation of residences and facilities for the aged, the infirm and those requiring special care, and in general the conservation of human resources by the provision of human services responsive to the welfare needs of the community, all without regard to or discrimination on account of nationality, sex, color, religious scruples, or prejudices.

Source: Bryson, King, Roering, and Van de Ven, 1986, p. 124.

2. The group should complete a stakeholder analysis using the worksheets (or modifications of them) in Resource Section A. Public and nonprofit organizations typically consist of shifting coalitions related to external networks of stakeholders. Organizational purpose should be crafted at least in part out of a consideration of these stakeholders' interests. Otherwise, successful agreement on organizational purposes is unlikely (Fisher and Ury, 1981).

3. After completing the stakeholder analysis the group should fill out the mission statement worksheets as individuals first, and then should discuss their answers as a group. The worksheets will be found in Resource Section A.

4. After the worksheets have been completed and discussed by the group, the task of developing a draft mission statement for discussion should be turned over to an individual. It is very important to allow sufficient time to debate the draft mission statement, particularly if any changes in mission are contemplated. Quick agreement may occur, but should not be expected. After an agreed-upon mission statement is developed, the group also may wish to brainstorm a slogan that captures the essence of the mission, or run a contest among organizational members for an appropriate slogan.

5. It is important not to get stalled by development of a mission statement. If the group hits a snag, record areas of agreement and disagreement, and then move on to the next steps. Return later to discuss the mission based on any additional information or solutions that turn up in future steps.

6. Indeed, strategic planning teams should expect to have to reexamine their draft mission statement as they move through the process, either to reaffirm the statement or to redraft it in light of additional information or reflection. Even if the organization already has a satisfactory mission statement, it still should expect to reexamine the statement periodically during the process.

7. Once agreement is reached on a mission statement, it should be kept before the strategic planning group as it moves through the planning process. The group should refer to the statement as it seeks to identify strategic issues, develop effective strategies, prepare a vision of success, and in general resolve conflicts among the team. The organization's mission provides a basis for resolving conflicts based on interests, not positions (Fisher and Ury, 1981).

8. Once general agreement is reached, the mission should be visibly set before all organizational members. It should be referred to in preambles to official organizational actions, should be posted on walls and in offices, and in general should become a *physical* presence. Otherwise it is likely to be forgotten at the very times it is most needed. Explicit reference to the mission should be the standard first step in resolving conflicts. The organization that forgets its mission will drift. Opportunism and the loss of integrity are likely to spread and perhaps become rampant (Selznick, 1957). Organizational survival itself, or at least the survival of its leadership, will then be in serious question.

9. Adoption of the mission should mark an important decision point. Agreement may not occur at the end of this step, however, for the draft mission may be revised during the planning process. Formal agreement on the organization's mission definitely should be reached by the end of the strategy development step.

Summary

This chapter has discussed the identification of mandates that the organization faces and the clarification of the mission it wishes to pursue. Mandates are imposed from the outside and may be considered the "musts" that the organization is required to do (although it may "want" to do them as well). Mission is developed more from the inside and identifies the purposes the organization wishes to pursue. Mission may be considered what the organization "wants" to do. Rarely is an organization so boxed in by mandates that there is room only for a mission that meets the mandates. This chapter has outlined a process for identifying and clarifying organizational purposes—both "musts" and "wants"—and for developing a mission statement that embodies these purposes.

Chapter 6

Assessing Strengths, Weaknesses, Opportunities, and Threats

You can observe an awful lot just by watching.
Yogi Berra

In nature, improbabilities are the one stock in trade. The whole creation is one lunatic fringe.
Annie Dillard

Instead of worrying about the future, let us labor to create it.
Hubert H. Humphrey

To respond effectively to changes in their environments, public and nonprofit organizations (and communities) increasingly must assess their external and internal environments. To use Yogi Berra's language, they must watch. But they must also interpret what they observe.

Purpose

The purpose of Steps 4 and 5 in the strategic planning process, therefore, is to provide information on the *internal* strengths and weaknesses of the organization in relation to the *external* opportunities and threats it faces. The approach to external and internal environmental assessments outlined in this chapter will set the stage for identifying strategic issues in Step 6, and will provide valuable information for the next step, strategy development. Strategic issues typically concern how the

117

organization (what is inside) relates to the larger environment it inhabits (what is outside). Every effective strategy will take advantage of strengths and opportunities at the same time it minimizes or overcomes weaknesses and threats.

The first chapter highlighted several major trends and events that are forcing sometimes drastic changes on governments, public agencies, and nonprofit organizations. Unfortunately, for various reasons, organizations typically are not very savvy about perceiving such changes quickly enough to respond effectively. Often a crisis has to develop before organizations respond (Wilson, 1967). This may open up significant "opportunity spaces," but for the *unprepared* organization many useful avenues of response typically will be closed off by the time a crisis emerges (Bryson, 1981; Smart and Vertinsky, 1977). Also, in crisis situations people typically stereotype, withdraw, project, rationalize, and oversimplify (Bryson, Van de Ven, and Roering, 1987). The result can be colossal errors (Tuchman, 1984). A major purpose of any strategic planning exercise therefore is to alert an organization to the various *external* threats and opportunities that may need a response in the foreseeable future. In other words, a major purpose of strategic planning is to prepare an organization to respond effectively to the outside world before a crisis emerges.

But any effective response to external threats and opportunities must be based on an intimate knowledge of the organization's internal strengths and weaknesses. Effective responses build on internal strengths and minimize or overcome internal weaknesses to take advantage of external opportunities and minimize or overcome external threats. Strategic planning, in other words, is concerned with finding the best or most advantageous fit between an organization and its environment based on an intimate understanding of both.

The desired outcomes, benefits, and process guidelines are much the same for Steps 4 and 5, so both steps are covered in this chapter; distinctions between the two will be noted. Resource Section B at the end of the book offers practical information on developing permanent external scanning operations.

Desired Outcomes

Steps 4 and 5 produce documented lists of external opportunities and threats and internal strengths and weaknesses. Ordered differently, these four lists constitute the classic SWOT analysis, a popular strategic planning tool.

First, however, it may be necessary to prepare various background reports on external forces and trends, clients, customers, and payers, competitors and collaborators, with additional reports on internal resources, present strategy, and performance. Once the four lists are prepared, it may be necessary to commission careful analyses of some listed items in relation to the overall strategic posture of the organization.

Another important outcome of these two steps may be specific actions to deal with threats and weaknesses. As soon as appropriate moves become apparent, key decision makers should consider taking action. A sharp temporal distinction between planning and implementation is not only unnecessary, it probably also is undesirable. As long as the contemplated actions are based on reasonable information, have adequate support, and do not foreclose important strategic options, serious consideration should be given to taking them.

Completion of Step 4 also should be an impetus for establishing a formal environmental scanning operation, if one does not exist already. It will need adequate staff, typically an in-house coordinator and volunteer in-house scanners; added staff may be needed for special studies. Scanning should result in a newsletter or some other form of regular report distributed widely within the organization. Special studies should produce detailed analyses that also may need to be distributed widely. Environmental scanning, however, never should be allowed to become a bureaucratic, paper-pushing exercise.

The most effective scanning operations will be part of a network of scanners from several organizations who exchange information and mutually develop scanning skills. If this network does not exist, it may be possible to create it.

Completion of Step 5 should prompt the organization to

develop an effective management information system (MIS) that
includes input, process, and output categories, if one does not
already exist. An effective MIS system usually is time consuming, but without it the organization will be unable to assess, ob-
jectively and unambiguously, its strengths, weaknesses, efficiency, and effectiveness. Again, the MIS system should not be
allowed to become excessively bureaucratic or cumbersome.

Thoughtful discussions among key decision makers and
opinion leaders about strengths, weaknesses, opportunities, and
threats is one of the most important outcomes. Such discussions,
particularly when they cross functional lines in the organization, provide important quantitative and qualitative insights into
the organization and its environment, and also prepare the way
for the identification of strategic issues in the next step.

Benefits

An effective external and internal environmental assessment should provide several benefits to the organization. Among
the most important is that it produces information vital to the
organization's survival and prosperity. It is difficult to imagine
that an organization can be truly effective over the long haul
unless it has an intimate knowledge of its strengths and weaknesses in relation to the opportunities and threats it faces (Quinn,
1980, pp. 155–162; Luttwak, 1977).

Said somewhat differently, Steps 4 and 5 allow the strategic planning team to see the organization as a whole in relation to its environment. This is usually one of the singular accomplishments of strategic planning. Such a view keeps the
organization from being victimized by the present. Instead, the
organization prepares itself to follow Hubert Humphrey's advice: to stop worrying about the future and begin the work of
creating it.

Steps 4 and 5 also clarify for the organization the nature
of the "tension fields" within which it exists. Wechsler and
Backoff (1987) suggest that every organization must manage
the tensions among its capacities and intentions, in relation to
the opportunities and threats it faces. A SWOT analysis clarifies

the nature of these tensions by juxtaposing two fundamental dimensions: good (strengths and opportunities) and bad (weaknesses and threats), present (strengths and weaknesses) and future (opportunities and threats) (R. W. Backoff, personal communication, 1985).

External and internal assessments also develop the boundary spanning skills of key staff, especially key decision makers and opinion leaders. Assessments draw attention to issues and information that cross internal and external organizational boundaries. In effect, key decision makers and opinion leaders are prompted to move beyond their job descriptions in their thinking and discussions, thereby increasing opportunities for creative and integrative insights that bridge the organization to its environment.

If reasonably routine and formal environmental scanning and MIS operations are established, then the organization will have routinized attention to major and minor external trends, issues, events, and stakeholders, and to internal inputs, processes, and outputs. The chances of encountering major surprises are reduced and the possibilities for anticipatory actions are enhanced. The world at times may still look like a "lunatic fringe," in Annie Dillard's words, but the organization that regularly scans its environment should at least be able to see improbabilities (as well as probabilities) coming.

But even if external scanning and MIS systems are not institutionalized, the organization will have become more externally oriented, even as it gains a better understanding of its internal strengths and weaknesses. In my experience, organizations tend to be extremely insular and parochial and must be forced to face outward. Unless they face out, they are virtually certain not to satisfy key external stakeholders.

Another major benefit of these two steps is that timely actions may be taken to deal with threats and weaknesses. As appropriate actions become apparent at any point throughout the process, they should be taken, as long as they are based on reasonable information, have adequate support, and do not prematurely close off important strategic avenues. As the final benefit of these steps, the organization is prepared to focus on key strategic issues, stemming from the convergence of an organization's mandates, mission, strengths, weaknesses, opportunities, and threats.

External Environmental Assessment

The purpose of Step 4 is to explore the environment outside the organization to identify the opportunities and threats it faces. Figure 1 (see Chapter Three) identifies three major categories that might be monitored: forces and trends; clients, customers, or payers; and actual or potential competitors or collaborators. These are the basic foci for any effective environmental scanning system.

Forces and trends usually are broken down into four categories: political, economic, social, and technological—sometimes designated PESTs. (Organizations may choose to monitor additional categories. For example, the University of Minnesota has added education; see Pflaum and Delmont, 1987.) The acronym PESTs aptly suggests the often painful changes forced on organizations by these forces and trends. Unfortunately, the acronym does not suggest the potential opportunities presented by environmental changes. Strategic planners must be sure they attend to both threats and opportunities.

What are the recent issues and trends affecting public and nonprofit sector organizations? Pflaum and Delmont (1987) identified six categories, based on their survey of external scanning in ten public and nonprofit organizations:

1. Revenue-related issues and trends. For example, redefining U.S. trade and investment policy (Congressional Clearing House); strategies for maximizing non-property-tax income (Hennepin County, Minnesota); taxing oil operations on state right-of-way (Council of State Planning Agencies); and creating university-industry partnerships in equipment purchase and entrepreneurial ventures (University of Minnesota).
2. Social and political value shifts. For example, how the values of the baby-boom generation might affect university enrollments (University of Minnesota); allowing for direct donor

options (United Way of America); and acknowledging and planning for an emerging political constituency (Florida Office of Planning and Budgeting).

3. Computation, communication, and information system trends. For example, developments in artificial intelligence and robotics (Congressional Clearing House); building industry ties to expand a niche in supercomputing (Minnesota); considering the hi-tech workplace (United Way); and the use of sensors and robotic technology in traffic monitoring (Minnesota Department of Transportation).

4. Increases in liability and risk-management costs. For example, developing strategies for reducing civil liabilities (Hennepin County); exploring the possibility of a regional consortium to pool risk and insurance costs (Toledo Council of Governments); and developing strategies to deal with threatened premium cost increases (Pennsylvania State University and Minnesota State Planning Agency).

5. Health care. For example, issues and trends in health care, particularly cancer and heart disease research (Congressional Clearing House); and contracting as an option for better provision of health care for employees and clients (Hennepin County).

6. Other issues. For example, disaster recovery and teen pregnancy (Hennepin County); the growing animal rights movement (University of Minnesota); public sector child care delivery (Florida); and reduced federal funds for highways (Minnesota Department of Transportation).

In addition to the PESTs, organizations might monitor important stakeholder groups, especially actual or potential clients, customers, and payers, and competitors and collaborators. Nursing Service, for example, found that its client population was becoming increasingly indigent. The trend posed a threat because Nursing Service could stretch its budget to serve them only by having a large number of paying clients. At the same time, Nursing Service also detected the emergence of private sector providers of home health care services who constituted a competitive threat because they aimed their services at the same paying clients.

In my experience, members of an organization's governing board, particularly if they are elected, are better at identifying threats and opportunities than are its employees. Partly this is a reflection of differing roles; unlike most employees, a governing board typically has formal responsibility for relating an organization to its external environment (Thompson, 1967). In the public sector, there is a further reason. Employees get their mandates from laws, rules, and policies. Elected officials primarily get their mandates from elections. There usually is a major difference between legal mandates and political mandates. Politicians pay most attention to the political ones, because they must. Indeed, they typically employ "external environmental assessors," called pollsters, to keep them informed of externally imposed mandates. So it actually may be easier to sell external scanning to elected officials than to planners and public administrators, since politicians live or die by how well they scan (R. C. Einsweiler, personal communication, 1986).

Even though the board may be better than staff at identifying external opportunities and threats, typically neither does a systematic or effective job of external scanning. Thus, both groups should rely on a more or less formal and regular process of external assessment. The technology is fairly simple, and allows organizations cheaply, pragmatically, and effectively to keep tabs on what is happening in the larger world that is likely to have an impact on the organization and the pursuit of its mission. Later in this chapter, a simple process for external assessment will be outlined. A more complicated (yet still simple) process is outlined in Resource B.

Internal Environmental Assessment

The purpose of Step 5 is to assess the internal environment of the organization in order to identify its strengths and weaknesses, those aspects that help or hinder accomplishment of the organization's mission and fulfillment of its mandates. The three major categories (see Figure 1 in Chapter Three) that should be assessed are the basic elements of a simple systems model: resources (inputs), present strategy (process), and performance (outputs). These are also the fundamental categories around which any effective management information system (MIS) should be built (Wetherbe, 1984). Indeed, organizations with effective MIS systems should be in a better position to assess their strengths and weaknesses than organizations without such systems.

In my experience, most organizations have the greatest volume of information about their inputs, such as salaries, supplies, physical plant, full-time equivalent (FTE) personnel, and so on. They have a less clear idea of what their present strategy is, either overall or by function. And they have little notion of outputs, let alone the effects those outputs have on clients, customers, or payers. For example, social welfare agencies can say a lot about their budgets, staff, physical facilities, and so on, but they can say very little about the effects they have on their clients (Flynn, 1986).

The relative absence of performance information presents problems both for the organization and for its stakeholders. Stakeholders will judge the worth of an organization by how well it does against the criteria they wish to use. For external stakeholders in particular, these criteria typically relate to performance. If the organization cannot demonstrate its effectiveness against the criteria, then stakeholders are likely to withdraw their support. Public schools, for example, now are finding their management, budgets, staffing patterns, and curricula judged by how well the schools' pupils score on standardized educational achievement tests. Schools that fail to produce "educated" students may be forced to do better or close their doors. If educational voucher schemes become widespread, public schools may even have to compete directly with one another for revenues, students, and staff, in the same way that private and nonprofit schools must compete with each other and with the public schools. In fact, some voucher schemes would allow public monies to be spent on education delivered in private and nonprofit schools, so that *all* schools, regardless of sector, might need to compete with one another.

The absence of performance information may also create, or harden, major organizational conflicts. Without performance criteria and information, there is no way to judge the relative effectiveness of different resource allocations, organizational designs, and distributions of power. Without such judgments, organizational conflicts are likely to occur unnecessarily, be more partisan, and be resolved in ways that undermine the organization's mission.

The difficulties of measuring performance in the public sector are well known (Flynn, 1986). Nevertheless, stakeholders will continue to demand that organizations demonstrate effective performance and thereby justify their existence. Again, the schools present an instructive example. If public schools cannot demonstrate that they are educating their students, then taxpayers will seek alternatives in the private and nonprofit sectors.

The technology for making internal assessments is relatively simple and cheap. A simple process (along with some elaborations) for making internal and external assessments will be presented in the next section.

The Assessment Process

Snow Card Technique

The "snow card" technique (Greenblat and Duke, 1981) is a very simple yet effective group process for developing a list of strengths, weaknesses, opportunities, and threats. Also referred to as the "snowball" technique (Nutt and Backoff, 1987), the method combines brainstorming—which produces a long list of possible answers to a specific question—with a synthesizing step, in which the answers are grouped into categories according to common themes. Each of the individual answers is written onto a white card (for example, a five-by-seven-inch index card) called a "snow card"; the individual cards then are taped to a wall according to common themes, producing several "snowballs" of cards.

The technique is extremely simple in concept, very easy to use, speedy, and remarkably productive. It is particularly useful as part of a SWOT analysis and as part of the strategy development step. In a SWOT analysis the technique would be used four times to focus on the questions:

1. What major external opportunities do we have?
2. What major external threats do we face?
3. What are our major internal strengths?
4. What are our major internal weaknesses?

The strategic planning team then very quickly would have before it four lists to discuss, compare, and contrast, both to determine actions that should be taken immediately and to prepare for strategic-issues identification in the next step. The SWOT analysis will also help the team prepare effective strategies in response to the issues.

Guidelines for using the snow card technique are:

1. Select a facilitator.
2. Form the group that will use the technique. The ideal group is five to nine persons (Delbecq, Van de Ven, and Gustafson, 1975), but the technique can still be effective with as many as twelve.
3. Have the members of the group seat themselves around a table in a room that has a nearby wall where the snow cards may be taped and read clearly from where the members sit.
4. Focus on a single question, problem, or issue.
5. Have the individuals in the group silently brainstorm as many ideas as possible in response to the question, and record them on their personal worksheets.
6. Have individuals pick out the five ''best'' items from their personal worksheets and transcribe them onto five separate index cards. Make sure people write legibly enough and large enough so that their items can be read when posted on a nearby wall.
7. Have group members attach a tape roll (drafting tape rolled sticky side out into a roll one inch in diameter) to the back of each of their snow cards.
8. Collect the cards (shuffling them if anonymity is important) and start taping them one at a time to a nearby wall, clustering cards with similar themes together. The tentative label for each cluster should be selected by the group. As an alternative, the group may wish to tape all the cards to the wall at once, and as a group rearrange the cards into thematic clusters.

9. Once the group agrees to a category's name, it should be written on a separate snow card and placed at the top of the items in the category. These label cards should be differentiated in some way, perhaps a different color card or ink, or by drawing a box around the category name.

10. Once all items are on the board and included in a category, the items should be rearranged and the categories tinkered with until the group thinks the results make the most sense. Categories might be arranged in logical, priority, or temporal order. New items may be added and old ones deleted as necessary. Subcategories should be added as needed.

11. When the group members are satisfied with the categories and their contents, they should discuss, compare, and contrast the results.

12. When the session is over, the cards should be collected in order, typed up in outline or spreadsheet form, and distributed to the group.

SWOT Analysis: An Example

Simply creating a list of strengths, weaknesses, opportunities, and threats is not enough. The lists must be carefully discussed, analyzed, compared, and contrasted; that is, a "SWOT analysis" must be performed. Planners should note specific implications for the formulation of strategic issues and effective strategies, as well as actions that might be necessary and might be taken before the end of the strategic planning process.

One of the fascinating features of most SWOT analyses is that strengths and weaknesses, and opportunities and threats, are often mirror images of one another. That is, an organization's greatest strengths may also be its greatest weaknesses. Strategic planning team members should not be surprised to see such relationships; indeed, they should expect them. The trick is to take advantage of the strengths and opportunities without being disadvantaged by the related weaknesses and threats. (They should also not be surprised to find *internal* opportunities and threats and *external* strengths and weaknesses.)

Central City's executive branch provides an interesting example of a SWOT list developed through the use of snow cards; see Exhibit 4. Only the main category headings will be discussed here, but they are enough to illustrate some of the points made above.

Exhibit 4. Central City's SWOT List.

Strengths

- Political leadership of mayor.
- Management professionalism, stability, and freedom of action.
- Orientation toward action and innovation.
- Work force dedication and morale.
- Strength in personnel programs.
- Organization—departmental independence and flexibility.
- Citizen support.
- Excellent citizen participation.
- Good labor relations.

Weaknesses

- Organization—too strongly organized along vertical lines without enough lateral overlays and external contacts.
- City Council—not an effective policy-making body.
- Lack of citywide management vision.
- No strategic planning.
- Mayor—a leader, not an effective manager.
- Outdated personnel system.
- Too much citizen participation.
- Legislative restrictions.
- Labor relations—too many unions that are too strong and make good management difficult.
- Funding—declining revenues.

Opportunities

- Access and transportation.
- Economic development.
- Organizational and service redesign as a result of funding shortages and other pressures.
- Relationships with institutions and stakeholders.

Threats

- Revenue loss.
- Poor national and regional economy.

Exhibit 4. Central City's SWOT List, Cont'd.

- Competition from other governments, regions, and the private sector.
- Economic base.
- Revenue demands.
- Uncooperative stakeholders.

A few observations about the SWOT list are in order. First, the lists involve Central City both as a government (organization) and as a place (community). Central City's executive branch, in other words, has blended strategic planning for itself as an organization and as a jurisdiction. Suburban City did the same thing. This blending should be expected of governments responsible both for themselves and for places. Unfortunately, however, most governments' strategic planning processes remain too divorced from their comprehensive community planning processes.

Second, there are many more strengths and weaknesses than opportunities and threats, probably because the members of the planning team as a group tended to be internally rather than externally focused. This is not surprising; most team members were line managers responsible for the day-to-day operations of their departments. Their jobs almost by definition precluded paying careful attention to external trends and events. Furthermore, there were no established occasions and forums for operating managers as a group to discuss external trends and their likely impact. Clearly the executive branch was in danger of being blindsided by external developments, unless it set up an external scanning operation and organized forums for managers as a group to discuss information developed through external scanning.

Third, weaknesses outnumber strengths. That may reflect a natural human tendency to focus more on the inhibitors of action than on what facilitates action. A less charitable explanation would be an equally familiar human tendency to blame or scapegoat as a way of avoiding action. Whatever the reasons, the executive branch should turn these weaknesses into challenges to be overcome.

Strengths. The executive branch strategic planning team identified a solid set of strengths. These can be built upon to make the executive branch a powerful engine for growth, development, change, innovation, and service. Unfortunately, of the three broad kinds of features of the internal environment— resources, present strategy, and performance—only the first is well represented in the list of strengths; very little can be counted as a strategy or as performance. Under resources, the list certainly identifies several "people" strengths, and there are hints of competencies, but nowhere is there a statement of what the executive branch is really good at. And there are other resource strengths that are not listed, such as Central City's relatively stable tax base. Central City has considerable information at its disposal, but it is not clear how much of that stockpile counts as a strength.

Under present strategy, there is reliance on a strong, responsive mayor and quasi-autonomous departments. Not clear, however, are present overall or functional strategies, or how well they work.

Most worrisome perhaps is the absence of performance outcomes among the strengths. There is no mention of any measurable successes tied to Central City's mission. Since external stakeholders will judge the executive branch primarily by its performance in the mission-related results category, the clear message is that the executive branch should develop a stronger sense of present strategy and a better performance monitoring system.

The fact that the list of strengths (and of weaknesses, opportunities, and threats noted below) is incomplete is to be expected; at least the list showed the executive branch where more information was needed. The quick snow card exercise by Central City's key executive-branch decision makers to create the SWOT list took only a few hours, and provided the basis for a number of decisions that helped improve the performance of the executive branch and moved its strategic planning process forward.

Weaknesses. The executive branch identified a fairly substantial set of weaknesses, some of which mirrored strengths.

For example, the effective, politically responsive mayor (a strength) often causes difficulties for the executive branch because he does not always think through the managerial implications of his decisions before saying "yes" (a weakness). While the executive branch has strong departments and flexibility within departments (a strength), the corresponding weaknesses are insufficient interdepartmental cooperation and coordination and the absence of a citywide vision among the departments' managers. While Central City is known for its excellent citizen participation mechanisms and process (a strength), the resulting weakness is the time-consuming nature of the mechanisms. Finally, while the executive branch has very good working relations with the various employee unions and associations (a strength), that produces three weaknesses: (1) long-standing labor practices are often inefficient and difficult to change; (2) the necessity of dealing with many unions results in time-consuming negotiations and difficulties in achieving fairness across agreements; and (3) many of the unions are very strong politically and make it difficult for managers to manage as they would like.

Fortunately, general solutions to many of the weaknesses are not difficult to find. The difficulties with the organization and with the absence of a citywide management vision can be ameliorated by establishing a cabinet of city department heads. That cabinet need not await completion of the strategic planning process; in fact, Central City's executive branch went ahead and formed a cabinet chaired officially by the mayor's executive assistant. The cabinet became the official body charged with overseeing the strategic planning process.

The executive branch felt that the city council was not an effective policy-making body. (As noted earlier, the city council strategic planning team agreed with this assessment and made a number of proposals to improve its effectiveness.) There obviously are real limits to what the executive branch can do about the council, given that Central City has a strong mayor form of government and the executive branch reports primarily to the mayor and not the council. It probably is most feasible for the executive branch to develop its own focus and vision, to which the council might respond by developing *its* own focus and vision. Collaboration with the council in development of a shared vision is clearly possible, but may be very difficult in practice.

Under the category of no strategic planning, the solution is obvious: begin a strategic planning process and find some way to institutionalize it. Central City did both—without waiting for completion of its first strategic planning process to institutionalize it.

A strong mayor who is responsive to external demands is obviously not an unmixed blessing for an executive branch, as, for example, when the mayor says "yes" to implementation of difficult (and perhaps unwise) proposals. On the other hand, a strong mayor, responsive to external demands, can provide the vision, authority, and political resources necessary to pursue the executive branch's mission. One possible way to gain from the mayor's strengths and minimize his weaknesses would be to convene a mayor-cabinet retreat, and include on the discussion agenda: "How can we reinforce the mayor's strengths and minimize or overcome any weaknesses?" The discussion obviously would be two-way, and very healthy.

Central City's personnel system was described as outdated. Obviously it should be updated. At the same time, the government invests very little in its managers and employees, even though the key decision makers in the executive branch believe that the government's employees are one of its greatest strengths. One possible solution would be a more extensive and focused manager and employee development effort, perhaps tied to strategic planning. Hennepin County, Minnesota, for example, found that one of the biggest payoffs from its strategic planning effort was employee—and organizational—development. Participation in Hennepin County's strategic planning task forces was a real source of employee growth, involvement, and excitement (Eckhert, Haines, Delmont, and Pflaum, 1988). Perhaps a strategic issue for Central City is "How best can we improve the training and development of our managers and employees?"

There is not too much to be said about the legislative restrictions category. In the funding category, revenue and dollar shortages simply must be turned into opportunities to the extent possible.

What seems to be missing from the list of weaknesses again are items that would fit under the large labels of resources (perhaps other than people), present strategy, and results. Missing are the details of Central City's people, economic, information, and competency resources. Missing are statements of the weaknesses of its current strategies. And missing are weaknesses in results. As with the list of strengths, Central City's executive branch now knows where it needs additional information. However, it has enough information now to push ahead with its first strategic planning effort.

Opportunities. The list of opportunities is surprisingly short, considering how many potential opportunities local governments have. A well-developed environmental scanning function clearly would help the executive branch identify more opportunities, as well as threats. Also needed are occasions, such as retreats, to discuss the results of scanning and implications for Central City.

As we have seen (Figure 1, Chapter Three), the three main sources of opportunities and threats are (1) forces and trends (political, economic, social, and technological); (2) clients, customers, and payers; and (3) competitors and collaborators. An environmental scanning function should help identify forces and trends that now affect Central City or soon will. A good MIS system should help Central City define its clients, customers, and payers. And a corporate strategic planning function, along with departmental efforts, should give Central City a clearer sense about its existing and potential competitors and collaborators.

In the economic development area there obviously are a number of potential opportunities. What needs careful analysis, however, is Central City's competitive advantages for industries and firms (see Chapter Two for a discussion of competitive analysis). To clarify the opportunities for redesign as a result of funding shortages, Central City planners should carefully explicate and analyze the forces that will lead to increases and decreases in revenues and demands. A continuous series of discussions about public service redesign also would be helpful.

Finally, in the relationships area, forums might be convened to discuss how these relationships might be used in pursuit of the various parties' missions and agendas. One such forum might be task forces charged with resolving strategic issues identified by the cabinet, if those task forces involve outsiders. Having outsiders at a cabinet retreat devoted to environmental scanning might be another approach. A citywide conference on collaboration in pursuit of Central City's mission is another forum, a very ambitious one.

Threats. The list of threats appears reasonable, but again it is very short. It does not tap all that it might in the areas of forces and trends; clients, customers, and payers; and competitors and collaborators. Again, an environmental scanning function, an MIS system, and a corporate planning function would help fill out the list.

In revenue loss and revenue demands, again, there is a need for studies of the forces and trends that will lead to increases and decreases in revenues and demands. While economic development may be an opportunity, Central City's existing economic base is a threat. The strategic planners should develop a clear description of what Central City's economic base is, what it should be, and what Central City can do to strengthen it. These statements are needed before an effective economic development strategy can be formulated.

Uncooperative stakeholders are the mirror image of the relationships category noted in the opportunities list. Political and managerial leadership must take advantage of what those stakeholders have to offer and minimize the impact of their uncooperativeness.

In sum, Central City's strategic planning team identified a number of strengths, weaknesses, opportunities, and threats through use of the snow card technique. Specific actions were suggested based on these lists, and the identification of strategic issues was facilitated. The lists are not exhaustive, however, and an important future task is completion of a more extensive SWOT analysis with more staff support.

Process Guidelines

One of the special features of strategic planning is the attention it accords external and internal environments. Coupled with attention to mandates and mission, external and internal environmental assessments give an organization a clear sense of its present situation and lay the basis for identifying strategic issues and developing strategies in the next steps. The following process guidelines may be helpful as an organization looks at its external and internal environments.

1. Keep in mind that simpler is likely to be better. Highly elaborate, lengthy, sophisticated, and quantified procedures for external and internal assessment are likely to drive out strategic thinking, not promote it. Assessment procedures must be kept simple and useful if line managers are to follow them. Otherwise, strategic planning will become the province of the technical analyst and will have little impact on decision making.

2. Consider using the snow card technique with the strategic planning team to develop an initial list of external opportunities and threats and internal strengths and weaknesses. The technique is very simple and allows users to develop and discuss a list of SWOTs easily in a half day. Be sure to save the snow cards so that they can be typed up and distributed to participants and other interested parties.

3. Always try, if possible, to get a strategic planning team to consider what is going on outside the organization before it considers what is going on inside. Organizations typically spend most of their time talking to themselves about internal happenings, and too little time talking about, and with, the outside environment. The result is a kind of organizational mental illness. Attending to the outside is crucial because the social and political justification for virtually every organization's existence is what it does, or proposes to do, about external social or political problems. Organizations should focus on those problems first, and on themselves second.

4. As part of the discussion of its SWOT list, the strategic planning team should look for patterns, important actions that might be taken immediately, and implications for strategic

issues. A facilitator can play an important role by constantly pushing the strategic planning team to identify patterns, necessary actions, and implications for issue identification. Since strengths and weaknesses and opportunities and threats frequently mirror each other, discussion should focus on these paired items and on what could be done to capitalize on the strengths and opportunities while minimizing or overcoming the weaknesses and threats. A facilitator also should prompt comparisons of inside with outside. Someone should take notes on the essence of these discussions.

5. A followup analysis of the SWOT list is almost always a good idea. It should focus on whether the appropriate categories have been identified or some regrouping is necessary, whether some categories need to be fleshed out, and whether some important categories have been missed. Also, actions that might be taken as a result of the analysis should be identified. Finally, implications for the identification of strategic issues should be noted. The followup analysis should be discussed at a subsequent team meeting and probably will become the basis for the SWOT section of the organization's strategic plan.

6. The organization should consider institutionalizing periodic SWOT analyses. The simplest way to do so is to schedule periodic meetings of the strategic planning team—say, once or twice a year—to do a snow card exercise and develop a SWOT list as a basis for discussion. In more elaborate form this would mean establishing a permanent environmental scanning function, along the lines proposed by Pflaum and Delmont (1987) and presented in Resource B; development of an MIS system that provides information on resources, present strategy, performance, and clients, customers, and payers; and institutionalization of strategic planning.

Summary

Steps 4 and 5 explore the organization's external and internal environments in order to identify the strengths, weaknesses, opportunities, and threats it faces. When combined with attention to mandates and mission, these steps lay the foundation for identifying strategic issues in the next step, and developing effective strategies in the subsequent step. Recall that every effective strategy will build on strengths and take advantage of opportunities while it minimizes or overcomes weaknesses and threats.

By far the most important strategic planning technique is group discussion. The snow card technique can be used to provide the basic SWOT list that would be the focus of group discussion.

Organizations should consider institutionalizing their capability to perform periodic SWOT analyses. They will need to establish an external scanning operation, develop a good MIS system, and undertake regular strategic planning exercises.

As with every step in the strategic planning process, simpler is usually better. Strategic planning teams and organizations should not get bogged down in external and internal assessments. Important and necessary actions should be taken as soon as they are identified, as long as they do not prematurely seal off important strategic options.

Chapter 7

Identifying the Strategic Issues Facing an Organization

When in doubt, talk.
Hubert H. Humphrey

Identifying strategic issues is the heart of the strategic planning process. Recall that a strategic issue is defined as a "fundamental policy choice affecting an organization's mandates, mission, values, product or service level and mix, clients or users, cost, financing, organization, or management." The purpose of this step therefore is to identify the fundamental policy choices facing the organization. The way these choices are framed can have a profound effect on decisions that define what the organization is, what it does, and why it does it.

As noted in Chapter Three, strategic issues are important because issues play a central role in political decision making. Political decision making begins with issues, but strategic planning can improve the process by affecting the way issues are framed and resolved. With carefully framed issues, subsequent decisions are more likely to be both politically acceptable and technically workable; in accord with the organization's basic philosophy and values; and morally, ethically, and legally defensible.

Identifying strategic issues typically is one of the most riveting steps for participants in strategic planning. Virtually every strategic issue involves conflicts: what will be done, why it will be done, how it will be done, when it will be done, where it will be done, who will do it, and who will be advantaged or

139

disadvantaged by it. These conflicts may draw people together or pull them apart, but in either case participants will feel heightened emotion and concern (Filley, 1975). If strategic planning is in part about the construction of a new social reality, then this step outlines the basic paths along which that drama might unfold (Mangham and Overington, 1987). As with any journey, fear and anxiety are as likely to be travel companions as excitement and adventurousness.

Desired Outcomes and Benefits

Two basic outcomes should be sought from this step. The first is a list of the strategic issues faced by the organization. The second is an arrangement of the issues on the list in some sort of order: priority, logical, or temporal.

The list should also contain information to help people consider the nature, importance, and implications of each issue. The administrators and planners of Hennepin County, Minnesota (the county that contains Minneapolis), for example, require three kinds of information: (1) a description of the issue, usually no more than a paragraph long, in which the issue itself is posed as a question the organization can do something about; (2) a discussion of the factors (mandates, mission, and internal and external environmental features) that make the issue strategic; and (3) a brief discussion of the consequences of failure to address the issue. They believe it should be possible to summarize the answers for each issue on one single-spaced, typewritten page. (Examples of strategic issues from Hennepin County and more information on the county's issue identification process will be presented later in the chapter.)

A number of benefits ensue from the identification of strategic issues. First, attention is focused on what is truly important. The importance of this benefit is not to be underestimated. Key decision makers in organizations usually are victimized by the 80–20 rule—they spend 80 percent of their time on the least important 20 percent of their jobs. When this is added to the fact that key decision makers in different functional areas rarely discuss important cross-functional matters with one another, the stage is set for shabby organizational performance.

It also helps to recognize that there are three different kinds of strategic issues: (1) issues where no action is required at present, but the issue must be continuously monitored; (2) issues that can be handled as part of the organization's regular strategic planning cycle; and (3) issues that require an immediate response and therefore cannot be handled in a more routine way.

A second benefit is that attention is focused on issues, not answers. All too often serious conflicts arise over solutions to problems without any clarity about what the problems are (Filley, 1975; Fisher and Ury, 1981). Such conflicts typically result in power struggles, not problem-solving sessions.

Third, the identification of issues usually creates the kind of useful tension necessary to prompt organizational change. Organizations rarely change unless they feel some need to, some pressure or tension that requires change to relieve the stress (Dalton, 1970). The tension must be great enough to prompt change, but not so great as to induce paralysis. Strategic issues that emerge from the juxtaposition of internal and external factors—and that involve organizational survival, prosperity, and effectiveness—can provide just the kind of tension that will focus the attention of key decision makers on the need for change. They will be particularly attentive to strategic issues that entail severe consequences if they are not addressed.

Fourth, strategic issue identification should provide useful clues about how to resolve the issue. By stating exactly what it is about mission, mandates, and internal and external factors that makes an issue strategic, one also gains some insight into possible ways that the issue might be resolved. In particular, if one follows the dictum that any effective strategy will take advantage of strengths and opportunities and minimize or overcome weaknesses and threats, one will gain insights into the nature and shape of effective solutions.

Fifth, if the strategic planning process has not been "real" to participants up until this point, it will become real for them now. For something to be real for someone there must be a correspondence among what the person thinks, how he or she behaves toward it, and the consequences of that behavior (Brickman, 1978; Boal and Bryson, 1987b). As the organization's situation and the issues it faces become clear, as the consequences of failure to face those issues are discussed, and as the behavioral changes necessary to deal with the issues begin to emerge, the strategic planning process will begin to seem less academic and much more real. The more people realize that strategic planning can be quite real in its consequences, the more seriously they will take it. A qualitative change in the tone of discussions often can be observed at this point, as the links among cognitions, behaviors, and consequences are established. Less joking and more serious discussion occur.

A typical result of this "real-ization" is that the group may wish to recycle through the process. In particular, the initial framing of strategic issues is likely to change as a result of further discussion among members who come to realize more fully the consequences of both addressing and failing to address the issues.

A further consequence of the realization that strategic planning may be all too real in its consequences is that key decision makers may wish to terminate the effort at this point. They may be afraid of addressing the conflicts embodied in the strategic issues. They may not wish to undergo the changes needed to resolve the issues. A crisis of trust or a test of courage may occur, and lead to a turning point in the organization's character. If at the completion of this step, the organization's key decision makers decide to push on, a final very important benefit therefore will have been gained: the organization's character will be strengthened. Just as an individual's character is formed in part by the way the individual faces serious difficulties, so too is organizational character formed by the way the organization faces difficulties (Selznick, 1957). Strong characters emerge only from confronting serious difficulties squarely and courageously.

Examples of Strategic Issues

It may help to present two examples of strategic issues. Both were prepared by Hennepin County's Office of Planning and Development as training aids to help key managers compile their list of strategic issues for the county's strategic planning process. The first, a historical example from the late 1960s and early 1970s, is an elaboration of the question: How should the county meet its long-term office space requirements? The second example, still current, poses the question: How should the solid waste produced in the county be handled?

In these examples, strategic issues emerge from the conjunction of internal and external environmental factors, externally imposed mandates, and the county's own policy objectives. The county does not have a mission statement per se, but its policy objectives serve the same purpose.

The issue of what to do about long-term space requirements was presented to county staff graphically (see Figure 6). The issue arose in an environment characterized by significant overcrowding, significant projected program and staff growth, a shortage of downtown office space in Minneapolis, rising lease costs, and a dysfunctional scattering of county office locations. On top of this, the county was mandated to take over Minneapolis General Hospital (which became the Hennepin County Medical Center), provide major administrative services as part of new Medicaid legislation, and develop new management organizations to run the various county manifestations of new federal programs. Given the changes in the environment and the new mandates, the county faced serious difficulties in achieving its relevant policy objectives, namely, to provide efficient and professional management of county operations, to provide convenient and quality public services, and to contain the cost of facilities. The issue of long-term space requirements was resolved by the construction in downtown Minneapolis of a striking twin-towered skyscraper, a large underground parking garage, and a spacious surrounding urban park.

The second issue of what to do about the solid waste also was presented graphically to county staff (Figure 7). In this case the environmental factors were large volumes of waste, rapidly increasing disposal costs, the reduction of existing landfill space, public opposition to new landfills, and the emergence of a number of potentially economical and environmentally safe technologies, such as recycling and incineration with co-generation of heat, steam, and electricity. The pressure to find a solution was increased by two recent mandates embodied in state legislation: each county was required to prepare a landfill abatement plan, and to recommend new landfill sites. The county does not

Figure 6. Example of a Strategic Issue: Long-Term Space Requirements.

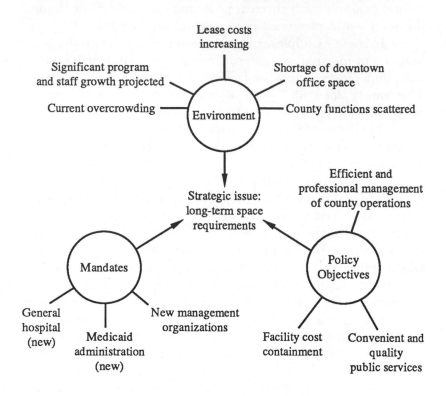

really have any policy objectives in this area other than a desire to find a solution that satisfies all key stakeholders. The issue has not been resolved, even though the county has contracted with an Alabama firm to construct a huge incineration and power generation plant just north of downtown Minneapolis. In spite of its large size, the new plant will not be able to handle all the solid waste now projected for the county.

How Should Strategic Issues Be Described?

Hennepin County's Office of Planning and Development (OPD) provided some extremely useful advice to its managers on what strategic issues are, how they arise, and how they should be described (Hennepin County, 1983). OPD argued that strategic

Figure 7. Example of a Strategic Issue: Solid Waste Management.

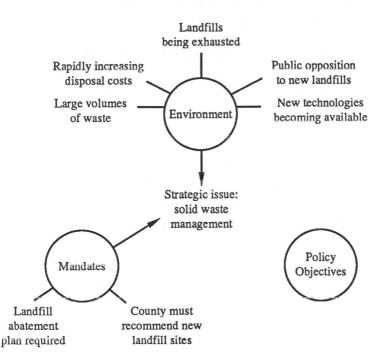

issues typically are *not* current problems or crises. (Even so, there are almost always strategic implications to the way current problems or crises are resolved.) OPD's point was that once a problem or crisis has emerged, it may be very difficult to deal with it strategically. Instead, OPD argued that strategic issues should be thought of as fundamental policy questions about what services the county should provide, to whom, by what methods, at what cost, and how they should be financed and managed. In other words, Hennepin County's definition of strategic issues is somewhat narrower than (although still compatible with) my own. OPD added that strategic issues typically *are* complex and potentially destructive if not satisfactorily resolved.

OPD argued that strategic issues arise in three kinds of situations. First, they can arise when events beyond the control of the organization make or will make it difficult to accomplish basic objectives affordably. These situations would probably be called threats. Second, they can arise when technology, cost, financing, staffing, management, or political choices for achieving basic objectives change or soon will. These situations might present either threats or opportunities. Last, they arise when internal or external events (I would add mission or mandates as well) suggest present or future opportunities to (1) make significant improvements in the quantity or quality of products or services delivered, (2) achieve significant reductions in the cost of providing products or services, (3) introduce new products or services, or (4) combine, reduce, or eliminate certain products or services.

OPD requested that Hennepin County managers provide three kinds of information when proposing a strategic issue (Hennepin County, 1984). First was a narrative statement of the issue, preferably no more than a paragraph long. Somewhere in that paragraph the issue was to be posed as a question that might have several answers and that the county might act upon. In other words, if the question only had one answer, then it probably was not an issue at all, but a choice of whether to pursue a specific solution. In addition, if people were forced to frame issues in such a way that there might be more than one answer, the chances were increased that strategic issues (fundamental policy questions) would not be confused with strategies (answers to those questions), and that innovative or even radical answers to those issues would be considered. The instruction to pose the question as something the county can do something about implies that if the county cannot do anything to answer the question, the issue is not a county issue. It may be an issue for someone, but not the county. The county should focus its most precious resource—the attention of key decision makers—on issues that the county can do something about.

Two examples of strategic issues that actually were addressed as part of the county's strategic planning process illustrate these points. The first was: What can the county do to ensure that the tax base will increase sufficiently to sustain growth in services without substantially raising property tax rates? The second was: In view of the projected growth in the size of the elderly population and the high costs of serving them, what changes should be made in the county's service delivery system for the elderly and its financing mechanisms to ensure responsiveness to future human needs and fiscal realities? In both cases the questions were posed so there were many possible answers.

OPD also wanted a brief review and discussion of evidence that the issue involved fundamental policy questions. In other words, OPD wanted to know what about mandates, policy objectives (or mission), internal or external trends, issues, or events made the issue strategic, as opposed to routine or operational. This information not only clarified the issue but also established the outlines of potential strategies to resolve the issue.

Last, OPD wanted managers to state the consequences of failure to address the issue. If there are no consequences, then the issue is not an issue. The issue may be interesting in an academic sense, but it does not involve an important or fundamental choice for the county. In more colloquial jargon, if it ain't broke (or likely to be broke in the future), then don't fix it.

Three Approaches to Strategic Issue Identification

Three approaches to the identification of strategic issues are possible: the direct approach, the goals approach, and the "vision of success" approach (Barry, 1986). Which approach is best depends on the organization's or community's characteristics. (Guidelines for the use of the three approaches will be presented in this section; guidelines for the whole strategic issue identification step will be presented in the following section.)

In the direct approach—probably most useful to most governments and nonprofit organizations—planners go straight from a review of mandates, mission, and SWOTs to the identification of strategic issues. The direct approach is best if (1) there is no agreement on goals, or the goals on which there is agreement are too abstract to be useful; (2) there is no preexisting vision of success, and developing a consensually based vision will be difficult; (3) there is no hierarchical authority that can impose goals on the other stakeholders; or (4) the environment is so turbulent that development of goals or visions seems unwise, and partial actions in response to immediate, important issues seem most appropriate.

The direct approach, in other words, can work in the pluralistic, partisan, politicized, and relatively fragmented worlds of most public (and many nonprofit) organizations, as long as there is a "dominant coalition" strong enough and interested enough to make it work. There must be a coalition committed to identifying and resolving at least some of the key strategic issues, even if they are not committed to developing a comprehensive set of goals or a vision of success.

In the goals approach—more in keeping with traditional planning theory—an organization first establishes goals and objectives for itself and then identifies issues or develops strategies to achieve those goals and objectives. For the approach to work, fairly broad and deep agreement on the organization's goals and objectives must be possible, and the goals and objectives themselves must be specific and detailed enough to provide useful guidance in the development of strategies. This approach also is more likely to work in organizations with hierarchical authority structures in which key decision makers can impose goals on others affected by the planning exercise.

The approach, in other words, is more likely to work in public or nonprofit organizations that are hierarchically organized, pursue narrowly defined missions, and have few powerful stakeholders. In contrast, organizations with broad agendas and numerous powerful stakeholders are unlikely to achieve the kind of consensus (whether "forced" or otherwise) necessary to use the goals approach effectively. For the same reasons, the approach is unlikely to work well for communities.

Finally, in the vision of success approach, the organization is asked to develop a "best" picture of itself in the future as it fulfills its mission and achieves success. The strategic issues then involve how the organization should move from the way it is now to how it would look and behave based on its vision of success. This approach is most useful if it will be difficult to identify strategic issues directly, if no preexisting goals and objectives exist and will be difficult to develop, and if drastic change is likely to be necessary. As conception precedes perception

(May, 1969), development of a vision of success can provide the concepts necessary in times of major change to enable organizational members to see what changes are necessary.

The vision of success developed in this step will be much sketchier than the more elaborate version called for in the last step in the strategic planning process. All that is needed here is a one-page idealized scenario of the future. This approach is more likely to apply to nonprofit organizations than to public organizations, as public organizations are more likely to be tightly constrained by mandates. The approach may also work for communities, but it is often very difficult for communities to develop effective strategies to achieve the vision.

Direct Approach. The following guidelines may prove helpful to organizations that use the direct approach.

After a review of mandates, mission, and SWOTs, strategic planning team members should be asked to identify strategic issues first as individuals by answering for each issue three questions on a single sheet of paper:

- What is the issue?
- What factors (mandates, mission, external and internal) make it a strategic issue?
- What are the consequences of failure to address the issue?

Sample worksheets in Resource Section A at the end of the book may help here.

It may be best to give individuals at least a week to propose strategic issues. The identification of strategic issues is a real art and cannot be forced. People may need time to reflect on what the strategic issues really are. Also, an individual's best insights often come in odd moments and not in group settings.

Each of the suggested strategic issues, phrased as a question the organization can do something about, then should be placed on a separate sheet of large paper and posted on a wall so that members of the strategic planning team may consider and discuss them as a set. The sheets may be treated as giant snow cards, with similar issues grouped together and perhaps recast into a different form on blank sheets held in reserve for that purpose.

When at least tentative agreement is reached on what the strategic issues are, prepare new single sheets that present each issue and answer the three questions. These new sheets will provide the basis for further discussion if necessary, or for the development of strategies to resolve the issues in the next step.

One technique that has proved useful is the SWOT Matrix, used by the giant multinational corporation Philips of Eindhoven in the Netherlands (Freedman and Van Ham, 1982, pp. 184–186). On one side of a two-by-two matrix are listed strengths and weaknesses; on the other side, opportunities and threats. Members of the strategic planning team then are asked to identify patterns in the resulting juxtaposition of SWOTs. Issues that are combinations of strengths and opportunities obviously are especially desirable, as the organization is positioned well to take advantage of the opportunities. On the other hand, issues that are combinations of weaknesses and threats are likely to be distressing, since the organization will be in a poor position to defend itself against the threats. Issues that are combinations of weaknesses and opportunities will be problematic because the organization will not be in a good position to take advantage of the opportunities, while issues that combine strengths with threats may not cause too much concern as long as the organization is strong enough to deal with the threats.

Nursing Service developed the set of strategic issues contained in Exhibit 5 after a review of mandates, mission, and SWOTs. The first issue in Part A asks what the mission of Nursing Service should be. After addressing that issue, and changing their mission statement as a result, Nursing Service's strategic planning team decided to scrap the rest of the issues in Part A and develop the new set presented in Part B. The new set focused directly on what Nursing Service (and the county government of which it was a part) had to do to fulfill its new mission. (The fact that Nursing Service rethought both its mission and strategic issues is not unusual and, indeed, should be expected.)

Goals Approach. The following guidelines are for organizations that choose the goals approach.

If the organization does not already have a set of goals, then after a review of mandates, mission, and SWOTs, members

Exhibit 5. Nursing Service's Strategic Issues.

Part A. The First Set of Issues

1. What business should we be in? The question is one of mandates, mission, and values.
2. How do we ensure an adequate funding base to fulfill our mission?
3. How do we organize and manage the agency in order to fulfill our mission effectively?
4. How do we influence public policy at the state and local levels to assure appropriate gatekeeping to, and quality of, public health services for the community?

Part B. The Second Set of Issues

1. What is the role of Nursing Service in ensuring the health of the citizens of the county?
2. How should Nursing Service deal with the growing health care needs for which there is inadequate or no reimbursement for services?
3. What is the role of Nursing Service (and the county) in ensuring quality in community-based health care?
4. What is the role of Nursing Service (and the county) in ensuring community planning and system development?

---

of the strategic planning team should be asked to propose goals for the organization as a basis for group discussion. Again, the snow card procedure is an effective way to develop and organize a set of possible goals quickly as a basis for further group discussion. More than one session may be necessary before the group can agree on a set of goals that are specific and detailed enough to guide the development of strategies in the next step.

It may not be necessary to identify strategic issues if this approach is used; rather, the team may move directly to the strategy development step. If strategic issues are identified, they are likely to pose questions such as: How do we gain the agreement of key decision makers on this set of goals? How do we establish priorities among these goals?

An alternative way to identify a set of goals for the organization is to assign one or more members of the strategic planning team the task of reviewing the past decisions and actions to uncover the organization's implicit goals. This approach can uncover the existing consensus in the organization about what its goals are. It also can uncover any divergences between this consensus and the organization's mandates, mission, and SWOTs. Dealing with the divergences may represent strategic issues for the organization.

Hennepin County staff reviewed the previous decisions and actions of the county board and administrative branch to uncover the implicit goals (they referred to them as policy objectives) of the county government. The countywide policy objectives developed in this way are presented in Exhibit 6. These objectives have the advantage of embodying an existing consensus on what the county should seek in the three areas of service delivery, finance, and management.

Exhibit 6. Hennepin County Policy Objectives.

Service Delivery Objectives

One of Hennepin County's primary goals is to provide services that are cost-effective, timely, and responsive to the changing needs of the county's citizens. It is the objective of the county to:

- Furnish mandated and optional public services in the areas of assessment, elections, public records, licenses, tax administration, transportation and environmental concern as provided in Minnesota statutes and in a cost-effective and coordinated manner.
- Protect life and property, administer justice, protect the rights of citizens and rehabilitate offenders through effective and appropriate use of its law enforcement, prosecution, legal defense, civil and criminal courts, and corrections programs.
- Maintain and improve the physical well-being of county residents by reducing the number of illnesses and disabilities, or by lessening their severity.
- Provide effective citizen access to informational and outdoor recreational resources.
- Protect from abuse, exploitation, and neglect county residents who are unable to assure themselves of basic rights and opportunities.
- Assist in achieving and maintaining basic levels of economic, social, and personal independence for individuals.
- Provide a permanent and stable family setting for all dependent children.
- Maximize the economic self-sufficiency of individuals and families by effectively, efficiently and humanely managing the federal and state aided economic assistance programs administered by the county.
- Provide legislative direction, administrative support, and general services for the efficient operation of county business and the effective management of county programs.

Exhibit 6. Hennepin County Policy Objectives, Cont'd.

Financial Objectives

The operating and capital budgets of the county are to be prepared annually according to law and reviewed in public meetings which provide for citizen input. The budget shall contain programs and capital projects that are responsive to the needs of the citizenry and that meet the requirements of federal and state mandates.

In financing the budget, property taxes are the funding source of last resort for the county. The level of property taxes required by the county is primarily dependent on the amount of federal, state and fee revenues available; and the level of property tax–related expenditures to be financed. It is the objective of the county to:

- Limit the rate of growth in the property tax levy to the rate of increase in the estimated market value of property in Hennepin County.
- Ensure that increases in county expenditures do not exceed the rate of inflation for the SMSA from May to May.
- Aggressively seek to ensure that state and federal program appropriations are sufficient to fully fund mandated services and statutory reimbursement formulas.
- Seek added federal and state support through general purpose revenue-sharing programs and local government aids.
- Aggressively seek grants and other private sources of funding for new and existing programs.
- Maximize fees for services based on the full cost of providing the service, or based on competitive market forces unless prohibited by law.
- Maintain a minimum cash position adequate to finance 60 days of operations for the county.

Management Objectives

The county considers management to have a progressive as opposed to a maintenance role. Improvements, innovation, and progress in administering the business of the county are to be encouraged, pursued, and achieved. It is the objective of the county to:

- Emphasize hiring practices that reflect the equal opportunity employment philosophy of the county.
- Maintain wage and benefit programs for employees that are competitive with the private sector and other units of government.
- Maintain a personnel policy that is designed and administered in a manner that provides adaptability and efficiency.
- Improve its productivity by 2 percent per annum.
- Actively consider alternative approaches for providing services whenever an alternative offers quality service at the levels needed in a more cost-effective manner.

Exhibit 6. Hennepin County Policy Objectives, Cont'd.

- Foster the development of intergovernmental cooperation agreements and joint ventures in order to improve service, enhance efficiency or reduce costs, and improve intergovernmental relations.
- Develop program evaluation and performance measurement standards for existing and new county programs.

Source: Hennepin County, 1983, pp. 3-2–3-5.

Whichever approach to the development of goals is used, specific objectives will be developed in the next step, strategy development. Strategies are developed to achieve goals; objectives should be thought of as specific milestones or targets to be reached during strategy implementation.

Vision of Success Approach. The following guidelines may help organizations develop a "vision of success."

After a review of mandates, mission, and SWOTs, each member of the strategic planning team should be asked as an individual to develop a picture or scenario of what the organization should look like as it successfully fulfills its mission and achieves its full potential. The visions should be no longer than a page in length, and might be developed in response to the following instructions: "Imagine that it is three to five years from now and your organization has been put together in a very exciting way. It is a recognized leader in its field. Imagine that you are a newspaper reporter assigned to do a story on the organization. You have thoroughly reviewed the organization's mandates, mission, services, personnel, financing, organization, management, etc. Describe in no more than a page what you see" (Barry, 1986, p. 41).

The members of the strategic planning team should then share their visions with each other. A facilitator can record the elements of each person's vision on large sheets. Either during or after the sharing process, similarities and differences among them should be noted and discussed. Basic alternative visions then should be formulated (perhaps by a staff member after the session) as a basis for further discussion.

At a subsequent session, planning team members should

rate each alternative vision or scenario along several dimensions deemed of strategic importance (such as fit with mandates and mission, stakeholder support, financial feasibility) and should develop a list of relative advantages and disadvantages of each vision. Discussion should follow to decide which vision is best for the organization.

Once agreement is reached among key decision makers on the best vision, the strategic planning team may be able to move on to the next step: developing strategies to achieve the vision.

Health Center pursued the vision of success approach. Its strategic planning team identified four possible scenarios: (1) continue as a division of the city's health department; (2) become a free-standing, nonprofit community health center; (3) become a free-standing, nonprofit "umbrella" community agency housing a variety of health and human service organizations; and (4) become a component of a free-standing, nonprofit health maintenance organization. After exploring these options with possible partners, Health Center's executive director and strategic planning team decided to pursue the second option.

The vision developed with this approach actually may constitute a "grand strategy" for the organization, the overall scheme for how best to "fit" with its environment. The strategy development step then would concentrate on filling in the detail for putting the grand strategy into operation.

The strategic planning team may decide to identify strategic issues first, however, before developing more detailed strategies for implementation. The strategic issues typically would concern how to gain broad acceptance of the vision and how to bridge the gap between the vision and where the organization is at present.

It is probably easier for nonprofit organizations with narrowly defined missions to develop a full-blown vision of success (that is, a vision that is more than the sketch called for in this step) than it is for large general-purpose governments. In my experience it is very difficult for a government or multi-function public agency to develop a detailed vision of success. The numerous stakeholders with their conflicting agendas, and the typically more numerous and constricting mandates, make development of a vision difficult. A vision probably can be developed only after a government or multi-purpose agency has gone through several cycles of strategic planning in which fairly broad and deep understanding and agreement have emerged about who the government is, what it should do, and why.

It is for this reason that the vision of success step has been placed at the end of the strategy formulation process in Figure 1. A vision of success, in other words, is more likely to guide the implementation of strategies than it is to guide their formulation. Further, it is not necessary to agree on a detailed vision, or even on goals, in order to agree on issues—fundamental policy choices—and effective strategies to deal with those issues. Since development of a vision of success may entail unnecessary conflict, it can be postponed until a vision emerges from the accumulated decisions and actions of key decision makers aimed at dealing with the fundamental policy choices facing the organization. Indeed, key decision makers may choose not to develop a vision of success at all if doing so would prove to be an impossible or excessively disruptive task.

It should be noted that the three approaches to the identification of strategic issues are interrelated (a point that will be brought out again in the next chapter). It is a matter of where you choose to start. For example, an organization can frame strategic issues directly and then in the next step can develop goals and objectives for the strategies developed to deal with the issues. Mission, strategies, goals, and objectives then can be used to develop a vision of success in the last step in the process. Or an organization may go through several cycles of strategic planning using the direct or goals approaches before it decides to develop a vision of success. Or it may start with the ideal scenario approach and then expand the scenario into a vision of success after it completes strategy development.

Process Guidelines

The following process guidelines should prove helpful as a strategic planning team identifies the strategic issues its organization faces:

1. Review the organization's (or community's) mandates, mission, strengths, weaknesses, opportunities, and threats. These external and internal elements provide a "map" of the organization in relation to its environment. Strategic issues involve fundamental choices facing the organization about how it should relate to its environment. The strategies that are developed to deal with these issues in effect define what the organization is, what it does, and why it does it in relation to its environment. Good strategies provide the best "fit" for the organization with its environment. But the place to begin this process of strategy development is the identification of strategic issues, and the place to begin that is with a review of the map of the organization and its environment. (Participants also may find it helpful to review Resource Section C at the end of the book.)

2. Select an approach to strategic issue identification that fits your situation: the direct approach, the goal approach, or the "vision of success" approach (Barry, 1986).

3. Once strategic issues have been identified, they should be sequenced in either a priority, logical, or temporal order as a prelude to strategy development in the next step. The attention of key decision makers probably is the resource in shortest supply in most organizations, so it is very important to focus that attention effectively and efficiently. Establishing a reasonable order among strategic issues allows key decision makers to focus on them one at a time. (Sometimes the issues may be so interconnected that they have to be dealt with as a set.)

The strategic implications of the chosen order should be considered carefully. For example, it may *not* be wise to have key decision makers focus first on the top priority issue, especially if they have had little prior interaction and little experience with constructive conflict resolution. In such circumstances it may be best to start the process of resolving strategic issues by focusing on the *least* important issue, so decision makers can gain experience in dealing with one another and with conflict when the consequences of failure are least.

4. It may be helpful to use a "litmus test" to develop some measure of just how strategic an issue is. The litmus test used by Hennepin County to screen strategic issues is presented in Exhibit 7. A truly strategic issue is one that scores high on

Exhibit 7. A Litmus Test for Strategic Issues.

Operational ←—————————————→ Strategic

	(1)	(2)	(3)
1. When will the strategic issues' challenge or opportunity confront you?	Right now	Next year	Two or more years from now
2. How broad an impact will the issue have on your department?	Single unit or division	Several divisions	Entire department
3. How large is your department's financial risk/financial opportunity?	Minor (less than $250,000 or 10% of budget)	Moderate ($250,000 to $1,000,000 or 10 to 25% of budget)	Major ($1,000,000 plus or more than 25% of budget)
4. Will strategies for issue resolution likely require:			
a. Development of new service goals and programs?	No		Yes
b. Significant changes in tax sources or amounts?	No		Yes
c. Significant amendments in federal or state statutes or regulations?	No		Yes
d. Major facility additions or modifications?	No		Yes
e. Significant staff expansion?	No		Yes
5. How apparent is the best approach for issue resolution?	Obvious, ready to implement	Broad parameters, few details	Wide open
6. What is the lowest level of management that can decide how to deal with this issue?	Line staff supervisor	Division head	Department head
7. What are the probable consequences of not addressing this issue?	Inconvenience, inefficiency	Significant service disruption, financial losses	Major long-term service disruption and large cost/revenue setbacks
8. How many other departments are affected by this issue and must be involved in resolution?	None	One to Three	Four or more
9. How sensitive or "charged" is the issue relative to community social, political, religious and cultural values?	Benign	Touchy	Dynamite

A note on use and interpretation: There is no absolute test to establish whether an issue is strategic or operational. There is a large gray area into which many issues will fall and the assessment of their strategic importance is a judgment that must be made by top management. To assist managers in making this judgment, it is suggested that the questions in the "litmus test" be applied to each identified issue. Generally speaking, major strategic issues will be characterized by answers that fall predominately in Column 2 and Column 3. Operational issues will tend to be characterized by answers in Column 1 and Column 2.

all dimensions. A strictly operational issue would score low on all dimensions.

Hennepin County's litmus test is designed for use by management. If the test is to be more generally useful, two additional questions should be added to the top of the list. First, Is the issue on the agenda of the organization's policy board (whether elected or appointed)? If an issue is already of concern to the board it is likely to be of more strategic importance. Second, Is the issue on the agenda of the organization's chief executive (whether elected or appointed)? Again, if it is, the issue is likely to be of more strategic importance. This is not to say that issues that are not on the two agendas are not strategically important. If an issue not on those agendas is judged by the strategic planning team to be of real strategic importance, then the team will have to develop a strategy to place it there.

5. There is a real art to framing strategic issues. Considerable discussion and revision of first drafts are likely to be necessary to frame issues in the most useful way. Nursing Service illustrates this point. After considerable discussion, Nursing Service concluded that its mission had to be revised. The revised mission then led the strategic planning team to conclude that the remaining issues in its first set were not focused enough to be useful, so they formulated a second set of strategic issues more pointedly aimed at implementing the mission. The main benefit of the first set therefore was to prompt Nursing Service to reexamine its mission; once that was done, the "real" strategic issues could be identified. The importance of Hubert Humphrey's advice—"When in doubt, talk"—should be apparent.

It is important to critique strategic issues to be sure that they really do usefully frame the fundamental choices the organization faces. The strategic planning team should ask itself several questions about the issues it identifies before it settles on a set of issues to address. Some useful questions include:

What is the issue, conflict, or dilemma?
Why is it an issue? What is it about mission, mandates, or SWOTs that makes it an issue?
Who says it is an issue?

What are the consequences of not doing something about it?

Can we do something about it?

Is there a way to combine or eliminate issues?

Should issues be broken down into two or more issues?

What issues are missing from our list?

It is especially important to remember that strategic issues framed in single-functional terms will be dealt with by single-functional departments or agencies. Strategic issues that are framed in multi-functional terms will have to be addressed by more than one department. Strategic issues that are framed in multi-organizational, multi-institutional terms will have to be addressed by more than one organization or institution. If one seeks to wrest control of an issue from a single department, then the issue must be framed multi-functionally. If one seeks to wrest control of an issue from a single organization, then it must be framed multi-organizationally. Strategic planners can gain enormous influence over the strategic planning process and its outcomes if the issues are framed in such a way that decision makers must share power in order to resolve the issues.

6. Remember that there are likely to be at least three kinds of strategic issues; each will need to be treated differently. The three are (1) those that require no action at present, but must be monitored; (2) those that can be handled as part of the organization's regular strategic planning cycle; and (3) those that require urgent attention and must be dealt with out of sequence with the organization's regular strategic planning cycle.

7. Focus on issues, not answers. The answers will be developed in the next step, strategy formulation. Those answers will be helpful only if they are developed in response to the issues that actually confront the organization. Put differently, an answer without an issue is not an answer.

8. Reach an agreement among key decision makers that a major fraction of their time together will be devoted to the identification and resolution of strategic issues. Without an agreement of this sort, it will be too easy to forget that when key decision makers get together one of their most important

tasks is to deal with what is most important to the organization. Central City's cabinet, for example, has agreed to spend a major fraction of every cabinet meeting on strategic issues. Hennepin County's cabinet meets every Monday for two hours to deal with strategic matters; if there are none to discuss, the cabinet doesn't meet.

9. Keep it light. As noted at the beginning of this chapter, this step in the strategic planning process can quickly become very serious and "heavy." It is important for members of the strategic planning team to keep their senses of humor and acknowledge and release tensions with good humored mutual solicitude. Otherwise, destructive conflict or paralysis may set in, and the group may find it difficult to agree on a set of strategic issues and move on to developing effective strategies to deal with the issues. Emotions may run high in this step and the group will have to acknowledge these emotions and deal with them constructively.

10. Agreement on strategic issues to be addressed in the next step is likely to mark an important organizational decision point. Remember that identifying strategic issues is the heart of the planning process. Identifying the fundamental policy questions the organization faces will have a profound effect on the actual choices made and ultimately on the viability and success of the organization.

11. Managing the transition to the next step in the process—strategy development—is crucial. Too often organizations quickly identify strategic issues and then back off from resolving them. The conflicts or choices embodied in the issues may seem too difficult or disruptive to address. Strong leadership and commitment to the strategic planning process must be exercised if the organization is to deal effectively with the basic issues it confronts.

Summary

The purpose of the strategic issue identification step is to identify the fundamental policy choices facing the organization concerning its mandates, mission, and product or service level and mix; clients, customers, or users; cost; financing; organization; or management. At the end of this step key decision makers should agree on a set of strategic issues to be addressed in priority, logical, or temporal order.

To return to the story metaphor, this step constitutes the framing of conflicts (issues). The climax of the story will be reached in the next step when these conflicts are resolved through the construction of effective strategies.

Three basic approaches to the identification of issues are: the direct approach, the goals approach, and the vision of success approach. In general, governments and nonprofit agencies will find the direct approach most useful.

The transition to the next step in the process—strategy development—is crucial and will require careful management. Too often strategic planning teams move quickly to the identification of strategic issues, but have difficulty in moving forward with the development and implementation of effective strategies. It is one thing to talk about what is fundamental, quite another to take action based on those discussions. Strong leadership and high morale will be required to keep moving ahead. Unless the team and organization push on, organizational effectiveness and stakeholder satisfaction are likely to suffer, and the organization will not fulfill its mission.

Chapter 8

Formulating Strategies to Manage the Issues

Every innovation is a failure in the middle.
Rosabeth Moss Kanter

The art of progress is to preserve order amid change,
and change amid order.
Alfred North Whitehead

Changes in degree lead to changes in kind.
Karl Marx

Strategy may be thought of as a pattern of purposes, policies, programs, actions, decisions, or resource allocations that define what an organization is, what it does, and why it does it. Strategy therefore is the extension of mission to form a bridge between an organization (or community) and its environment. Strategies typically are developed to deal with strategic issues, that is, they outline the organization's response to fundamental policy choices. (If the goal approach to strategic issues is taken, strategies will be developed to achieve the goals; or, if the vision of success approach is taken, strategies will be developed to achieve the vision.)

This definition of strategy is purposely very broad. It is important to recognize patterns across organizational policies, decisions, resource allocations, and actions large and small. General strategies will fail if specific steps to implement them are absent. Further, strategies are prone to failure if an organization has no consistency among what it says, what it pays for, and what it does. The definition of strategy offered here calls attention to the importance of this consistency.

Rosabeth Kanter observes that "every innovation is a failure in the middle" (1983). They are failures in the middle because they *must* be. By definition, they have never been tried before (at least by the organization), and success can be determined only after they are implemented. The broad definition of strategy is used to help assure that strategic changes (a kind of innovation), while they may be failures initially, are successes in the end.

Also, according to this definition every organization already *has* a strategy; that is, for every organization there is already some sort of pattern across its purposes, policies, programs, actions, decisions, or resource allocations. The pattern just may not be a very good one. It may need to be refined or sharpened or changed altogether for it to be an effective bridge from the organization to its environment.

Strategies also can vary by level and time frame. Four basic levels include:

1. Grand strategy for the organization as a whole.
2. Strategic public planning unit (SPPU) or strategic nonprofit planning unit (SNPPU) strategies. Note, however, that if the organization as a whole and the SPPU or SNPPU are synonymous, the first two categories will be the same; if not, SPPUs or SNPPUs may be divisions, departments, or units of larger organizations.
3. Program or service strategies.
4. Functional (such as financial, staffing, facilities, and procurement) strategies.

Strategies also may be long-term or fairly short-term.

Strategies are different from tactics. Tactics are the short-term, adaptive actions and reactions used to accomplish limited objectives. Strategies provide the "continuing basis for ordering these adaptations toward more broadly conceived purposes" (Quinn, 1980, p. 9).

Purpose

An example of a strategy statement for an organization is presented in Exhibit 8. The organization is the Amherst H.

Wilder Foundation of St. Paul, Minnesota, a large nonprofit operating foundation active in health and welfare. In 1984 the foundation had an endowment and assets worth more than $170 million, spent more than $5 million of trust income, employed 950 people, and served more than 38,000 people (Bryson, King, Roering, and Van de Ven, 1986). The strategy statement outlines the grand strategy for the foundation during 1982–1986, but also includes aspects of program, service, and functional strategies. The statement is short and to the point. It is easily communicated and understood. And it provides guidance for decision making and action at higher levels within the organization.

Exhibit 8. Wilder Foundation 1982–1986 Strategy Statement.

As a board and staff, for the next five years the Foundation will:

1. *Continue as an operating, direct service, health and welfare agency,* 90% in the greater St. Paul metropolitan area with minor emphasis on support services such as: consultation, training, and community-wide cooperative approaches.
2. *Provide direct services for primary areas:* (1) outpatient and residential psychiatric services to children; (2) residential and home services to elderly; (3) correction services to children and adults; (4) administration of housing.
    In addition, special emphasis will be placed on training, education, consultation, and research through Wilder Forest, Office of Research and Statistics, and Management Support Services to other agencies.
3. *Within direct services for primary area:*
    a.   direct service to members of low- and moderate-income families;
    b.   a gradual change to working with groups in comparison to one-to-one relationships;
    c.   direct service to a large range of persons: clients, members, participants, residents, attendees;
    d.   increased use of volunteers;
    e.   programs funded through: (1) leveraging income ($3 of outside funds for $1 of trust income) to increase impact, and (2) investing in comparison to direct use (grants) of trust income;
    f.   cooperation with other organizations.
4. *General policies will include:* annual funding of liabilities, balancing budgets, and perpetuity of trust.

Source: Bryson, King, Roering, and Van de Ven, 1986, p. 133.

Unfortunately, very few governments, public agencies, or nonprofit organizations have such a clear strategy statement, whether explicit or implicit. As a result, there is usually little more than an odd assortment of policies to guide decision making and action in pursuit of organizational purposes. In the absence of such direction, the sum of the organization's parts can be expected to add up to something less than a whole.

The purpose of the strategy development step therefore is to create a set of strategies that effectively link the organization and its constituent parts to the external environment. Typically these strategies will be developed in response to strategic issues, but they also may be developed to achieve goals or a vision of success.

Two resources sections at the end of the book supplement material in this chapter. Resource D outlines several concepts that may help the strategic planning team think about strategy and its implementation. Resource E presents in detail the strategies selected by Suburban City to deal with one of its strategic issues. Suburban City used the five-part process outlined here to develop these strategies.

Desired Outcomes and Benefits

Several desired planning outcomes may come from this step. First are various strategy statements. The organization might seek a grand strategy statement for itself. It also might want SPPU or SNPPU, program or service, and functional strategy statements for its constituent parts. A complete set of these statements is probably warranted if the organization has chosen the vision of success approach; the set would be necessary to clarify strategies for achieving the vision. On the other hand, the organization may have more limited aims. If it has chosen the direct approach it may simply want a statement of how it will deal with each issue. Or if it has chosen the goal approach, it may want statements that clarify how it will achieve each goal.

Second, the organization may or may not wish to have a formal strategic plan at the end of this step. Remember that what is important about strategic planning is strategic thinking and acting, not necessarily preparation of a strategic plan.

The plan, if it is developed, probably would include the organization's mission statement; mandates to be met; SWOT analysis (at least as an appendix); strategic issues, or goals, or vision of success; and strategies (grand, SPPU or SNPPU, program or service, or functional), including guidance for implementation. Possible contents of a strategic plan will be discussed further later in this chapter.

Third, at the conclusion of this step, planners may seek formal agreement to push ahead. If a strategic plan has been prepared, this agreement may include formal adoption of the plan. Formal agreement may not be necessary, but it usually enhances legitimacy of strategic actions and provides an occasion for communicating widely the intent and content of such actions.

Finally, as is true throughout the process, actions should be taken when they are identified and become useful or necessary. Otherwise, important opportunities may be lost or threats may not be countered in time. It is also important to ease the transition from an old reality, whatever that may have been, to the new reality embodied in the emerging strategies. If the transition can be broken down into a small number of manageable steps it will be easier to accomplish than if it requires a major leap.

Ten benefits of the strategy development step can be identified.

1. A fairly clear picture will emerge—from grand conception to detailed implementation—of how the organization can meet its mandates, fulfill its mission, and deal effectively with the situation it faces. This picture provides the measure of clarity about where an organization is going, how it will get there, and why, that is an important part of most successful change efforts (Dalton, 1970; Kanter, 1983). A new reality cannot be fully realized until it is named and understood (May, 1969).

2. This new picture should have emerged from a consideration of a broad range of alternative strategies, which in itself should enhance organizational creativity and overcome the usual tendency of organizations to engage in simplistic, truncated, and narrow searches for solutions to their problems (Cyert and March, 1963).

3. If actions are taken as they become identified and useful to achieve the new reality, that new reality will emerge in fact, not just in conception. If the strategic planning exercise has not become "real" for team members and key decision makers, it certainly will become real now (Boal and Bryson, 1987b).

4. Early implementation of at least parts of major strategies will facilitate organizational learning. The organization will be able to find out quickly whether its strategies are likely to be effective, and they can be revised or corrected before being fully implemented.

5. Emotional bonding to the new reality can occur as it emerges gradually through early and ongoing implementation efforts. To return to the story metaphor, no drama can reach an effective and satisfying conclusion without a catharsis phase in which the audience is allowed time to break its emotional bonds with an old reality so that it can forge new bonds to the new reality. This bonding process is likely to fail if the gap between old and new realities is too large and not bridged in a series of "acts" and "scenes" (Hostager and Bryson, 1986; Quinn, 1980).

6. Heightened morale among strategic planning team members, key decision makers, and other organizational members should result from task accomplishment and early successes in the resolution of important issues. If the organization is pursuing an important mission and dealing with the fundamental questions it faces, it can expect involvement and excitement from key actors (Selznick, 1957).

7. Further strategic planning team development (and indeed broader organizational development) should result from the continued discipline of addressing fundamental questions constructively (Eadie and Steinbacher, 1985). Improved communication and understanding among team (and organizational) members should occur. Strategic thinking and acting are likely to become a habit.

8. If key internal and external stakeholder interests have been addressed successfully as part of the strategic planning process, a coalition is likely to emerge that is large enough and strong enough to agree on organizational strategies and to pursue their

implementation. If a formal strategic plan is prepared, there is likely to be a coalition large enough and strong enough to adopt it, implement it, and use it as an ongoing basis for decision making.

9. Organizational members will have the permission they need to move ahead with implementation of strategies. Those who wish to preserve the status quo will find themselves fighting a rearguard action as the organization mobilizes to implement adopted strategies.

10. If all these benefits are achieved, the organization will have achieved progress in an effective and artful way. Following Alfred North Whitehead, the organization will have preserved order amid change, and change amid order. It will have built new and more effective bridges from itself to its environment, and from its past to its future. And people will be able to cross those bridges relatively easily and painlessly.

A Five-Part Process

I favor use of a five-part strategy development process, in which planners answer five questions about each strategic issue. (The approach is adapted slightly from one developed by the Institute of Cultural Affairs.) The questions themselves would be changed somewhat depending on whether the strategic issues, goal, or vision of success approach is used. The questions are:

1. What are the practical alternatives, "dreams," or "visions" we might pursue to address this strategic issue, achieve this goal, or realize this scenario?
2. What are the barriers to the realization of these alternatives, dreams, or visions?
3. What major proposals might we pursue to achieve these alternatives, dreams, or visions directly, or to overcome the barriers to their realization?
4. What major actions with existing staff must be taken within the next year to implement the major proposals?
5. What specific steps must be taken within the next six months to implement the major proposals and who is responsible?

The process begins conventionally by asking strategic planning team members to imagine grand alternatives to deal with the specific issue. Then comes an unconventional step—enumerating barriers to realization of the alternatives, instead of developing major proposals to achieve the alternatives directly. The listing of barriers at this point helps ensure that implementation difficulties are dealt with directly rather than haphazardly.

The next step asks for major proposals either to achieve the alternatives directly, or else indirectly through overcoming the barriers. Many organizations find that they must spend considerable time overcoming barriers before they can get on with achieving an alternative. For example, Central City found it had to spend time and resources modernizing its personnel system before it could seriously consider major proposals aimed directly at achieving its preferred alternatives for service delivery, economic development, and financial management. Other organizations may be able to move directly to achieve their preferred alternatives.

The answer to the fourth question will essentially be a one- to two-year work program to implement the major proposals. Note that the work will be done by existing staff within existing job descriptions. This question begins to elicit the specificity necessary for successful strategy implementation. The question also conveys the notion that any journey must begin where one is. For example, if full-blown implementation of the strategy will require more staff and resources, this question will ask strategists to be clear about what can be done, using existing staff and resources, to get *more* staff and resources. The question also begins to force people to "put their money where their mouths are." As the precise shape and content of strategy implementation emerges, it will become quite clear who is willing to go ahead and who is not.

The final question asks strategists to be even more specific about what must be done and who must do it. The implications of strategy implementation for organizational members will become quite real at the conclusion of this step. The specificity of actions and assignment of responsibilities to particular individuals are requisites of successful strategy implementation

(Dalton, 1970). In addition, such specificity often will determine *exactly* what people are willing to live with and what they are not.

I have found that a strategic planning team can use the snow card process to answer each question. The technique allows for great creativity and at the same time facilitates development of organization-specific categories to hold the individual ideas. The categories that emerge will identify, in order, practical alternatives, barriers, major proposals, major actions, and specific steps. Suburban City, for example, developed its strategies to deal with its strategic issues using the five-part process and the snow card technique. The strategies for one strategic issue are reproduced in Resource E.

Using this five-step process in conjunction with the snow card technique has several advantages. First, it keeps people from jumping immediately to solutions, a typical failing of problem-solving groups (Johnson and Johnson, 1987). Second, it keeps people from overevaluating ideas; it keeps idea creation and evaluation in a reasonable balance. Third, it forces people to build a bridge from where they are to where they would like to be. Fourth, it forces people to deal with implementation difficulties directly.

Finally, a particular advantage of the technique is that a great deal of unnecessary conflict is avoided simply because items proposed in answer to one question will drop out if no one suggests a way to handle them in the next step. For example, instead of struggling over the advantages and disadvantages of some major proposal to realize an alternative, the process simply asks the group what has to happen in the next year or two with existing staff within existing job descriptions to implement the proposal. If no one can think of reasonable responses, then an unnecessary struggle never happens. Of course, the group needs to make sure answers in previous steps are linked to answers in subsequent steps to keep some proposals from dropping from sight unintentionally.

It may not be necessary to answer all the questions; some groups find that they can collapse the last three into two or even one question. The important point is that the specifics of implementation must be clarified as much as necessary to allow effective evaluation of options and to provide detailed guidance for implementation. Recall that a strategy has been defined as a *pattern* of purposes, policies, decisions, actions, or resource allocations that effectively link the organization to its environment. The purpose of the questions, whether all five or only three are used, is to get the organization to clarify exactly what the pattern has to be and who has to do what if the link is to be truly effective.

Some organizations (and communities), particularly larger ones, find it effective to have their strategic planning team answer the first two questions using the snow card technique and then delegate to task forces, committees, or individuals the task of developing answers to the last three questions. These answers are then brought back for review and perhaps decisions by the team. Alternatively, the entire task of developing answers to all five questions may be turned over to a division, department, task force, committee, or individual who then reports back.

Yet another alternative is to use the two-cycle strategic planning process outlined in Chapter Three (or Hennepin County's three-cycle process discussed in the same chapter). In the first cycle, divisions, departments, or smaller units are asked to identify strategic issues (or goals, or scenarios) and to prepare strategies, using the five-part process, within a framework established at the top. The strategies are then reviewed by cross-divisional or departmental strategic planning coordinating committees, including perhaps a cabinet. Once the cabinet, or in some cases a governing board, agrees to specific strategies, detailed operating plans may be developed. These plans would involve a detailed elaboration of answers to the last two questions.

Once answers have been developed to deal with a specific strategic issue (or goal or scenario), the strategic planning team is in a position to make judgments about what strategies actually should be pursued. (The team may rely on one or more of the concepts presented in Resource D to inform its judgments.) In particular, the team needs to ask:

1. What is really reasonable?
2. Where can we combine proposals, actions, specific steps?
3. Do any proposals, actions, or specific steps contradict each other, and if so what should we do about them?
4. What are we really willing to commit ourselves to over the next year?
5. What are the specific next steps that we *will* pursue in the next six months?

The process also helps with ongoing strategy implementation. Once specific strategies have been adopted and are in the process of implementation, the organization should work its way back up the original set of five questions on a regular basis. Every six months the last question should be addressed again. Every year or two the fourth question should be asked again. Every two or three years the third question should be asked. And every three to five years, the first two questions should be addressed again.

Strategic Plans

Strategic plans can vary a great deal in form and content. The simplest form of strategic plan may be nothing more than an unwritten agreement in the minds of key decision makers about the organization's mission and what it should do, given its circumstances. This is the most common form of strategic plan and clearly reflects a basic premise of this book—that strategic thinking and acting are what count, not strategic plans in and of themselves.

But coordinated action among a variety of organizational actors over time usually requires some kind of formal plan so that people can keep track of what they should do and why (Van de Ven, 1976a, 1976b). For one thing, people forget, and the plan can help remind them of what has been decided. The plan also provides a baseline for judging strategic performance. It also serves a more overtly political purpose: it usually amounts to a "treaty" among key actors, factions, and coalitions. Finally, the plan (perhaps not in all its details) can serve as a communications and public relations document for internal and external audiences.

The simplest form of written strategic plan, perfectly acceptable although somewhat crude, would consist of the final versions of several of the worksheets included in Resource A at the end of this book:

Mission statement
Mandates statement
SWOT analysis
Strategic issues (or a set of goals, or a scenario outlining the ideal future)
Strategies—practical alternatives, "dreams," or "visions"; barriers; major proposals; major actions; and specific steps
Vision of success, if one has been prepared

Most organizations will prefer, however, to use the final versions of the worksheets as background material for a written strategic plan. The worksheets might be attached as appendices. If this approach is taken, a table of contents might include the following headings (Barry, 1986):

Mission statement
Mandates statement
Grand strategy statement
Subunit (SPPU or SNPPU) strategy statements (if applicable)
Functional strategy statements
Program, service, or product plans, including strategy statements, goals, and target markets
Staffing plans, including full-time, part-time, and volunteers needed
Financial plans, including operating budgets for each year of the plan, plus any necessary capital budgets or fundraising plans
Implementation plans, including work programs

The mission and strategy statements in effect should constitute an executive summary of the plan. The plan itself need not—and should not—be overly long. If it is, it will be put aside or forgotten by key staff. However, a number of other sections may be included in the plan if necessary (Barry, 1986):

1. A statement of needs, problems, or goals to be addressed.
2. A vision of success, or picture of what the organization (or community) would look like if it fulfilled its mission and achieved its full potential.
3. The organization's structure, either current, proposed, or both.
4. Governance procedures (current, proposed, or both).
5. Key organizational policies (current, proposed, or both).
6. Relationships with key stakeholders (current, proposed, or both).
7. Assumptions on which the plan is based.
8. Marketing plans.
9. Facilities plans.
10. Contingency plans to be pursued if circumstances change.
11. Any other sections deemed to be important.

The task of preparing a first draft of the strategic plan usually should be assigned to a key staff person. Once the draft is prepared, key decision makers, including the strategic planning team, the governing board, and possibly several external stakeholders, should review it. Several modifications are likely to be suggested by various stakeholders, and if modifications improve the plan, they should be accepted. After a final review by key decision makers, the revised plan will be ready for formal adoption. The planning team then will be ready to move on to implementation, although many implementing actions may have occurred already as they have become obvious and necessary over the course of the planning process.

Process Guidelines

The following guidelines should be kept in mind as a strategic planning team formulates effective strategies to link the organization with its environment.

1. Remember that strategic thinking and acting are more important than any particular approach to strategy formulation or the development of a formal strategic plan. The particular way strategies are formulated is less important than how good they are and how well they are implemented. Similarly, whether or not a formal strategic plan is prepared is less important than the effective formulation and implementation of strategies.

2. Members of the strategic planning team may wish to review Resource Section D, "Advanced Concepts for Strategy Formulation and Implementation," at the end of this book. It is very important that a variety of creative, even radical, options be considered during the strategy formulation process. The broader the range of alternative strategies the team considers, the more likely they will find effective strategies. Constant awareness of the variety of options available will help assure that a diverse set of possible strategies are considered before final choices are made.

Another way of making this point is to argue that an organization should *not* engage in strategic planning unless it is willing to consider alternatives quite different from "business as usual." If the organization is only interested in minor variations on existing themes, then it is wasting its time on strategic planning. It might just as well engage in traditional incremental decision making, or "muddling through" (Lindblom, 1959).

3. Incremental decision making, however, can be very effective if it is tied to a strategic sense of direction. Incrementalism uninformed by a strategic sense of direction is simply "muddling through," but when guided by a sense of mission, small decisions can accumulate over time into major changes. Quinn (1980) argues that most strategic changes in large corporations are in fact small changes that are guided by, and result in, a sense of strategic purpose. Karl Marx is perhaps the progenitor of this line of thought with his observation that changes in degree lead to changes in kind.

In effect there are two polar opposite strategies: big wins and small wins (Weick, 1984). The strategic planning process outlined in this book, because it highlights what is fundamental, may tempt organizations always to go for the "big win."

But the big-win strategy may be a mistake. While big-win moves should be considered, the organization also should consider how a whole series of small wins might add up to big wins over time, with less risk and greater ease of implementation.

Consider what may seem to be an unusual example (Weick, 1984): the performance of the Pittsburgh Steelers in their first 115 games under head coach Chuck Knox. Through 1980 the Steelers gained a reputation of near invincibility and went on to win the Super Bowl several times. Their record—eighty-eight wins and twenty-seven losses—is particularly interesting if it is compared to opponents' records. Against opponents who won more than half of their games, the Steelers won twenty-nine and lost twenty-six, or slightly more than half (53 percent). But against opponents with less than .500 records, the Steelers won an astounding fifty-nine against one defeat, for a winning percentage of 98 percent.

So the Steelers gained their reputation for sheer power by winning all the easy ones. The lesson is that you can achieve great things not only through the big win (although big wins clearly can help) but also—perhaps necessarily—through a sequence of small wins. In other words, you may not be in a position to achieve big wins, or the big wins might not even count for much, if they are not built on a series of small wins.

4. Effective strategy formulation can be top down or bottom up. The organizations that are best at strategic planning indeed seem to combine these two approaches into an effective strategic planning system (Lorange and Vancil, 1977). Usually some sort of overall strategic guidance is given at the top, but detailed strategy formulation and implementation typically occur deeper in the organization. Detailed strategies and their implementation may then be reviewed at the top for consistency across strategies and with organizational purposes. Hennepin County, Minnesota (Eckhert, Haines, Delmont, and Pflaum, 1988) and the 3M Corporation (Tita and Allio, 1984), for example, have such systems.

5. Planners should select a preferred approach: should strategies be formulated in response to strategic issues, to achieve goals, or to realize a vision of success? Most organizations prob-

ably will choose the strategic issues approach, at least at first. The goals or vision of success approaches are more suitable for smaller, single-function, or hierarchically organized organizations, or organizations that have engaged in strategic planning for some time, and more useful for nonprofit organizations than governments or public agencies.

It is important to repeat a point made in the previous chapter: the three approaches are interrelated. For example, an organization can start with the strategic issues approach and then develop goals based on its strategies. Goals, in other words, represent desired states in relation to specific strategies. Mission, goals, and strategies then can be used as the basis for developing a vision of success. Alternatively, an organization may go through several cycles of strategic planning using the direct or goals approaches before it decides to develop a vision of success, if indeed it ever chooses to do so. Or an organization may start with the ideal scenario approach and expand the scenario into a vision of success after it completes the strategy development step.

No matter which approach is chosen, the five-part process outlined in this chapter provides an effective way to formulate strategies, particularly if the snow card technique is employed in each step. The questions will change only slightly depending on approach. The strategic planning team may wish to assign different questions to different groups or individuals. If, for example, the team wishes to identify major alternatives and barriers to their achievement, it might ask task forces to develop major proposals and work programs to achieve the alternatives or to overcome the barriers. Hennepin County, Minnesota, used more than thirty different task forces to develop strategies to deal with strategic issues (Eckhert, Haines, Delmont, and Pflaum, 1988).

6. Strategies should be described in enough detail to permit reasonable judgments about their efficacy and to provide reasonable guidance for implementation. Hennepin County (1983) provides a useful example. The planning team asked the various task forces to describe proposed strategic alternatives with regard to:

Principal components or features
Intended results or outcomes
Timetable for implementation
Organizations and persons responsible for implementation
Resources required (staff, facilities, equipment, training)
Costs (startup, annual operating, capital)
Estimated savings over present approaches
Flexibility or adaptability of strategy
Effects on other organizations, departments, or persons
Rule, policy, or statutory changes required
Effects outside the county
Other important features

7. Alternative strategies should be evaluated against agreed-upon criteria prior to selection of specific strategies to be implemented. Those involved in strategy formulation probably should know in advance what criteria will be used to judge alternatives. Again, Hennepin County provides an interesting example. The cabinet of top administrative officials use the following set of criteria to evaluate strategies before adopting any or referring any to the county board for adoption (P. Eckhert, personal communication, 1986):

Acceptability to key decision makers, stakeholders, and
    opinion leaders
Acceptance by the general public
Technical feasibility
Consistency with mission, values, and philosophy
Relevance to the issue
Cost and financing
Long-term impact
Staff requirements
Cost-effectiveness
Flexibility or adaptability
Timing
Client or user impact
Coordination or integration with other programs and
    activities

Facility requirements
Training requirements
Other appropriate criteria

8. The organization should consider developing a formal strategic plan. Such a plan may not be necessary, but as the size and complexity of the organization grow, a formal, written strategic plan is likely to be increasingly useful. The strategic planning team should first agree on major categories and on general length so that the actual preparer has some guidance. Indeed, a general agreement on the form of the strategic plan probably should be reached during the negotiation of the initial agreement (Step 1), so that key decision makers have some general sense of what the effort is likely to produce and surprises are minimized.

It is conceivable, of course, that preparation and publication of a formal strategic plan would be unwise politically. Incompatible objectives or warring external stakeholders, for example, might make it difficult to prepare a "rational" and publicly defensible plan. Key decision makers will have to decide whether a formal strategic plan should be prepared, given the circumstances the organization faces.

9. Even if a formal strategic plan is not prepared, the organization should consider preparing a set of interrelated strategy statements describing grand strategy; subunit (SPPU or SNPPU) strategies; program, service, or product strategies; and functional strategies. To the extent they are agreed upon, these statements will provide extremely useful guides for action by organizational members from top to bottom. Again, however, it may be politically difficult or dangerous to prepare and publicize such statements.

10. A normative process should be used to review strategy statements and formal strategic plans. Drafts typically should be reviewed by planning team members, other key decision makers, the governing board, and at least selected outside stakeholders. Review meetings themselves need to be structured so that the strengths of the statements or plan are recognized and modifications that would improve on those strengths are iden-

tified. Review sessions can be structured around the following
agenda (Barry, 1986):

1. Overview of plan.
2. General discussion of plan and reactions to it.
3. Brainstormed list of plan strengths.
4. Brainstormed list of plan weaknesses.
5. Brainstormed list of modifications that would improve on
   strengths and minimize or overcome weaknesses.
6. Agreement on next steps to complete the plan.

11. It is very important to discuss and evaluate strategies
in relation to key stakeholders. Strategies that are unacceptable
to key stakeholders probably will have to be rethought. Strategies
that do not take stakeholders into consideration are almost certain to fail. Strategists should use techniques such as Nutt and
Backoff's "Classifying the Stakeholder" matrix (see Resource
D) to design winning coalitions for strategy adoption and implementation.

12. The organization should have budgets and budgeting
procedures in place to capitalize on strategic planning and
strategic plans. Hennepin County, Minnesota, for example,
makes sure that monies tied to implementation of strategic plans
are flagged so that they always receive special attention and treat-
ment. They also are attempting to develop a special contingency fund to allow "bridge" funding, so that implementation of
strategies can begin out of sequence with the normal budgeting
process.

Most important, however, is the need to make sure strategic thinking precedes, rather than follows, budgeting. Unfortunately, the only strategic plans most organizations have are
their budgets, and those budgets typically have been formulated
without benefit of any strategic thought. Attention to mission,
mandates, situational assessments, and strategic issues should
precede development of budgets.

13. It is important to allow for a period of catharsis as
the organization moves from one way of being in the world to
another. Strong emotions or tensions are likely to build up as

the organization moves to implement new strategies, particularly if these strategies involve fairly drastic changes. Indeed, the buildup of emotions and tensions may prevent successful implementation of the strategies. These emotions and tensions must be recognized and people must be allowed to vent and deal with them (Dalton, 1970; Hostager and Bryson, 1986). Such emotions and tensions must be a legitimate topic of discussion in strategic planning team meetings. Sessions that review draft statements can solicit modifications that will deal effectively with these emotional concerns.

14. The strategy formulation step is likely to proceed in a more iterative fashion than previous steps because of the need to find the best fit among elements of strategies and of different strategies and levels of strategy with one another. Strong process guidance and facilitation, along with pressure from key decision makers to proceed, probably will be necessary to reach a successful conclusion to this step. Process champions, in other words, will be especially needed if this step is to result in effective strategies.

15. If the organization will not go on to develop a vision of success, some sense of closure to the strategic planning process must be provided at the end of the strategy formulation step. Formal adoption of a strategic plan can provide such a sense of closure. But with or without a strategic plan, some sort of ceremony and celebration probably is required to give participants the sense that the strategic planning effort is finished for the present and that the time for sustained implementation is at hand (Bryson, Van de Ven, and Roering, 1987).

16. Completion of the strategy development step is likely to be an important decision point. The decision will be whether to go ahead with strategies recommended by the strategic planning team. Actually, a number of decision points may result. Proposed strategies to deal with different strategic issues are likely to be presented to the appropriate decision-making bodies at different times. Thus, there would be an important decision point for each set of strategies developed to deal with each strategic issue.

Summary

This chapter has discussed strategy formulation. Strategies are defined as a *pattern* of purposes, policies, programs, actions, decisions, or resource allocations that defines what an organization is, what it does, and why it does it. Strategies can vary by level, function, and time frame; they are the way an organization (or community) relates to its environment.

A five-part process for developing strategies was outlined, and suggestions were offered for the preparation of formal strategic plans. It was again emphasized that strategic thinking and acting are important, not any particular approach to strategy formulation, or even preparation of a formal strategic plan.

Chapter 9

Establishing an Effective Organizational Vision for the Future

Eighty percent of success is showing up.
Woody Allen

Where there is no vision, the people perish.
Proverbs

If you want to move people, it has to be toward a vision that's positive for them, that taps important values, that gets them something they desire, and it has to be presented in a compelling way that they feel inspired to follow.
Martin Luther King, Jr.

The purpose of the final step in the strategic planning process is to develop a clear and succinct description of what the organization or community should look like as it successfully implements its strategies and achieves its full potential. This description should be the organization's vision of success. Typically, this vision of success is more important as a guide to implementing strategy than it is to formulating it.

While few public and nonprofit organizations have a clear and useful mission statement, fewer still have a clear, succinct, and useful vision of success. Part of the reason is that a vision, while it includes mission, goes well beyond it. Mission outlines organizational purposes, while vision goes on to describe how the organization should look when it is working well (Lonnie Helgeson, personal communication, 1986). Developing this description is more time consuming than formulating a mission statement. It is also more difficult, particularly because most

184

organizations are coalitional (Pfeffer and Salancik, 1978), and thus the vision usually must be a treaty negotiated among rival coalitions.

Other difficulties may hamper construction of a vision of success. People are afraid of how others will respond to their vision. Professionals are highly vested in their jobs, and to have their vision of excellent performance criticized can be trying. People may also be afraid of that part of themselves that can envision and pursue excellence. First of all, we can be disappointed in our pursuit, which can be painful. Our own competence can be called into question. Second, being true to the vision can be a very demanding discipline, hard work that we may not be willing to shoulder all the time.

To construct a compelling vision of success, key decision makers must be courageous. They must listen to their best selves. They must envision their best selves in order to envision success for the organization as a whole. And they must be disciplined enough to affirm the vision in the present, to work hard to make the vision real in the here and now (Lonnie Helgeson, personal communication, 1986).

It may not be possible therefore to create an effective and compelling vision of success. The good news, however, is that although a vision of success may be very helpful, it may not be *necessary* for improved organizational performance. Fortunately, people do not have to agree on a vision to agree on next steps, as international arms control negotiators, labor-management relations specialists, and used-car buyers and sellers all know (Fisher and Ury, 1981; Cleveland, 1985). Simply finding a way to frame and deal with a few of the strategic issues often markedly improves organizational effectiveness. As Woody Allen notes facetiously, "Eighty percent of success is showing up." If people can deal with a few important issues after they have shown up, so much the better.

Desired Outcomes and Benefits

While it may not be necessary to have a vision of success in order to improve organizational effectiveness, it is hard to imagine a truly high-performing organization that does not have at least an implicit and widely shared conception of what success looks like and how it might be achieved. Indeed, it is hard to imagine an organization surviving in the long run without some sort of vision to inspire it, as the quote from Proverbs implies. Assuming key decision makers wish to promote superior organizational performance, three outcomes might be sought in this step.

First, a vision of success might be prepared. If it is to provide suitable guidance and motivation, it should probably include:

1. Mission.
2. Basic philosophy and core values.
3. Goals, if they are established.
4. Basic strategies.
5. Performance criteria.
6. Important decision rules.
7. Ethical standards expected of all employees.

The vision should emphasize purposes, behavior, performance criteria, decision rules, and standards that are public serving, rather than self-serving. The guidance offered should be specific and reasonable. The statement of the vision should include a promise that the organization will support its members in pursuit of the vision. The vision should be relatively short—no more than ten double-spaced typewritten pages—and inspiring.

Second, the vision should be widely circulated among organizational members and other key stakeholders after appropriate consultations, reviews, and signoffs. A vision of success can have little effect if organizational members are kept in the dark about it.

Third, the vision should be used to inform major and minor organizational decisions and actions. Preparing the vision is a waste of time if it has no behavioral effect. If, on the other hand, copies of the vision are always on the table at formal meetings of key decision makers, for example, and performance measurement systems take explicit cognizance of the vision, then it can be expected to affect organizational performance.

A number of benefits flow from a clear, succinct, inspiring, and widely shared vision of success.

1. Organizational members are given specific, reasonable, and supportive guidance about what is expected of them and why. They see how they fit into the organization's big picture. Too often the only guidance for members, other than hearsay, is their job descriptions (necessarily focused on the parts and not on the whole). In addition, key decision makers are all too likely to issue conflicting messages to members, or simply tell them, "Do your best." A widely accepted vision of success records enough of a consensus on ends and means to channel members' efforts in desirable directions while at the same time providing a framework for improvisation and innovation in pursuit of organizational purposes (Taylor, 1984).

2. As Kant argued, conception precedes perception (May, 1969). People must have some conception of what success and desirable behavior look like before they can actually see them; only when success and desirable behavior are envisioned will they be seen and therefore made more likely. A vision of success provides the conception that people need to discriminate among preferred and undesirable actions and outcomes, to produce more of what is preferred, and to fashion expectations and reward systems in line with what is preferred.

3. If there is agreement on the vision, and if clear guidance and decision rules can be derived from it, the organization will gain an added increment of power. Less time will be expended on debating what to do, how to do it, and why, and more time can be devoted to simply getting on with it (Pfeffer and Moore, 1980).

4. The two things that most determine whether goals are achieved appear to be the extent to which they are specific and reasonable, and the extent to which people are supported in pursuit of them (Locke, Shaw, Saari, and Latham, 1981). It seems reasonable to extend the same argument to a vision of success and claim that the more specific and reasonable the vision, and the more supported organizational members are in pursuit of the vision, the more likely the vision will be achieved or realized.

5. A vision of success provides a way to claim or affirm

the future in the present, and thereby to invent one's own preferred future. If the future is what we make it, then a vision outlines the future we want to have and forces us to live it—create it, real-ize it—in the present. One therefore does not predict the future, a hazardous enterprise at best—one *makes* it.

6. A clear yet reasonable vision of success creates a useful tension between the world as it is and the world as we would like it. If goals are to motivate, they must be set high enough to provide a challenge, but not so high as to induce paralysis, hopelessness, or too much stress. A well-tuned vision of success can motivate the organization's members to pursue excellence.

7. An inspiring vision of success can supply another source of motivation: a calling. If a vision of success becomes a calling, an enormous amount of individual energy and dedication can be released in pursuit of a forceful vision focused on a better future. Consider, for example, that most remarkable of nonprofit organizations, the Society of Jesus, the Jesuits, founded in 1534 in Paris by Ignatius Loyola. Their vision was first formulated in Ignatius's *Spiritual Exercises* (Guibert, 1964). Their worldwide success as missionaries, teachers, scholars, and spiritual directors is a tribute to how much they have been guided by, and how close they have remained to, their ideal: to be a disciplined force on behalf of the Roman Catholic Church. The fact that they have succeeded so often in the face of incredible odds and trials is in part due to the power of their vision.

8. A well-articulated vision of success will at least implicitly help people recognize the barriers to realization of the vision and thereby assist in overcoming them. In this the vision acts in much the same way as the first step in the strategy formulation process outlined in Chapter Eight. In that process, people are first asked to formulate practical alternatives, dreams, or visions to deal with specific strategic issues, or to achieve specific goals, or to realize a preferred scenario (or vision of success); to identify barriers to those alternatives; and then to make proposals to achieve the alternatives directly or else indirectly through overcoming the barriers.

9. A clear vision of success provides an effective substitute for leadership (Kerr and Jermier, 1978; Manz, 1986). People

are able to lead and manage themselves if they are given clear guidance about directions and behavioral expectations. More effective decision making then can occur at a distance from the center of the organization and from the top of the hierarchy.

10. While constructing a vision of success may be difficult in politicized settings, the task may nonetheless be worth the effort. An agreed-upon vision may contribute to a significant reduction in the level of organizational conflict if the vision establishes a set of superordinate goals that can rechannel conflict in useful directions (Filley, 1975; Fisher and Ury, 1981).

11. To the extent that the vision of success is widely shared, it takes on a moral quality that can infuse the organization with virtue. It is not particularly fashionable to talk about virtue, but most people wish to act in morally justifiable ways in pursuit of morally justified ends (Frederickson, 1982). A vision of success provides important permission, justification, and legitimacy to the actions and decisions that accord with the vision, at the same time that it establishes boundaries of permitted behavior. The normative self-regulation necessary for any moral community to survive and prosper is facilitated (Kanter, 1972).

Two Brief Examples

Two examples may help clarify what is meant by a vision of success. The first is the Dayton Hudson Corporation's 1982 "Statement of Philosophy." This brief document—only ten pages long, with no more than 200 words per page—is packed with information and presents a model vision of success. The document has helped guide the emergence of the corporation as a U.S. retailing giant with 1986 sales of over $6.5 billion.

The document begins with a statement of the corporation's mission. The company is "a diversified retailing company whose business is to serve the American consumer through the retailing of fashion-oriented merchandise." Then comes a list of the corporation's key stakeholders or constituencies: customers, employees, shareholders, and the communities in which the company operates. The document lists the purposes the company pursues in relation to each stakeholder group. For example, with respect to customers, the company's primary purpose is ''to serve as the consumers' purchasing agent in fulfilling their needs and expectations for merchandise and services.'' Five specific subpurposes are listed under this major purpose.

Under the next heading of ''corporate objectives,'' the statement declares that ''our primary objective is to be premier in every facet of our business.'' Then come nine specific areas in which the company seeks premier performance, ranging from consistency of performance to public image.

Next is a discussion of the corporation's merchandising philosophy, which includes an emphasis on merchandise and market preeminence, quality, fashion, and value to the customer. The company's real estate philosophy—as vital to its success as its merchandising strategy—is discussed next.

The next major section outlines the decision-making process for the company. Roles, rules, and decision areas are given for the corporate headquarters and for the operating companies. The final two sections of the statement of philosophy outline the corporation's growth philosophy and the ethical standards and business conduct expected of employees.

The document provides an amazing amount of specific and reasonable advice to company employees and indicates that the company will support and reward employees who act in accord with the philosophy. Because Dayton Hudson's success depends on actions and decisions taken at a considerable physical distance from the corporate headquarters, the importance of wide circulation of, and agreement on, this document is hard to overestimate. It is also worth noting that the company actually behaves in accord with its philosophy. The philosophy is no mere public relations ploy; it is a serious statement of the way Dayton Hudson's leaders try to live their business lives.

The other example is from the public sector. Nursing Service has prepared an ideal vision of public health nursing in its county for the 1990s. The vision is reproduced in Exhibit 9. The vision is not as long or as detailed as the Dayton Hudson Corporation's, but it covers a number of the same topics. In particular, basic purposes are emphasized, key strategies are

Exhibit 9. The Ideal Vision of Public Health Nursing in the County for the Nineties.

The county will have a community-based public health nursing system that will provide disease prevention, health restoration, health maintenance, and health promotion services to the population as a whole, with programs focused particularly on those population groups who are at highest risks for health problems.

Public health nursing stations will be in community centers in order to assist communities to identify their own health problems and to develop programs to better meet the community's health needs. An example of this joint effort with communities is the Block Nurse Program where volunteer recruitment and training have been developed and services provided in a joint venture between the community and the public health nursing agency. Services are delivered in a cost-effective way in such a program and outreach is enhanced.

Linkages between community services such as public health nursing, hospitals, physicians, community clinics, social service agencies, day care, community education, housing, senior centers, and transportation will be enhanced in order to provide beneficial, coordinated, comprehensive services to the population, and to encourage distribution of information about available services.

The public health nursing program will ensure at least a minimum level of health services in each community for vulnerable populations by working collaboratively with other organizations such as day-care associations and the department of community human services to ensure the delivery of appropriate and coordinated services.

Funding for services will be a mixture of fees, grants, and the county tax levy. Private organizations will be encouraged to replicate public health nursing services for their employees or members or to contract for service with public health nursing programs. The importance of providing nursing services that include concepts of disease prevention, health restoration, health maintenance, and health promotion will be generally accepted by the large corporations providing health services to their enrolled populations. If the corporations provide their own nursing services, nursing personnel will be hired who have expertise in public health nursing practice and will have management control of the service delivery. A nursing system of public and private providers will collaborate to ensure safe, effective care for populations.

Priority actions to realize the Ideal Vision scenario:

1. Collaborations with community organizations to develop a community based health protection system for vulnerable populations. Vulnerable populations are defined as:
    a. Parents and children at risk for infant and child mortality and morbidity who need:
        (1) day care
        (2) prenatal/postpartum/child care services

Exhibit 9. The Ideal Vision of Public Health
Nursing in the County for the Nineties, Cont'd.

---

      (3) outreach to isolated parents
  b. Elderly at risk for nursing home placement, or at risk for mortality
      and morbidity in community settings, who need:
      (1) preadmission screening
      (2) outreach to isolated individuals
  c. Mentally ill, retarded, and chemically dependent individuals residing
      in community settings.
2. Provision of information to others in the health care system of the need
    for health services by the population at risk and the services public health
    nursing can offer most effectively.
3. Consultation to other organizations and communities to encourage them
    to plan to meet their population's health needs more effectively.
4. Provision of quality services as a model incorporating disease preven-
    tion, health restoration, health maintenance, and health promotion con-
    cepts in the delivery of all services to individuals and groups.
5. Provision of quality professional educational experience to students.
6. Collaboration on research with [the local university] to further develop
    the practice of public health nursing.

---

outlined, and the emphasis throughout is on excellence. Using
the ideal vision as a starting point, Nursing Service over time
will be able to prepare a vision of success that includes all
the key content areas outlined above in the section on desired
outcomes.

Process Guidelines

The following guidelines are intended to help a strategic
planning team formulate a vision of success.

1. Remember that in most cases a vision of success is not
necessary to improve organizational effectiveness. Simply developing and implementing strategies to deal with strategic issues
can produce marked improvement in the performance of most
organizations. An organization therefore should not worry too
much if it seems unwise or too difficult to develop a vision of
success. On the other hand, it seems unlikely that an organization can achieve truly superior performance without at least an
implicit, widely shared, vision of success.

2. Most organizations should wait until they have gone through several cycles of strategic planning before they try to develop a vision of success. Most organizations need to develop the habit of thinking and acting strategically—thinking about and acting on the truly important aspects of their relationships with their environment—before a collective vision of success can emerge. In addition, the consensus on key decisions and the ability to resolve conflicts constructively (both necessary to develop an effective vision of success) are likely to emerge only after several cycles of strategic planning.

This guideline may not apply if the organization has decided to proceed with strategic planning using the idealized scenario or goals approaches, and if it has developed and is implementing effective strategies based on those approaches. If capacity for consensus is already adequate for use of the scenario or goals approaches, then the organization also may succeed in developing a viable, detailed vision of success.

3. A vision of success should include the items listed earlier in the chapter under desired outcomes. The vision itself should not be long, no more than ten double-spaced typewritten pages.

4. A vision of success should grow out of past decisions and actions as much as possible. Past decisions and actions often are the record of a consensus about what the organization is and should do. Basing a vision on a preexisting consensus avoids unnecessary conflict. Also, the organization, through its vision, should be effectively linked to its past. Realization of a new future is easier if it can be shown to be a continuation of the past and present (Weick, 1979).

However, a vision of success should not be merely an extension of the present. It should be an affirmation in the present of an ideal and inspirational future. A vision of success should create an image of an ideal future and then map back to the present to show organizational members how their daily actions can help the organization (and themselves) achieve success.

5. A vision of success should be inspirational. It will not move people to excel unless it is. And what inspires people is a clear description of a desirable future backed up by real

conviction. An inspirational vision has the following attributes (Kouzes and Posner, 1987):

> It focuses on a better future.
> It encourages hopes and dreams.
> It appeals to common values.
> It states positive outcomes.
> It emphasizes the strength of a unified group.
> It uses word pictures, images, and metaphors.
> It communicates enthusiasm and kindles excitement.

Just recall Martin Luther King, Jr.'s "I Have a Dream" speech and you will have a clear example of an inspirational vision of success, focused on the better future of an integrated society.

6. An effective vision of success will embody the appropriate degree of tension to prompt effective organizational change. Too much tension will likely cause paralysis. The vision therefore should be toned down to reduce excessive tension. On the other hand, too little tension will not produce the challenge necessary for outstanding performance. If there is not enough tension, the vision should be recast to raise organizational sights.

7. A useful way to begin constructing a vision of success is to have strategic planning team members as individuals prepare draft visions, then share and discuss their responses. After the discussion, the task of drafting a vision of success should be turned over to an individual; an inspirational document rarely is written by a committee. The team may find it useful to review Resource F before starting the drafts.

Special sessions may be necessary to develop particular elements of the vision of success. For example, the organization's performance criteria may not be fully specified. They might be developed out of the stakeholder analysis, the strategy statements, or use of the snow card technique. Wherever there are gaps in the vision, special sessions may be necessary to fill them.

8. A normative process should be used to review the vision of success. Drafts typically are reviewed by planning

team members, other key decision makers, governing board members, and at least selected outside stakeholders. Review meetings need to be structured so that the strengths of the vision are identified and modifications that would improve on those strengths are listed. Review sessions can be structured according to the agenda suggested for the review of strategic plans (see Chapter Eight).

9. Consensus on the vision statement among key decision makers is highly desirable, but may not be absolutely necessary. It is rarely possible to achieve complete consensus on anything in an organization, so all that can be realistically hoped for is a fairly widespread general agreement on the substance and style of the vision statement. Actual deep-seated commitment to any vision statement can emerge only slowly, over time.

10. For a vision of success to help guide organizational decisions and actions it must be widely disseminated and discussed. The vision statement probably should be published as a booklet and given to every organizational member and to key external stakeholders. Discussion of the statement should be made a part of orientation programs for new employees, and periodically it should be discussed in staff meetings.

A vision of success can become a living document only if it is referred to constantly as a basis for discerning and justifying appropriate organizational decisions and actions. If a vision statement does not regularly inform organizational decision making and actions, then its preparation probably was a waste of time.

Summary

This chapter has discussed development of a vision of success for the organization. A vision of success is defined as a description of what the organization should look like as it successfully implements its strategies and achieves its full potential. A vision statement should include the organization's mission, basic philosophy and core values, basic strategies, performance criteria, important decision rules, and ethical standards expected of all employees. The statement should emphasize the important social purposes that the organization serves and that justify its existence. It should also be short and inspirational.

For a vision of success to have a strong effect on organizational decisions and actions it must be widely disseminated and discussed, and it must be referred to frequently as a means of discerning and justifying appropriate responses to the various situations that confront the organization. Only if the statement is used as a basis for organizational decision making and action will it have been worth the effort of crafting it.

PART III

Implementing Strategic Planning Successfully

Strategic planning does not implement itself. People who want to use strategic planning to strengthen and sustain organizational achievement must address four key barriers to effective strategic planning: the *human* problem of attention and commitment, the *process* problem of turning strategic ideas into good currency, the *structural* problem of part-whole relations, and the *institutional* problem of appropriately exercising transformative leadership. Chapter Ten discusses these barriers—or challenges—and ways to overcome them.

In Chapter Eleven the four major examples of strategic planning used throughout the book—Central City, Suburban City, Nursing Service, and Health Center—are summarized and discussed. Then a number of process guidelines are presented to help organizations get started with their own strategic planning process.

Chapter 10

Overcoming Barriers to Strategic Planning

Previous chapters detailed eight specific steps in the strategic planning process. This chapter will take a different tack and discuss four challenges to the management of strategic change in any organization or community. These challenges must be effectively met if strategic planning is to help bring about major changes in the way an organization or community relates to its internal and external environments. The challenges will be confronted in each step of the strategic planning process. If the challenges are addressed successfully, strategic planning is likely to be successfully implemented. Strategic planning, management, and governance will have joined to produce successful change.

The four challenges are (Bryson, Van de Ven, and Roering, 1987):

1. The human problem is the management of attention and commitment. The attention of key people must be focused on key issues, decisions, conflicts, and policy preferences at key places in the process and the organizational hierarchy.
2. The process problem is the management of strategic ideas into good currency. Unconventional wisdom must be turned into conventional wisdom.

3. The structural problem is the management of part-whole relations. Internal and external environments must be linked advantageously.
4. The institutional problem is the exercise of transformative leadership. The most difficult problems strategic planning must deal with can be solved only through institutional transformation. Such transformations cannot happen without strong leadership. (Reprinted by permission of the Curators of the University of Missouri.)

Readers are encouraged to examine Van de Ven (1985), which explores the challenges in the context of the management of innovation, and Klay's insightful paper, "The Future of Strategic Management" (1987).

The Human Problem

The attention of key people must be focused on key issues, decisions, conflicts, and policy preferences at key places in the process. When necessary, commitments to past courses of action must be severed and new ones established.

The management of attention and commitment is a problem for individuals, groups, organizations, and communities. At each level, the problem has a different texture.

Individuals. Consider the following characteristics of individuals:

People have limited abilities to handle complexity.
Individuals are highly adaptive and do not recognize gradual change.
Individuals withdraw, project, and rationalize in crises.
Individuals lose consciousness and concentration as they gain competence and repeat tasks.
Commitment increases as people take public, binding, and irrevocable actions.

People have limited abilities to handle complexity. The normal adult can handle seven ideas at a time, plus or minus two (Miller, 1956). Beyond that number most people begin to stereotype. The difficulties this basic fact presents for strategic planning are obvious. Most stakeholder analyses, SWOT analyses, strategic issues, and strategies consist of more than seven items, plus or minus two. This means that people either will not appreciate fully the information that is presented to them, or else they will stereotype many of the factors and incorrectly diagnose the situation. Special care must be taken not to overload people involved in strategic planning with too much information (Feldman and March, 1981). Planners should always attempt to focus the attention of key decision makers on a few truly important issues, decisions, or actions.

Consider, for example, the Central City executive branch SWOT analysis discussed in Chapter Six. There were twenty-nine categories, each with several items; the total number was over one hundred. The twenty-nine categories actually represent the consultant's recategorization of the original list created by the top decision makers. To handle the volume of material, the managers had created categories that actually were too large, included too many items, to be useful at later stages in the process.

Individuals are highly adaptive; they typically do not recognize gradual change. Consider, for example, what happens to frogs. If you put a frog in a boiling pan of water, it will jump out. The frog does not want to get burned. But if you put the frog in a cold pail of water, put the pail on the stove, and turn up the heat gradually, the frog will not jump out; it will burn to death—slowly. The frog will slowly adapt to its changing environment without knowing it is in serious trouble.

In some ways, people are like frogs. They do not notice gradual changes, or their strategic implications (Starbuck, Greve, and Hedberg, 1978; Wildavsky, 1979b). Over time problems can swell to crisis proportions without anyone realizing what was happening all along. Once a crisis has developed, the opportunities for making dramatic changes may be enhanced, but so are a host of concomitant dangers (Bryson, 1981).

One characteristic of individuals makes it particularly important to avoid crises if at all possible: the tendency to project, stereotype, blame others, and freeze up in crisis situations. We all know the story of the Cuban missile crisis, and can be very thankful nuclear missiles were not unleashed by top decision makers who projected, blamed others, or simply froze (Allison, 1971). We need better mechanisms for assessing the strategic implications of small changes, and need to be more diligent in making the small decisions that will help us to avoid disasters and crises. An annual or biennial strategic planning process can be such a mechanism; it routinizes attention to small (and large) changes and routinizes the making of small (and large) decisions and actions in response to the changes.

At the opposite extreme from crisis situations, but just as problematic for effective strategic planning, is the fact that people engaged in repetitive tasks do not pay attention to what they are doing (Langer, 1978). For example, most people have had the unnerving experience of driving home and not being sure how they got there; the trip itself is a blur. The point is, we think the least about what we are best at and do the most. On the other hand, what we think about most is what we will do in the near future. In other words, we spend maybe 80 to 90 percent of our time doing things out of habit while we think of other things.

If strategic planning becomes a routine task, people can be expected to lose consciousness and concentration, and the purpose of strategic planning will be negated. Methods must be found to make strategic planning very "special" so that people pay attention and take it seriously. Special retreats or occasions are two possibilities. In addition, people will not view strategic planning as "real," as worth taking seriously, unless real consequences—such as performance reviews, important decisions, and budgetary allocations—flow from it (Brickman, 1978; Peters, 1978).

Commitment increases as people engage in important, explicit, public, and irrevocable actions (Salancik, 1977; Tokunaga and Staw, 1983). This is true even when the strategy implied by the course of those actions seems disastrous to an outside observer (Staw, 1976; Staw and Ross, 1978). Strategic planning, if it is to be effective, must include a consideration of how to break unproductive commitments at the same time that it seeks to bind people to new courses of action (Nystrom and Starbuck, 1984).

One important way to reduce commitments to unproductive courses of action is to redefine what is meant by an "error." If the consequence of making an error is to lose one's job, then people will either hide their errors or continue to make them while calling them a success. On the other hand, if people are encouraged to make errors as a way of learning, but are rewarded for correcting the errors, not for persisting in them, then it will be easier to change directions and augment organizational knowledge and change-management skills. Successful companies seem to be quite effective at error detection and correction, and at not punishing people for making "honest mistakes" (Peters and Waterman, 1982).

The public sector is a particularly hard place for people to take risks—and therefore to learn—without punishment. Accountability often has been interpreted to mean the minimization of mistakes, rather than learning how best to achieve desired outcomes effectively and efficiently. The wise course of action for public leaders and managers therefore appears to be a strategy of small mistakes. Public organizations and their employees must systematically make enough small mistakes so that they can learn, but not enough big mistakes so that they are punished.

Groups. A number of characteristics of groups pose problems for strategic planning:

Groups impose strong pressures to conform.
Groups try to minimize internal conflict.
Groups become homogeneous in two to three years.

Individuals tend to conform to the established norms of any group, both because they have a strong desire to fit in and because the group imposes strong pressure to conform (Shaw, 1971). If the group's norms do not promote frequent reexamination of current practices in light of their strategic implications, then the group will be ill prepared to deal with future strategic difficulties. A norm of strategic thinking can be established, but it will take time, effort, and commitment (Johnson and Johnson, 1987).

Groups also try to minimize internal conflict. Since talking about strategic issues almost certainly prompts serious disagreements, the unfortunate tendency of most groups will be to suppress the discussion. Group harmony will be a higher priority than serious discussion of the group's future and the fundamental choices it faces. Norms that promote free inquiry and discussion focused on strategic issues must be established, and people must possess good conflict resolution skills, if the heart of the strategic planning process is to be handled properly. Fortunately, a great deal is known about conflict resolution, and training in the appropriate skills is widely available (Filley, 1975; Fisher and Ury, 1981; Folger and Poole, 1984).

Finally, heterogeneous groups working together daily will acquire a homogeneous outlook in two to three years (Pelz and Andrews, 1966). That is helpful when the goal is to develop cohesive work groups, but not so helpful if it means the group always will approach problems in the same way and will not question accepted conceptions and practices. It may then become extremely difficult for the group to think strategically and purposefully about its future. A norm of incorporating divergent perspectives into the strategic planning process must be established if groups are not to blind themselves to other perspectives and approaches. Using cross-departmental, cross-level, multi-disciplinary strategic planning task forces (for organizations) or broadly representative task forces (for communities) is one way to get divergent perspectives into the process.

Organizations. Several characteristics of organizations also pose problems for strategic planning:

Strategic planning systems often drive out strategic thinking.
Readers of MIS and environmental scanning statistical reports become numb to the messages in them.
Specialization filters perception and constrains behavior.
Structures and systems become substitutes for leadership.

Another paradox of organizational life is that strategic planning systems can drive out strategic thinking. In the same way that repetition and competence can lead to lack of concentration and consciousness and thus to serious difficulties for individuals, so too can formalized and repetitive planning systems cause the very problems they seek to avert (Bryson, 1984; Bresser and Bishop, 1983). Strategic planning must always remain "special" if it is to be successful. Finding a way to directly involve the many constituencies who are served by a government is one way to create external expectations that will keep strategic planning a conscious and focused activity. Oak Ridge, Tennessee, pursued this approach as it developed a strategic plan for the city (King and Johnson, 1988). Another potential solution is to follow the example of some excellently run private corporations by assigning strategic planning not to staff planners but to line managers, the people who must live with the plans (Tita and Allio, 1984).

The average adult, remember, can handle seven, plus or minus two, pieces of information at one time. In contrast, the average MIS or environmental scanning report is loaded with pages and pages of numbers and graphs. What normally happens is that people become numb to the messages in these reports. As a result, they make decisions based not on data—the kind of data in a typical report—but on individual stories in which people were personally confronted with the need to make something different happen (Fisher, 1984).

Numerical data by itself is not likely to be helpful in formulating and implementing strategies. People must be exposed directly to situations in which they personally have to confront issues and have to think about how to make something happen. Role plays, case studies, simulations, and discussions with others who have faced similar problems will all help. But there is no substitute for constantly exposing the people in charge of strategic planning to occasions in which they can share stories with each other and subordinates, and in which stories from elsewhere can be shared and discussed.

Another attentional difficulty is that specialization filters perception and behavior (Lawrence and Lorsch, 1967). Because of the way we structure organizations, people get only certain kinds of information and pursue narrower aims than the organization as a whole does. The result is widespread suboptimization, in which people develop the best solutions possible within their own narrow world. Occasions must be developed to break people out of their normal circumstances, and to have them interact with other people in other areas so that more people can get a larger sense of the whole (Dalton, 1970). Task forces and retreats that bring together people from different parts of the organization are two conventional methods of doing this.

Finally, all too often structures and systems become substitutes for leadership. Structures and systems exist primarily to protect current practices—which in the longer run may not best serve the interests of the organization or its shareholders. When managers are preoccupied with administration and systems, they are not providing leadership, which is concerned with figuring out new ways of doing things. A key task of leadership is to identify new directions, thrusts, strategies, priorities, and ideas—in other words, strategic planning. Effective performance of strategic planning and effective leadership are inextricably intertwined.

Communities. Communities as well have a number of characteristics that pose serious problems for strategic planning:

> Communities are composed of individuals, groups, and organizations, and therefore represent an accumulation of the characteristics and difficulties discussed previously.
>
> Most organizations in any community represent solutions to "old" problems.
>
> No organization in any community is likely to contain any important problem.
>
> In most communities no one person, group, or organization is in charge.

Communities are very complex systems comprising individuals, groups, and organizations (Long, 1958; Rider, 1983). All the characteristics and difficulties cited so far therefore apply to communities as well. Consider, for example, the point that "specialization filters perception and constrains behavior."

What is true for individual organizations means that there is virtually *no one* in any community whose job it is to look out for the community as a whole, except perhaps the mayor or council president. Theoretically, of course, it is every citizen's job to look out for the community as a whole; practically, however, because it is everyone's job, it is no one's job. As a result, special committees or task forces must be forged and charged with looking out for the community as a whole, typically through strategic planning, and to educate the citizenry about their responsibility to care for the community.

Most organizations in any community represent solutions to old problems, institutionalized solutions that became dated as soon as the problems changed (Schon, 1971). The organizations typically represent inappropriate solutions to new problems. And to the extent people defend the inappropriate solutions that the organizations pursue, the organizations have become an end in and of themselves.

The question then becomes, how does one get to a new solution to a new problem when the organizational base is in an old solution to an old problem? The answer is through networks of concerned individuals. Networks will form around new definitions of problems and new solutions in response to those new definitions. New organizations (or reorganizations of old ones) will then institutionalize those new problem definitions and solutions. The formation of strategic planning task forces or committees is often an important first step in developing the networks that will form around new problem definitions and solutions.

No organization in any community is likely to contain any important problem; problems spill over organizational boundaries. People, groups, and organizations therefore typically focus on only a piece of any important problem, such as employment, health, or education. Again, the formation of strategic planning task forces or committees is usually the only way to constitute a body—a temporary organization, if you will—that can attend to the dimensions of important problems. Indeed, many smaller task forces or committees may be necessary to deal with specific problems (Rider, 1983; King and Johnson,

1988). When the time comes for implementation, it may be necessary to form a new organization to attend to the overall implementation task. For example, the Greater Philadelphia First Corporation (GPFC) was formed in the Philadelphia area to oversee the implementation of the region's strategic plan, known as the Philadelphia Investment Portfolio. GPFC is a consortium of the region's major economic development agencies, civic institutions, and the Greater Philadelphia Area Chamber of Commerce, along with an executive staff (Bryson, Freeman, and Roering, 1986).

In most communities, no one person, group, or organization is in charge, yet typically many persons, groups, and organizations are involved or affected by any strategic planning effort, or have a partial responsibility to act. Communities, in other words, represent "shared-power" situations (Bryson and Einsweiler, 1988a). The work lives of most leaders, managers, and planners are lived out in a shared-power world, where attention to what one wants is earned, not granted automatically. Persuasion, negotiation, bargaining, mediation, hassle, and haggling are the order of the day (Mintzberg, 1973; Bryson and Delbecq, 1979; Cleveland, 1985). Successful strategic planning in such situations depends on attention to issues important to key stakeholders in such a way that they are satisfied with the outcome. These issues typically must be raised and resolved in forums, arenas, and courts where no one is completely in charge. Leaders, managers, and planners therefore must work laterally at least as much as vertically, if not more, if they wish to see issues raised and resolved to the satisfaction of key stakeholders in a no-one-in-charge world (Cleveland, 1973, 1985). Successful strategic planning for a community is a *collective* enterprise.

The Process Problem

The most important process problem in strategic planning is the management of strategic ideas into "good currency" (Schon, 1971). In other words, how do you sell new ideas to enough people that unconventional wisdom is turned into conventional wisdom? Two basic issues are involved: (1) What is the life cycle of ideas? (2) How do you manage ideas over time?

Schon (1971) has presented an extremely interesting conception of the life cycle of policy-relevant ideas (also discussed in Resource C). First, some threatening or disruptive event stimulates people to act. They begin to articulate diagnoses of the problems and suggest solutions. Some solutions achieve public visibility. But nothing comes of these solutions until networks and coalitions begin to form around them. The ideas are then propelled into the realm of political debate. One or more of these ideas triumphs in the political contest and is adopted and legitimized as *the* solution to the problem. Solutions eventually become institutionalized and taken for granted. Eventually their potency declines. Regimes built on old ideas eventually will be supplanted (see also May and Wildavsky, 1978; Anderson, 1979; Nelson, 1984; Mandelbaum, 1984).

Throughout the United States, the desirability of deinstitutionalizing the residents of various state institutions (such as mental hospitals and corrections facilities) has passed through much of this cycle. The idea is that actual or potential residents of these facilities would be much better served if they lived in normalized settings (normal communities or "least restrictive" environments). Censuses in many state institutions therefore are way down as residents have been transferred to community settings. Unfortunately, there often are not adequate community facilities to handle the deinstitutionalized residents, so complete implementation of the idea has yet to come. Whether the idea will become outmoded is unclear, although some might argue that it has gone too far in some cases.

Several principles emerge for managing the life cycle of ideas:

1. Necessity and threat, but also opportunity, are the mothers of invention.
2. Ideas flourish in organized anarchies, but implementation of those ideas is difficult.
3. Ideas are the rallying point for collective action. They transcend isolated people and organizations. People and structures are the byproducts of changing ideas.
4. Ideas times resources equals power.
5. After a good idea dies, give it a funeral or a wake.

How do you get people's attention? The answer, in general, is through necessity and threat; these are what stimulate people and governments to action (Dalton, 1970; Allison, 1971; Van de Ven and Hudson, 1985). Strategic planning cycles typically begin with an appreciation and articulation of necessity and threat.

But opportunity also can capture people's attention, though it seems to do so less frequently than necessity and threat. A special virtue of strategic planning is that it promotes appreciation and articulation of opportunities.

The public and nonprofit sectors are good places in general to find possible solutions to strategic issues, because the organizations in both (especially the public sector) consist of "organized anarchies" (March and Olsen, 1979). Preferences are inconsistent, technologies are unclear, and participation is fluid. But those qualities that make the public and nonprofit sectors good producers of ideas also make them all too frequently poor implementors of ideas.

For strategic planning *and* implementation to be successful in the public and nonprofit sectors, organizations must become ambidextrous—both good producers and implementors of ideas (Duncan, 1976). Such organizations will be less formal and centralized, but more complex, when solutions need to be produced; and more formal and centralized, but less complex, when specific solutions need to be implemented. In other words, they will be more like a university when they need ideas, and more like an army when they implement them. One of the virtues of a strategic planning task force or committee as an overlay across regular organizational or community hierarchies is that it creates the kind of fluidity characteristic of universities; new important ideas are likely to be brought to the surface and discussed. Then, once strategic ideas are adopted, they can be implemented by regular "line" organizations, the organizational or community equivalent of armies.

Schon argues it is more important to manage ideas rather than people or structures, because ideas are the rallying points of collective action. As Figure 1 in effect illustrates, the essence of strategic planning is the management of strategic ideas through the states of appreciation, articulation, adoption, institutionalization, and decay. Furthermore, the process of developing strategic ideas transcends isolated individuals and organizations. In doing so, it establishes the foundation for coalitions large enough to create the collective action that is the hallmark of effective strategic action. In other words, ideas times resources (people, money, time, expertise, attention) equals power, including the power to effect useful strategic change.

But something more should be said about managing the "decay" of strategic ideas. People and organizations are attached to ideas. In fact, organizations, agencies, institutions, programs, products, and services are all organized around ideas, many of which are outmoded. We have not learned very well how to terminate organizations and activities whose animating ideas are outmoded (Kaufman, 1976; Behn, 1983). Since strategic planning, if it is to be effective, is often about replacing the way we are doing things now with other ways, we must find better ways to manage the transition from the old ways to the new ones. In everyday life, funerals and wakes are used to manage the transition from a time when a person was with us to a time when he or she is not. Perhaps, as my colleague Stuart Albert notes, we must construct funerals and wakes to commemorate the death of outmoded ideas as part of the transition to new ones.

The Structural Problem

The structural problem in strategic planning is linking internal and external environments across levels advantageously. This problem involves four important issues:

1. Is the whole greater than or less than the sum of the parts?
2. How can we manage transitions better?
3. How can we make sure that impeccable micro-logic does not add up to macro-nonsense?
4. How can we deal with the collective, rather than individual, nature of strategic planning?

Is the whole greater than or less than the sum of its parts? When an organization or community is working well, the resulting whole is usually greater than one would expect simply by adding up the constituent parts. The public sector offers several examples of monumental successes that have far transcended the sum of their individual parts. On the other hand, all too often public efforts have been dismal failures. The failures are perhaps most discussed (other than in the popular press) in the rather disheartening policy implementation literature, in which well-intentioned but disastrously implemented policies decompose into their ill-conceived or mismatched constituent parts (Pressman and Wildavsky, 1973; Hall, 1980; Mazmanian and Sabatier, 1983).

The challenge for strategic planners is to make sure that the whole resides in the parts; that is, they must use a holographic rather than a compositional approach. Planners should try to place the whole *in* each of its parts, so that the parts represent the whole. If this could be done, then each part of the system would have the essential ingredients for reproduction of the total system. Moreover, each part could, in the words of Harlan Cleveland (1985, p. 205), "think globally while acting locally."

A related difficulty is how to manage transitions better. Part of the problem arises from our penchant for sequential rather than simultaneous coupling across levels and between inside and outside. Thus we habitually treat planning and policy making as separate from implementation, rather than as part of a single gesture. Too often we make policy at one level or in one sector and expect other levels or sectors to embrace and implement the policy wholeheartedly. Too often planners plan and implementors implement and neither group talks to the other. Some of the difficulties highlighted in the implementation literature are a predictable result. Strategic planning is likely to be successful only if (1) planning and implementation are thought about simultaneously, (2) planners and implementors are involved simultaneously across levels and inside and outside, and (3) implementation begins before the planning is complete.

When part-whole relationships are flawed, another problem is likely to be present: organizational and community systems will be based on impeccable micro-logic that makes macro-nonsense (Peters and Waterman, 1982; Schelling, 1978). Our accountability systems, for example, will involve so many sign-offs and oversight mechanisms that innovation, entrepreneurship, and responsiveness will be driven out. We will have systems of rules and regulations that all make perfect sense individually, but that collectively make the total system so complicated that it cannot fulfill its mission. In short, we must find ways to ensure that the perfectly rational decisions reached in our highly decentralized system of "public" decision making (the interacting public, private, and nonprofit spheres; see Lindblom, 1977) do not add up to overall irrational results.

Finally, it should be recognized that the formulation and implementation of strategies is a collective achievement, not an achievement of individuals or small groups. There are heroes and heroines in the public and nonprofit worlds whose individual achievements are astounding (see Humphrey, 1976; Lewis, 1980; Addams, 1981; Oates, 1982), but behind every successful hero and heroine is a collective enterprise. When it comes to the formulation and implementation of strategies, we must involve a variety of people in a variety of roles: sponsors, entrepreneurs, champions, orchestrators, technicians, clients and users, and decision makers (Maidique, 1980; Bolan, 1971; Bryson and Delbecq, 1979).

The management of part-whole relations can be made much easier if the organization has a widely agreed-upon mission, even easier if it has a widely agreed-upon vision of success. Agreement on mission and vision will embed the whole into the parts, make the management of transitions easier, assure that a concern for the whole will limit macro-nonsense, and will facilitate the achievement of the collective success that effective strategic planning always is.

The Institutional Problem

The most difficult problems in strategic planning involve the transformation of institutions. Again, a number of issues emerge:

How are institutions transformed?
What are the central responsibilities of institutional leaders?
What happens in the absence of institutional leadership?

What we call institutions are in essence highly stable patterns of interaction (Giddens, 1979) organized around important ideas. The interaction patterns in public and nonprofit organizations become "institutions" when they become infused with value and character. Institutional character unfolds as a historical product, involves an integrated pattern, is purposeful, and is dynamic (Selznick, 1957). Communities also become infused with value and character as a result of history and purposeful, dynamic integration.

The development of an institution's or community's character (or culture, to use the current buzzword) is largely a leadership responsibility (Schein, 1985). As Selznick (1957) has pointed out, the central tasks of institutional leadership are the definition of the institution's mission, the embodiment of purpose into its structure and systems, the defense of its integrity, and the ordering of internal conflict. Community leaders have the same responsibilities.

It follows then that the tasks of "transformative leadership" (Burns, 1978) are the redefinition of purpose, the embodiment of new purposes into structures and systems, the establishment of new defenses in light of the new purposes, and the reordering of internal conflict. These obviously are not easy tasks, and their successful performance makes tremendous demands on the leaders involved.

If the leaders fail at the tasks of transformative leadership, the institution's or community's integrity will be in question. The loss of institutional integrity causes organizational drift. When people lose their purpose, their compass, illegitimate opportunism is likely, and with it further loss of integrity. Finally comes the loss of distinctive competence. Drift, illegitimate opportunism, and incompetence are reasons for abandoning the institution altogether, or for revolution in the community. When it comes to strategic planning for organizations or communities, there is simply no substitute for effective leadership.

Summary

This chapter has outlined four major categories of problems with which strategic planners must deal: (1) the human problem of the management of attention, (2) the process problem of the management of strategic ideas into good currency, (3) the structural problem of the management of part-whole relations, and (4) the institutional problem of the appropriate exercise of transformative leadership. These four categories of problems will be present across the eight steps of the strategic planning process and must be addressed persistently if the process is to reach a successful conclusion. If the problems are not addressed, the process will be prone to failure, and people will be unwilling to try strategic planning again in the future. If the problems are addressed successfully, strategic planning will be merged with management and governance to produce effective strategic change.

Chapter 11

Getting Started with Strategic Planning

Previous chapters presented an overview of strategic planning, an introduction to my preferred strategic planning process, detailed guidance on working through the process, and an overview of the challenges strategic planning must deal with if it is to be effective. This chapter will present a number of guidelines on how organizations and communities interested in strategic planning might proceed.

The Four Examples Revisited

How have our four examples—three public organizations and one nonprofit—fared with strategic planning? Each has achieved some success, and most also have encountered challenges to their ability to think and act strategically. A number of lessons can be drawn from each organization's experience. The lessons have been discussed before, particularly in the process guidelines in Chapters Four through Nine and in the challenges to effective strategic planning in Chapter Ten, but here they become more concrete in relation to specific cases.

Central City. The executive branch of Central City did form and institutionalize a cabinet. It is chaired by the mayor's executive assistant and includes the heads of the departments of community services, finance and management services, fire and safety services, planning and economic development, police, and public works, and the general manager of the water utility. The cabinet outlined a number of strategic issues and agreed to meet periodically to review progress on resolving them and to make any important decisions related to them.

Three achievements of Central City's executive branch stand out. First, the city government's top administrators have now established the precedent (one hopes the ingrained habit) of talking to one another about what is most important for the city as a whole. Second, the cabinet has now twice presented the mayor with a group-endorsed budget; the cabinet reviewed the budget in light of what is best for the city in two consecutive budget cycles and then made its budget recommendations to the mayor. Third, many individual departments (police and fire, for example) have now institutionalized strategic planning processes and produced strategic plans. Others, such as the public library, are about to engage in strategic planning.

The mayor's "Better Neighborhoods Program," while not a direct achievement of the strategic planning process, certainly must count as an important spinoff. The program is a major initiative of the mayor's, in cooperation with the planning division of the city's department of planning and economic development. The program promotes neighborhood self-improvement schemes in which the city also participates to the extent it can. Attempts are made to integrate employment, housing, and social service concerns in the schemes. The program is another example of the ways in which strategic planning for an organization, in this case the city government, can overlap with strategic planning for places, in this case neighborhoods.

The first budget the cabinet recommended actually included $2 million of additional cuts beyond what the mayor requested. The most remarkable feature of these cuts is that they were unevenly distributed across departments, in keeping with a strategic assessment of what was best for the city as a whole. Anyone familiar with the usual practice of public budgeting (*never offer cuts greater than what is requested, and always spread the* pain evenly [Wildavsky, 1979a]) has to be impressed. One might expect budgeting to drive out strategic thought and action on behalf of the city as a whole, but here budgeting has followed, rather than led, strategic planning.

Nonetheless, progress in dealing with the strategic issues identified by the cabinet has been slow. The two most important reasons are the shortage of skilled staff to deal with the issues, and the mayor's unsuccessful bid for statewide elective office. In line with the recent conservative trend in national, state, and local politics, Central City has trimmed its budget and staffing levels significantly, at the same time that it has held down the rise in local tax levies. As a result, there simply are not enough skilled staff to deal with some of the strategic issues, while still handling all the day-to-day operations of the city. Even so, one can criticize Central City for not devoting staff resources to what is truly important—presumably, strategic issue resolution—even if it means some falloff in the performance of day-to-day duties. If the citizens squawk too loudly, it is up to the mayor as a leader to tell the public why the minor reallocation of resources is needed. Such advice may seem naive, but what is the alternative, really? The alternative is to let the routine, important though it may be, drive out the truly important. In the end, the citizenry will not be well served and their leaders will have failed them.

The second reason for slow progress is probably more significant, and that is the mayor's decision to run, unsuccessfully, for statewide office about six months after the cabinet was formed. Not only did the mayor continue as mayor during the campaign, but his executive assistant became the campaign's director of research while continuing to serve as the mayor's assistant. With the mayor's tenure uncertain, and with the attention of the cabinet's chair elsewhere, it is no wonder little effort was put into the resolution of strategic issues. Now that the mayor has lost the statewide election, his attention is back on the city. Cabinet members expect him to continue as mayor for some time. As long as the mayor stays, and if his new executive assistant continues to believe in the importance of strategic planning, strategic issues are likely to be handled more expeditiously. (The previous executive assistant, the one who championed the process initially, recently resigned to accept a post in another state.)

The lessons from the Central City executive branch experience seem clear. First, unless the top decision makers are fully committed to strategic planning, it is unlikely to succeed in the organization as a whole. Second, strategic planning can succeed in those parts of the organization where the key decision makers want it to work. Third, staff must be assigned to work on what is truly important. Fourth, if strategic discussions precede budgeting, budgets may be prepared and reviewed in light of their consequences for the city as a whole. Fifth, perhaps the biggest innovation that strategic planning produced is the bringing together of key decision makers to discuss what is truly important. There is simply no substitute for such discussions when it comes to decision making for an organization as a whole.

Central City's city council has been less successful in its efforts to become a more effective policy-making body. So far not enough of its seven members have been willing to do what is necessary for the council to become more effective at policy making. (Recall that characteristics of effective policy-making bodies were discussed in the process guidelines section of Chapter Four.) Unless a very solid majority—say, five—are convinced, there is little real hope that the council will change its behavior. On the other hand, there is a real possibility that an upcoming election will result in a solid majority of five in favor of strategic planning.

Remember that the reason the council undertook strategic planning was its realization that if the executive branch really got its act together, through forming a cabinet and addressing strategic issues, the council could be reduced to a purely reactive body. The council would have little or no influence on which issues were addressed and how. The executive branch would take the lead on all important issues and would present fully worked-out proposals to the council for a yes or no decision. If the council said no, it might seem not only reactive but reactionary. Now that the executive branch is prepared to act strategically, this scenario may be increasingly likely unless a solid majority of council members also become committed to strategic action.

In the meantime, and to the council's credit, a number of steps have been taken to improve its effectiveness as a policy-making body. The council has adopted a strategic plan (endorsed publicly by the press) for improving its effectiveness. As part of that plan the council has identified six goals for itself, a time line for development of specific strategies to achieve each goal, and council members and staff who will take the lead in organizing efforts to achieve the goals. (As is the case with much government strategic planning, the goals bridge planning for the governmental unit and planning for the unit's jurisdiction.) The goals are:

1. To develop a strategy for safer, better neighborhoods.
2. To implement an effective complaint resolution process.
3. To improve housing conditions in the city.
4. To improve council communications with the public.
5. To initiate a continuous review of Central City revenue and budget commitments.
6. To create civic education programs to meet the needs of Central City's youth and children.

Again, the lesson from the city council's effort is obvious. There is simply no substitute for the commitment of key leaders and decision makers to strategic planning; they must be committed, or the process will fail.

Suburban City. Recall that Suburban City has a reputation for being extremely well managed and highly responsive to citizens' needs and desires. The assistant city manager initiated and headed the strategic planning effort with the support of the city manager and at least the nominal support of the city council. The city manager and a council member were active participants on the strategic planning team.

A number of strategic issues were identified through the process. Detailed strategies were then developed to deal with the four most important issues, using the five-part process outlined in Chapter Eight. The city staff then began implementing the aspects of the strategies that did not require city council approval.

But then a very strange thing happened. Every time the

assistant city manager and city manager wanted to present the results of the strategic planning effort to the council, the council postponed the presentation to deal with what it considered more pressing business. Unfortunately, the more pressing business all too often involved an investigation and criticism of various (often trivial) management activities. In other words, the council was becoming a second group of managers, and was gradually relinquishing its real role as policy maker. The strategic planning process thus highlighted a deteriorating situation that the city manager and assistant city manager had not fully recognized: one of the major strategic issues facing Suburban City (like Central City) was how to make the city council a more effective policy-making body.

The city manager and assistant city manager then began to discuss the issue with key council members, who agreed with the assessment that somehow the council had allowed itself to become overly involved in implementation detail and not involved enough in policy making. These council members then convinced others that the council needed some training on what it means to be a policy-making body and how a policy-making body should behave.

A consultant was hired to take the council through two training sessions on how to become an effective policy-making body. The council has been quite receptive and has begun to change its behavior. An upcoming election may result in the replacement of two council members with new people particularly interested in improving the council's policy-making effectiveness. The two top managers are now reasonably sure that a new strategic planning effort will be undertaken with full council involvement and ownership. (They also believe that most of the previously developed strategies will be adopted by the council.) Suburban City thus can have some confidence that it will maintain, and even enhance, its reputation as a well-managed and well-governed city.

The lessons from this example are also important. First, if strategic planning is to be really effective in an organization that has a governing board, the board itself must understand and "own" the process. Second, the board must understand what it means to be an effective policy-making body and must act the part. Third, strategic planning is an iterative process that can lead to surprising understandings and to new and more effective rounds of strategic thought and action. Fourth, strategic planning by itself is not enough. The key decision makers in the system (in this case the top managers and certain council members) must be willing to take effective political action to promote strategic thought and action.

Nursing Service. Nursing Service, like Suburban City, also discovered that strategic planning can be an iterative process. Recall that Nursing Service threw out most of its first list of strategic issues to come up with a more useful second set. To deal with the new list, the service developed strategies redesigning the agency so that it can be more responsive to the public health nursing needs of the community and the needs of the service's clients and employees. These strategies were well on the way to full implementation by the end of 1987.

The first strategy calls for a differentiation and clarification of the line and staff functions of nurse supervisors and administrators so that role ambiguity and conflict can be reduced. The line function is defined as staff supervision, while the staff function is seen as program development and program management. As part of the service's restructuring plan, the roles of all personnel have been clarified and management training provided to help people fulfill those roles.

The second strategy is definition and implementation of a process for regular program development and change, to replace the more haphazard process followed until recently. The strategy is designed to clarify how program priorities will be changed, new programs added, and old programs deleted. The process involves three major steps: (1) identification of a problem or need to be addressed, (2) development of a program plan, and (3) management of the program to address the problem or need.

The third strategy is an organizational redesign that will help the agency respond efficiently and effectively to the needs of communities as well as individuals and families. The redesign will not actually change the organization chart significantly, but will shift responsibilities in line with a more effective division of labor and sharing of work loads and decision making.

Several similar lessons can be gleaned from this case. First, there is no substitute for commitment to the strategic planning process on the part of key decision makers, and particularly *the* key decision maker. After some initial concerns about the purpose of the process were addressed, the director wholeheartedly embraced the process and pushed ahead. She was assisted by a skilled health planner assigned by the director of the public health department to assist the process. The planner, too, had some initial reservations but also came to believe in the process and kept things moving. Her persistence and expertise were essential to the success of the process, even though she took another job before the strategies were implemented. If the director had not been fully committed, the process might have died when the in-house planner left.

Second, strategic planning can help organizations cope with a variety of unexpected situations. As noted, initially some Nursing Service staff members thought strategic planning might be used against it. But when the county executive director was forced to resign, Nursing Service suddenly saw a marvelous opportunity to figure out what it really wanted and to be ready with compelling plans and arguments when a new executive director was hired. In other words, the strategic planning process conditioned Nursing Service to think and act strategically, to address both threats and opportunities.

Third, operational detail can overwhelm strategic planning efforts. Even though Nursing Service has been successful at strategic planning, it still took two years to progress from an initial agreement to approved strategies. (Strategy implementation has been swift.) This was due in part to uncertainty about how to proceed through the process, uncertainty about the intentions of the county's executive director and the county board, and the fact that strategic planning was an add-on to an already overworked staff.

Now that Nursing Service has gone through the process once, it will have less uncertainty about how to proceed in the future and it does not need to worry as much about the intentions of superiors. But timely strategic planning will still be difficult unless the new organizational design and program management process reduces the work demands on the staff, especially through helping staff set priorities and manage their time. An analysis of the work loads of the twelve key decision makers in the agency before the redesign indicated that each was operating at 125 percent of capacity, working fifty hours a week. Professionals typically overwork, but something clearly is wrong when such overwork keeps staff from dealing with what is *truly* important to the long-term viability and success of the agency.

Health Center. Health Center's strategic planning effort has been a straightforward success, and virtually all the strategic plan has been implemented. Health Center is now a free-standing nonprofit agency striving to improve the health status of the residents in the surrounding community. It offers primary medical, dental, and related services to community residents, especially those most in need.

The center has established a new and clearer identity, expanded its service area, and expanded its target group to include middle-class clients. Plans are well along for building a new main facility, and other organizations with complementary services (mental health, financial counseling, and day care) have been invited to locate in the new building. The center has established and maintains relationships with a range of area hospitals, community clinics, and human service providers. Staff has increased, and the funding base has expanded. The center appears to be financially viable for the long term.

Four lessons stand out from this case. First (again), leadership at the top is vital if an entire organization is to be changed. Second, quicker really can be better. If Health Center had taken two years to develop acceptable strategies, it would have been bankrupt before the strategies could have been implemented. Third, simpler can be better, too. Health Center did not use an elaborate strategic planning process. The planning team managed their time and attention effectively by focusing on their most critical issues and pushed ahead until they developed effective answers. The process was not "data heavy" (although some important financial projections had to be developed); it was heavy on strategic thinking.

Finally, if the consequences of failure are severe—bankruptcy, for example—strategic planning can help an organization move quickly, simply, and effectively to formulate and implement effective strategies. Put negatively, if there is no real reason to plan strategically, no major threats or important opportunities, then perhaps strategic planning is a waste of time. "Muddling through" may work acceptably until strategic planning does become necessary.

Getting Started

These four cases, plus the others cited in the book, indicate that strategic planning can help governments, public agencies, and nonprofit organizations fulfill their missions and satisfy their key stakeholders more effectively. These cases also indicate that a number of difficulties and challenges must be overcome if strategic planning is to fulfill its promise for organizations. Let me conclude with some advice about how to get started with strategic planning.

1. Start where you are, and where the other people who might be involved in or affected by the process are. This is one of the most important principles for organizing collective action (Kahn, 1982). You can always undertake strategic planning for the part of the organization you control. Whatever you are in charge of—a unit, department, division, or a whole organization—you can always start there. But wherever you start, you must also keep in mind where the participants are. Other involved or affected parties are likely to need some education about the purposes, processes, and products of strategic planning. If they are important for the formulation or implementation of strategies, you will have to bring them along so that they can be effective supporters and implementors.

2. You need a compelling reason to undertake strategic planning. Otherwise the process is not likely to be worth the effort, or to reach a satisfactory conclusion. The obverse of this lesson is that people can create an infinite number of reasons *not* to engage in strategic planning, even when it would be the best thing for the organization or community; such reasons may be nothing more than excuses.

The reasons that might be compelling are numerous. The organization or community may be performing well, but key decision makers may want to do even better. That was the case with Suburban City, and to a lesser extent with the Central City executive branch. Or the organization may feel threatened by the emergence of strong rivals. That was the case with Central City's city council. Or the organization may be confronting a real turning point in its history, a point that might lead to success or extermination. That was the case with Health Center. Or the organization may feel the need for something like strategic planning, but not engage in the process until asked to do so by decision makers farther up the hierarchy. That was the case with Nursing Service. But whatever the compelling reason, organizational or community members, and especially key decision makers, must see some important benefits from strategic planning, or they will not be active supporters and participants. And if they do not support and participate, the process is bound to fail.

3. There is no substitute for leadership. Unless the process is sponsored (ultimately, if not initially) by important and powerful leaders and decision makers, it is likely to fail. Only key decision makers who are also effective leaders will be able to motivate and guide their organizations through a successful strategic thinking and acting process. Leadership from the key decision makers is absolutely necessary if the organization itself must be changed as a result of strategic planning.

4. You need a process champion. Strategic planning will not succeed unless someone champions the process. This person should believe in the process and see his or her role as facilitating the effective thinking, deciding, and acting of key decision makers. A process champion does not have a preconceived set of answers to the important issues the organization faces, but wants instead to facilitate a process that will produce effective answers. It certainly helps if the process champion is at the top of the organization chart. That was the case in the Central City executive branch and city council, Suburban City, Nursing Service, and Health Center. But it does not hurt to have other champions from other levels. Indeed, the process

is likely to be more effective if more than one champion is involved.

5. Tailor the process and the planners' roles to the organization or community and situation. The generic strategic planning process outlined in this book must be applied with care, so that it clearly fits the situation, even if the ultimate aim of the process is to change the situation (Bryson and Delbecq, 1979; Galloway, 1979; Christensen, 1985). The roles played by planners in that process also will be contingent on the situation. In most cases involving cross-unit or cross-level strategic planning within an organization, or strategic planning for a community, planners will need to act as facilitators of strategic planning by key decision makers. But in some situations planners also will be called upon to serve as technical experts.

6. The big innovation in strategic planning is having key decision makers talk with one another about what is truly important for the organization or community as a whole. A strategic planning process is merely a way of helping key decision makers think and act strategically. The process can in no way substitute for the presence, participation, support, and commitment of key decision makers to raise and resolve the critical issues. Initiation and institutionalization of the process, however, can provide the occasions and justification to gather key decision makers together to think and act strategically on behalf of the organization or community. All too often, in all too many organizations and communities, such occasions and justifications do not exist. Organizational and community performance and stakeholder satisfaction suffer accordingly.

7. The resource most needed to undertake strategic planning is not money, but the attention and commitment from key decision makers. Strategic planning is not expensive in dollar terms, but it is expensive when it comes to the resources that typically are scarcest in most organizations and communities— the attention and commitment of key decision makers. For organizations, strategic planning may take up to 10 percent of the ordinary work time of each key decision maker each year. That may not seem like much. (Indeed, one might argue that decision makers unwilling to devote 10 percent of their work

time to what is truly important for the organization are either incompetent or disloyal and ought to be fired!) But realistically, it is hard to persuade key decision makers to commit that time to strategic planning. It may be even more difficult to get substantial blocks of time from community leaders for community strategic planning. An effective strategic planning process therefore is likely to be one that is simple (''simpler is better''), quick (''quicker is better''), and always treated in a special way, so that key decision makers will give the time and attention that are needed when they are needed.

8. Remember that the biggest payoffs from strategic planning may come in surprising ways or from surprising sources. Hennepin County, Minnesota, for example, found that organizational development, team building, and heightened morale throughout the organization were among the greatest benefits of its strategic planning process. In Suburban City, the process led surprisingly to the city council's commitment to become better policy makers. And Nursing Service found that strategic planning not only was not a weapon that might be used against it, but was a force that could help the service satisfy key stakeholders even better. There is no telling, really, what will happen as a result of the process. The organization or community open to surprises, however, may create and take advantage of its own opportunities.

9. Outside consultation and facilitation can help. Often organizations and communities need some consultation, facilitation, and education from outsiders. Central City, Suburban City, Nursing Service, and Health Center each relied on outside help at various points throughout the strategic planning process. If help is needed, try to get it.

10. If the going gets tough, keep in mind the potential benefits of the process. Recall that strategic planning can help organizations and communities

> Think strategically and develop effective strategies.
> Clarify future direction.
> Establish priorities.
> Make today's decisions in light of their future consequences.

Develop a coherent and defensible basis for decision making.

Exercise maximum discretion in the areas under organizational control.

Make decisions across levels and functions.

Solve major organizational problems.

Improve organizational performance.

Deal effectively with rapidly changing circumstances.

Build teamwork and expertise.

But it may not be easy to achieve those benefits. The faith of process champions often can be sorely tried, particularly if the organization is engaged in strategic planning for the first time. For example, the process seems particularly prone to disintegrate in the middle, the strategic issue identification and strategy development steps. But remember the words of Rosabeth Moss Kanter (1983), "Every innovation is a failure in the middle." The big payoffs may take a long time to achieve. For instance, it may take several years to know if some important strategy has worked or not. In the meantime, therefore, try to label as much as possible that comes out of the process a success, and work hard to improve the process along the way.

To maintain enthusiasm for the process until successes tied directly to implemented strategies began to appear, Hennepin County emphasized, even celebrated, the achievements and benefits of the process as they occurred (Eckhert, Haines, Delmont, and Pflaum, 1988). Achievements were highlighted through special meetings of all 300 managers, newsletters, glossy brochures, special meetings of the county board, even a theatrical pantomime show. Achievements included forming a cabinet of top administrators, developing strategic planning educational materials and guidebooks, identifying thirty-two strategic issues, developing alternative strategies to deal with specific issues, and creating innovative strategies. Thus, the process was managed so that it was "successful" long before any actual strategies were implemented.

11. Finally, keep in mind that strategic planning is not right for every organization or community. Barry (1986) believes that in the following situations, strategic planning perhaps should not be undertaken:

If the roof has fallen.

If the organization or community lacks the necessary skills, resources, or commitment of key decision makers to produce a good plan.

If costs outweigh benefits.

If the organization or community prefers to rely on the intuition and skill of extremely gifted leaders.

If "muddling" is the only process that will work.

If implementation of strategic plans is extremely unlikely.

On the other hand, while there may be reasons not to undertake strategic planning, those reasons all too easily can become excuses for not paying attention to what is really important for the organization or community. An organization or community that gives in to excuses has suffered a failure of hope and courage.

Strategic planning can help organizations fulfill their missions and satisfy their key stakeholders. But it will work only if people want it to work. This book was written to help all those who want their organizations and communities to survive, prosper, and fulfill important missions. I hope it will prompt more than a few of these people to proceed with strategic planning.

Resource Sections

Six resource sections are included. The first consists of a set of sample strategic planning worksheets. The second presents an ongoing approach for identifying external threats and opportunities. The third offers advanced concepts for identifying strategic issues, while the fourth presents advanced concepts for strategy formulation and implementation. The fifth is a detailed sample of strategies developed to deal with a strategic issue. The final resource section offers advanced concepts for establishing an effective organizational vision of the future.

Resource A

Sample Strategic Planning Worksheets

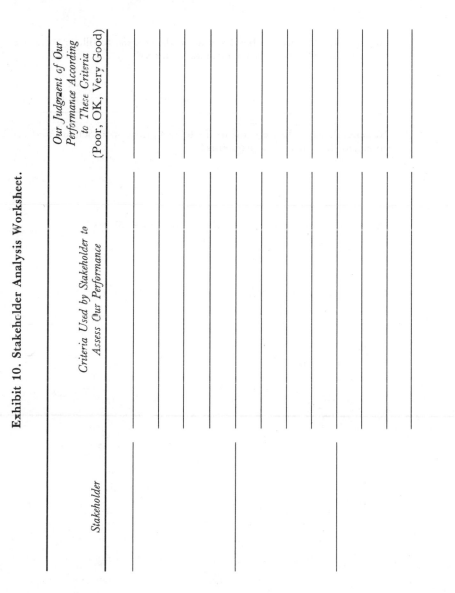

Exhibit 10. Stakeholder Analysis Worksheet.

Stakeholder	Criteria Used by Stakeholder to Assess Our Performance	Our Judgment of Our Performance According to These Criteria (Poor, OK, Very Good)

Exhibit 11. Mission Statement Worksheet.

1. Who are we?

2. In general, what are the basic social needs we exist to fill (or what are the basic social problems we exist to address)?

3. In general, what do we want to do to recognize or anticipate and respond to these needs or problems?

4. What should our responses be to our key stakeholders?

   a.

   b.

   c.

   d.

Exhibit 11. Mission Statement Worksheet, Cont'd.

e.

f.

g.

h.

i.

j.

5.   What is our philosophy and what are our core values?

6.   What makes us distinctive or unique?

Exhibit 12. External Opportunities Worksheet.

Opportunity #_____

Opportunity #_____

Opportunity #_____

Exhibit 13. External Threats Worksheet.

Threat #_____

Threat #_____

Threat #_____

Exhibit 14. Internal Strengths Worksheet.

Strength #_____

Strength #_____

Strength #_____

Exhibit 15. Internal Weaknesses Worksheet.

Weakness #_____

Weakness #_____

Weakness #_____

Exhibit 16. Strategic Issue Identification Worksheet.

1. What is the issue? Be sure to phrase the issue as a question about which your organization can take some sort of action.

2. Why is this an issue? What is it about the conjunction of mission and mandates, external opportunities and threats, or internal strengths and weaknesses that makes this an issue?

3. What are the consequences of not addressing this issue?

Exhibit 17. Practical Alternatives, Dreams, or Visions Worksheet.

What are the practical alternatives, dreams, or visions we might pursue to address this strategic issue?

Practical alternative, dream, or vision #_____

Practical alternative, dream, or vision #_____

Practical alternative, dream, or vision #_____

Exhibit 18. Barriers Identification Worksheet.

What are the barriers to the realization of these alternatives, dreams, or visions?

Barrier #_____

Barrier #_____

Barrier #_____

Exhibit 19. Major Proposals Worksheet.

What are the major proposals we might pursue either to achieve the practical alternatives, dreams, or visions directly or to overcome the barriers to their realization?

Strategy #_____

Strategy #_____

Strategy #_____

Exhibit 20. Major Actions Worksheet.

What major actions with existing staff and within existing job descriptions must be taken within the next year to implement the strategies or proposals?

Major action #_____

Major action #_____

Major action #_____

Exhibit 21. Action Steps Worksheet.

What action steps must be taken in the next six months to implement the proposals and who is responsbile for the action step?

Action step #_____   Person responsible:_____

Action step #_____   Person responsible:_____

Action step #_____   Person responsible:_____

Resource B

An Ongoing Approach for Identifying External Threats and Opportunities

Public and nonprofit organizations should consider establishing a regular scanning operation to routinely monitor the external environment for opportunities and threats. If the external scanning function is *not* routinized, almost certainly they will be in a reactive, rather than an anticipatory, position; important opportunities will be missed, and threats will not be recognized until it is too late or at least until many important strategic options are foreclosed.

Pflaum and Delmont (1987) have proposed an inexpensive, pragmatic, and effective approach to external scanning for public and nonprofit organizations. They believe that external scanning is basically a three-part function:

1. Identification of key issues and trends that pose actual or potential threats or opportunities.
2. Analysis and interpretation of the issues and trends.
3. Creating information that is useful for decision making.

241

Purpose, Participants, and Time

There are several reasons to undertake scanning, and those purposes should be clarified at the outset. Scanning can:

1. Provide information on emerging issues and trends.
2. Develop networks and partnerships among scanners and their organizations.
3. Educate the participants about the scanning function and about specific issues and trends.
4. Provide useful information for strategic planning.

An organization interested in strategic planning probably should do regular external scanning for all four purposes.

Pflaum and Delmont argue that scanning is most cost-effective if it is undertaken by a group or network of organizational insiders interested in scanning and willing to devote part of their work time to it. The group should be coordinated by a lead person. Outside consultants might be used as needed. The efforts of the insiders may be enhanced if they are part of a network of scanners in other organizations.

Time commitments are important to the success of scanning. If volunteers are to be involved, the organization must try to keep time demands to the necessary minimum. Pflaum and Delmont propose three options for meetings: annual or quarterly meetings lasting half a day to a full day; monthly sessions lasting two to three hours; and twice-monthly meetings lasting two hours. In addition to meetings, time must be spent reading and preparing short scanning reports, possibly on a one-page scanning form. Most professionals spend a portion of their time reading anyway, so scanning may not involve any additional reading time, though the reading itself may be redirected.

Identify Key Issues

Once purposes, participants, and time commitments are clarified, the next step is to carry out major scanning activities. Pflaum and Delmont identify these as:

1. Select issues and trends categories (for example, political, economic, social, and technological).
2. Identify appropriate sources, such as professional journals, newsletters, conference proceedings, key informants.
3. Understand issues cycles (discussed in Resource C and Chapter Ten).
4. Ask key questions:
    Is the issue or trend new?
    Does it come from a surprising source?
    Does it contradict prevailing wisdom?
    Is there a pattern to the issue or trend?
5. Develop a simple recordkeeping system, such as one-page scanning report forms or more elaborate computerized keyword systems.

Analyze Issues

Analysis and interpretation of the strategic importance of issues and trends can be accomplished by a number of techniques, but the simplest and best is group discussion. There is no substitute for the collective wisdom likely to emerge from a probing discussion by an experienced and heterogeneous group of people.

Additional techniques—the simpler the better—may be used to inform judgments about the meaning and implications of particular issues and trends. Brainstorming (Johnson and Johnson, 1987), the nominal group technique (Delbecq, Van de Ven, and Gustafson, 1975), and the snow card technique discussed in Chapter Six are simple yet effective techniques that can be used with groups (brainstorming for creating ideas, NGT for creating and ranking ideas, and snow cards for creating and synthesizing ideas into categories).

Scenarios (Amara and Lipinski, 1983; Linneman and Klein, 1983) also are relatively simple to construct and can be used to present an array of options for discussion. Scenarios are stories that pose alternative futures for the organization based on assumptions about trends and events. Usually a best case, a worst case, and a case somewhere in between are developed to map out the range of possible futures the organization might face.

Another useful technique is the impact network (Pflaum

and Delmont, 1987). Impact networks are constructed by brainstorming secondary or tertiary impacts, trends, or events that might follow from some primary impact, trend, or event. Another simple technique is an impact/probability matrix (Pflaum and Delmont, 1987). This matrix has two dimensions: the likely impact of an issue, trend, or event (high, medium, or low) and the likelihood that it will occur (high, medium, or low). Issues, trends, or events are mapped onto the matrix so that planners may judge which to monitor most closely and to make contingency plans for. Additional techniques can be found in Nutt (1984) and Nutt and Backoff (1987).

The final step in the analysis and interpretation process is to decide on the next steps. Possible next steps might include deciding which issues and trends to monitor more closely, which to act upon or refer to appropriate decision makers for consideration, and which to drop.

Report Information

The reporting and referral process produces information that is useful for decision making. Several approaches might be used to produce such information. Planners might prepare brief issue or trend summaries, often called "scans," which condense onto a single page the essence of an issue or trend. Three- to five-page policy papers might be developed that explore specific issues or trends in further depth. Comprehensive environmental scans that cover a range of issues and trends might be put together. Seminars or forums on specific issues or trends might be organized for particular stakeholder groups. Finally, a regular newsletter might cover a changing selection of issues and trends.

The basic idea is that for environmental scanning to be useful it must become a regular and expected part of several persons' jobs within an organization, must not place excessive demands on their time, and must produce useful information for decision making. When information produced by environmental scanning is coupled with information produced on an organization's actual or potential clients, customers, and payers, and competitors and collaborators, the organization is in a good position to identify external opportunities and threats in a timely way.

Resource C

Advanced Concepts for Identifying Strategic Issues

Strategic issues are fundamental policy questions affecting an organization's (or community's) mandates; mission and values; or product or service level and mix, clients, users or payers, cost, financing, management, or organizational design. Basically strategic issues emerge from the way organizations choose to, or are forced to, relate to their internal and external environments. The issues define the choices the organization faces over exactly what the "fit" with its environment will be.

This section will concentrate on several sources of what might be termed "generic" strategic issues for governments and, to a lesser extent, nonprofit organizations. The purpose of the section is to provide readers with more understanding of what strategic issues are and where to look for them.

Strategic issues can be expected to emerge from the nature of the public sector environment, issue cycles, agendas, the nature of public policies, and the use of the various tools that can help identify issues, such as environmental scanning and SWOT analyses (Ring, 1988).

The Nature of the Public Sector Environment

An appreciation of the important differences between the public and private sectors must lie behind any appropriate application of private sector approaches to strategic planning to the public (or nonprofit) sectors (see Chapter Two). One important difference is the institutional context of the public sector, a context characterized in the United States by a federal system of government (the formal sharing of power by state and local governments through dual sovereignty; see Glendening and Reeves, 1977) and extensive intergovernmental relations (Wright, 1978). Strategic issues of several kinds might be expected to emerge from such a system of government (Ring, 1988). Some issues might be expected to emerge at the boundaries between laterally related governments. For example, how will the legislators in one state react to changes in the tourism promotion plans of a neighboring state? Other issues might be expected to emerge around issues of coordination, responsibility, and shared resources for program operations and outcomes across vertically related levels of government. These issues are typical of many health, education, and social service programs that are initiated, regulated, and funded at levels other than that which implements them. Still other issues might emerge involving policy or program focus, responsibility, effort, and financing in situations where no one apparently is in charge (Cleveland, 1973).

Ring and Perry (1985) point out additional differences between the public and private sectors. First, they argue that the ill-defined nature of much public policy creates conflict over organizational goals or purposes. While key decision makers may not actually make the policies, they often are charged with implementing them without clear guidance about what to implement. Second, public organizations are more open to their external environments and, third, they serve a more diverse group of stakeholders. As a result, it often is more difficult to manage the development of an issue and the strategies used to deal with it. Fourth, the artificial time constraints in the public sector, particularly those imposed by periodic elections, can create strategic issues, such as the need for elected officials to demonstrate tangible accomplishments in a restricted time frame. Finally, Ring and Perry note the shaky coalitions that characterize political decision making in the public sector. As a result, creating and maintaining the coalitions necessary to adopt and enact a set of initiatives may itself become a strategic issue.

Finally, Ring (1988) points out that the interactions of public organizations with private organizations may generate strategic issues. Particularly important in this regard are the actions of public bodies to regulate or otherwise influence the activities of private sector bodies, and the concomitant efforts by private sector bodies to influence public policies and actions. As in most market-based societies, a major fraction of the attention of government is devoted to controlling the activities of the marketplace and to correcting the failures of the market. Indeed, the primary rationale for government intervention in the workings of society is to do what markets either cannot do, will not do, or do badly (Moore, 1978). Strategic issues thus will arise for governments over if, when, and how to intervene in market operations.

In the relatively recent past if government determined that a market was failing in some fashion, the normal response would be to replace the market with a public bureaucracy (Schultze, 1977). Now the trend is to rely on less drastic interventions that involve more marketlike public policy tools, such as vouchers, taxes, subsidies, insurance schemes, and contracting with public, private, or nonprofit organizations to provide services; but the strategic issues over if, when, and how to correct market failures still remain (Savas, 1982).

Issue Cycles

Issue cycles are another source of strategic issues. Schon (1971) has pointed out that there is a life cycle to issues and the attention they receive from organizations and the public. The cycle begins with a threatening or disruptive event that leads to public awareness that a problem exists. Solutions to the problem are then articulated, and networks or coalitions organize to advocate the different solutions. A political debate ensues and a solution is adopted and legitimized. The solution is then institutionalized and eventually taken for granted. Finally, as the problems change, the institution, and the policy solution it symbolizes, decays and becomes outmoded.

Strategic issues might emerge for an organization at any

point in the cycle (Bryson, Van de Ven, and Roering, 1987). Issues might concern, for example, how to widen the appreciation of a problem, which solutions to advocate, how to gain adoption of favored solutions, how to institutionalize solutions, and how to dismantle outmoded regimes.

Strategic planning can be seen as a way to routinize attention to policy-relevant ideas, so that the organization can take action early in the cycle when it may have a greater impact on the way events unfold. If an organization is to act quickly, however, it must have an effective environmental scanning system that focuses organizational attention on the strategic significance of threatening or disruptive events, new environmental trends, or emerging opportunities. Strategic planning also may help organizations realize when the time has come to change solutions and the organizations designed to implement them. To repeat a point from an earlier chapter, organizations must always be seen as a means to an end, as a solution to a problem—not as an end in themselves.

Agendas

Cobb and Elder (1972) identify two types of agendas: systemic and institutional. The systemic agenda "consists of all issues that are commonly perceived by members of the political community as meriting public attention and as involving matters within the legitimate jurisdiction of existing governmental authority" (p. 85). The institutional agenda is "that set of items explicitly up for active and serious consideration of authoritative decision makers" (p. 85). Items on either agenda potentially may be strategic for a public organization, but only become so when fundamental policy choices for the organization are involved.

The important point is that governmental decision making is governed by agendas, often quite formal ones, such as the legislative agenda of a governing body, and that some issues are seen as legitimately within the purview of government and others are not. If some issue requires formal action, typically the choices must be placed on the organization's agenda, and the issue itself must of course be seen as within the legitimate purview of government. Similarly, action can be avoided on an issue if it is kept off the institutional or systemic agendas.

Cobb and Elder argue that whether or not an issue appears on the institutional agenda depends upon relationships among three sets of factors: triggering devices, initiators, and gatekeepers. Triggering devices include natural catastrophe, unanticipated human events (such as riots or assassinations), technological changes, actual imbalances or bias in resource allocations, and ecological changes. Initiators find the issues they wish to pursue in the effects of the triggering devices. Whether or not the initiators are able to place the issue on the institutional agenda depends primarily on their access to institutional gatekeepers or key decision makers such as executives or legislators. The strategic planning process presented in this book is designed to routinize attention to triggering devices and to involve initiators and gatekeepers directly in the process so that there is a clear link to the institutional agenda.

The Nature of Public Policies

Public policies may be both the source of strategic issues (Wildavsky, 1979b) and the strategies used to resolve them. Types of public policies and their implementability, therefore, are of special concern. We will deal with policy types first, because the kind of policy involved is likely to influence how the issues are framed, what solutions are proposed, and how implementable those solutions are.

Lowi (1966) has argued that there are three basic categories of policy: distributive, regulatory, and redistributive. Distributive policies produce tangible results, such as those resulting from traditional "pork barrel" politics, most public land and resource policies, rivers and harbors legislation, research and development contracts, defense procurement programs, and labor, business, and agricultural "clientele" services. They are in effect patronage policies. As a result, the policies are almost not policies at all, but simply the aggregated effects of numerous highly individualized decisions. The policies benefit many individuals or organizations and result from an accumulation of uncommon interests in a "log-rolling" fashion. Winners and losers never need to come into direct contact with one another. Decisions usually are made by legislative committees or public agencies in which the power structure consists of stable, non-conflicting elites along with associated support groups. The policies are then implemented by an agency, typically a primary functional unit, or bureau.

Regulatory policies control the activities of specified populations or uses to which various resources might be put. They therefore cannot be disaggregated to the level of individuals or specific organizations the way distributive policies can, because implementation must be through application of a general rule and with reference to the broader standards of law. Regulatory policies thus can be disaggregated only down to sector levels, such as, for example, all bus companies, or food preparation facilities, or households of a certain kind. It is fairly clear who is helped and hurt by the regulatory decisions, at least in the short run. The policies are the outcome of a struggle among competing groups, or coalitions, with something to gain or lose from regulatory decisions—the classic "pluralist," or group struggle, form of decision making (Dahl, 1984). The coalitions usually are unstable, meaning that many regulatory decisions are made on the floor of legislative bodies, not in committee. Once decisions are made, implementation usually is delegated to an appropriate agency.

Redistributive policies involve shifting benefits away from one group toward another as, for example, first the shifting of federal spending away from defense toward social programs in the 1960s, and now, under Reagan, a shift back in the other direction. Redistributive policies thus are like regulatory policies in their impacts, except that the categories of impact are much broader, approaching social classes. Issues involving redistribution therefore activate interests in what are roughly class terms, and those interests are expressed by "peak associations," such as the U.S. Chamber of Commerce and the National Association of Manufacturers. The competing coalitions involve elites and counterelites and usually are quite stable. Key decisions typically are made within the peak associations and the executive

branch. Implementation occurs toward the top of some major
agency; that is, above the bureau level. Implementation of the
1986 federal tax reform, for example, is the responsibility of
the Internal Revenue Service as a whole.

In framing and resolving strategic issues, planners should
take account of the different actors, power structures, dynamics,
decisional loci, and implementation vehicles typically involved
in each policy type. Planners also should realize that policy types
can overlap in a given strategic issue.

A number of authors have explored public policy implementation in detail (Pressman and Wildavsky, 1973; Van Meter
and Van Horn, 1975; Bardach, 1977; Mazmanian and Sabatier,
1983). Their research indicates that policy implementation can
be problematic, giving rise to a number of strategic issues (Ring,
1988).

Mazmanian and Sabatier (1983) offer a model of the policy implementation process that indicates three specific sources
of strategic issues: the tractability of the problem, the statute
or other policy vehicle used to structure the course of implementation, and nonstatutory variables that may affect the course
of implementation. The tractability of the problem will determine whether or not measurable progress can be made in addressing the issue and, therefore, whether or not key stakeholders
can be satisfied in the long run. Tractability decreases as technical difficulties or the diversity of proscribed target group behavior increases, the larger the target group is as a percent of
the population, and the greater the extent of behavioral change
required.

Mazmanian and Sabatier describe seven features of statutes or other policy vehicles used to structure implementation
that may affect implementation success. Each feature in fact
might produce strategic issues or choices. First, are the policy
objectives clear and consistent? Second, has an adequate causal
theory been incorporated into the statute? Third, what allocation of resources is involved? Fourth, what degree of hierarchical
integration within and among competing institutions is needed
to achieve the policy objectives? Fifth, what decision rules will
be used? Sixth, how will implementation officials and staff be

recruited? Finally, how much formal access will outsiders have to the implementation processes?

The third element of their model is a set of nonstatutory variables that may affect the course of implementation. These include general socioeconomic and technological conditions; the extent of public support; attitudes and resources of constituency groups; support from sovereigns; and the commitment and leadership skill of implementing officials.

Mazmanian and Sabatier's model provides a useful check-list of areas in which strategic issues may emerge, and their checklist offers guidance on how to design public policies so that implementation difficulties may be avoided in the first place. Since the factors included in the model probably affect the implementation of programs, projects, products, or services (see Bryson, Boal, Poole, and Terrell, 1979; Bryson and Delbecq, 1979), the checklist also is useful in identifying strategic issues emerging from those other implementation efforts. Similarly, the model helps planners avoid difficulties in implementing programs, projects, products, or services.

Tools

The final generic source of strategic issues is the tools that might be used to identify the issues. Different tools can be expected to uncover different kinds of issues, so that one should not expect any single tool to uncover all the potentially fundamental issues facing an organization. The tools that will be discussed briefly in this section include stakeholder analyses, environmental scanning, competitive analysis, portfolio methods, scenarios, and SWOT analyses. Each of these tools is relatively simple in concept and use. The reader interested in other, typically more complicated tools, should consult Nutt and Backoff (1987) and Nutt (1984).

Stakeholder analyses are likely to uncover issues related to the satisfaction of key stakeholders, and to areas in which stakeholders' criteria for evaluating organizational performance are complementary, in conflict, or nonexistent. Environmental scanning will detect issues, trends, and events in the categories in which searches occur. Competitive analysis will focus attention on the forces affecting the level of returns in specific industries and on specific firms within those industries. Portfolio methods will array entities of some sort against dimensions thought to be of strategic importance. If the resulting array is unsatisfactory, strategic issues will concern what to do about it. Scenarios will present pictures or stories to the organization of various possible futures. Strategic issues are likely to emerge as a result of the distance or tension between where the organization is now and what the scenario describes as a likely or possible future.

Stakeholder analyses, environmental scanning, competitive analysis, portfolio methods, and scenarios each can feed into more formal SWOT analyses. The snow card technique is a particularly inexpensive and effective way to uncover SWOTs. The strategic issues identified as a result of a SWOT analysis will concern how to take advantage of the strengths and opportunities while minimizing or overcoming the weaknesses and threats.

Not all of the tools need to be used as part of every strategic planning effort, but at a minimum, stakeholder and SWOT analyses should be undertaken. Neither has to take much time, and yet each is likely to have a profound effect on which strategic issues are identified and how they are framed.

Advanced Concepts for Strategy Formulation and Implementation

A number of different concepts may prove useful to the strategic planning team members as they formulate strategies for the organization or community. Several will be presented in this section, including: Kolderie's public service redesign matrix (1986); typologies of strategies developed by Miles and Snow (1978; Boschken, 1988), Wechsler and Backoff (1987), Rubin (1988), Nutt (1984), Barry (1986), and Porter (1980); my own service management concept; a brief review of the portfolio approaches discussed in earlier chapters; and the implementation approaches of Nutt and Backoff (1987) and Mazmanian and Sabatier (1983).

Concepts Related to Organizational Role

Two of the concepts—Kolderie's public service redesign matrix and Miles and Snow's typology of strategy types—relate primarily to the organization's conceptualization of its role. Kolderie (1986) has developed a two-by-two matrix for understanding the relationships between public and private sectors, on the one hand, and the decisions about what will be provided and how it will be produced, on the other hand. One dimension is public versus private, the other is provision versus production.

The distinction between provision and production at first may seem obscure, but it is important and should be kept in mind. According to *The Oxford Reference Dictionary* (1986, p. 668) to provide means "to cause (a person) to have possession or use of something; to supply, to make available." Provision therefore is quite different from production, the actual creation of a good or service. For example, a parent may provide for children's education through payment of taxes or tuition, but not actually produce the education. Production is handled by school administrators, teachers, and the children themselves.

The distinction between provision and production is important precisely because it all too often is not made. Typically, once governments decided that something should be provided, they established a traditional public bureaucracy to produce it (Schultze, 1977). In the case of fire and police protection perhaps it was wise to assume that the government would not only provide the service but produce it as well. But even in these cases a number of governments are now experimenting with a variety of different modes of production, from contracting for service with public, private, or nonprofit producers to promoting protection schemes organized and financed by citizen groups.

Education offers a particularly interesting example of the importance of the distinction. State governments typically require compulsory education for all children under the age of sixteen and agree to provide the money for the education. That education is then produced, typically, in publicly owned, operated, controlled, and financed schools. Parents and students usually have little choice about which schools they attend and what is taught there (although parents with enough money can send their children to private or nonprofit schools of the parents' choice). Government, in other words, has a monopoly on the production of public education and dictates where, when, and under what conditions it will be received.

Various educational voucher schemes have been advanced to break this government monopoly, expand parental (and student) choice, and force schools to improve their performance because they will have to compete for students and the voucher monies that come with the students. In simplest terms, these schemes would give the parents of school-age children vouchers to be used in the schools of their choice to pay for their children's education. Vouchers would allow a choice of programs within the schools, and under some schemes even would be good for use in for-profit or nonprofit—not just public—schools (Peek, Duren, and Wells, 1985). What the educational voucher schemes are about therefore is not whether public education will be provided (because the compulsory education laws and voucher monies assure that it will), but instead breaking up the government's monopoly control over the *production* of education. Vouchers would allow parents (and perhaps students) far greater choice over what education will be produced by whom, how, when, and where.

Kolderie goes on to emphasize that the crucial role for government in all cases is to decide what will be publicly provided. A far less important role is to act as the actual producer of a good or service. Government may choose to be a producer, or to compete with other producers, but production is not central to government's role; the choice of what will be provided is.

Miles and Snow (1978) offer a different way of thinking about the role of an organization, not just of government. Actually, they were concerned primarily with private sector organizations, but Boschken (1988) in a study of West Coast port authorities has demonstrated the applicability of their typology to public sector enterprises.

Miles and Snow developed a strategic behavior typology. Along half of the scale are proactive behavior types, the "prospector" and the "analyzer." The prospector actively scans the environment for opportunities and develops a wide range of relations with external actors. The prospector is also an active innovator. The analyzer, on the other hand, while also proactive, is not as active a scanner and innovator as the prospector. Instead the analyzer watches the prospectors and adopts or adapts innovations after they have proved their effectiveness. While prospectors are more concerned with strategic effectiveness than with operational efficiency, the analyzers show a balanced concern for both.

On the other side of Miles and Snow's scale are two reactive strategic behavior types, the "defender" and the "reactor." These two types resist change, protect against any infringements of their turf, and actively scan the environment for threats while they often overlook opportunities. The difference between the two is that at least the defender has a consistent strategy while the reactor does not. The reactor just responds to events inconsistently and with little or no vision of the future.

Boschken found in a paired-comparison test of six West Coast port authorities that the prospectors and analyzers consistently outperformed the defenders and reactors. One is reminded of the old adage that "the best defense is a good offense." Ironically, because of their reactive strategic behavior, the defenders and reactors faced losing precisely what they sought to preserve.

Boschken found a number of additional factors that correlated with high performance. The prospectors and analyzers tended to emphasize strategic effectiveness, while the defenders and reactors highlighted operational efficiency. The leaders of the prospectors and analyzers played a catalytic, proactive role. While turnover was low among their chief administrative officers (CAOs), prospectors and analyzers also tended to have a larger number of civil service–exempt staff than did defenders and reactors. In contrast, the leaders of the defenders and reactors took a more "political" role (in the negative sense), or even relied on cronyism. Turnover among CAOs tended to be higher. Similarly, port authority commission members in prospectors and analyzers had a higher average tenure than commission members in defenders and reactors.

Prospectors and analyzers relied much more on mutual exchange in their involvements with other governments, while defenders and reactors relied more on power struggles or submission. The organizational designs and operations, particularly the strategic planning capacities and functions, of the prospectors and analyzers were oriented much more toward active harbor development than were those of the defenders and analyzers.

Within their strategic planning functions, prospectors and analyzers relied much more on matrix (or dual authority) relations than did defenders and reactors, who relied more on a uniform hierarchical command structure. Finally, prospectors and analyzers tended to be much more autonomous organizations requiring fewer political approvals by other officials or bodies than their worse-performing rivals required.

A Potpourri of Strategies

This section will present the strategy typologies developed by Wechsler and Backoff (1987), Rubin (1988), Nutt (1984), Barry (1986), and Porter (1980). Each provides a useful way to think about alternative strategies.

Wechsler and Backoff identified three patterns of strategy in their study of several Ohio state agencies. The patterns were labeled *developmental, political,* and *protective.* The patterns bear some resemblance to Miles and Snow's role types. The advantage of Wechsler and Backoff's typology is that it graphically points out the interaction between an agency's understanding of its environment and its efforts to make strategy. Decision makers and planners rarely can do all they wish strategically, but with careful thought and effective action, they can achieve as much as their situations allow—and in some cases can change their situations.

A developmental strategy attempts to improve the organization's status, capacity, resources, and influence. It also seeks to create a new and better future for the organization. Formal planning systems can play an important role in guiding the deployment of existing resources to build capacity. The organization must have support from the external environment for a developmental strategy to work.

Political strategies come in two types. The first is a response to changing environmental conditions and seeks to accommodate the balance of power among external stakeholders. The strategy is not totally reactive, as key decision makers can still exercise some control over the organization's direction. The second type of political strategy involves the organization as one of the spoils of partisan political contests. Organizational positions, structure, policy, and program changes are viewed as rewards for individual supporters and important constituencies. This type of strategy occurs most frequently after changes in governmental regimes.

Protective strategies are formulated by organizations with limited capacities in response to a hostile or threatening environment. This type of strategy attempts to maintain the organizational status quo while accommodating strong external pressures. This strategy is the most reactive in the set, as decisions are made and actions taken in response to external stakeholders, and may actually be dictated by them. Indeed, insiders may be led to question the skill and commitment of the organization's leaders.

Rubin (1988) has developed a typology of public sector strategies based on whether the time horizon is short or long and whether the context of change involves reaction to a disruptive present or the fashioning of a future quite different from the past. Rubin's typology is reprinted in Figure 8.

Sagas are a pattern of actions taken over the long term to reestablish a set of core values, goals, or institutions that have been lost, or are in danger of being lost, due to environmental changes or to the inadequacies of institutional or managerial capacities. The idea is not to reestablish the past, but to regain the lost qualities of the past through strategic responses to new or changed circumstances. The saga thus is the organizational analogue of Homer's great literary saga, *Ulysses,* which recounts the hero's efforts to return to Greece at the end of the Trojan War. Rubin identifies three kinds of sagalike strategies: (1) restorative, aimed at restoring lost qualities through the design of new policies and a reorientation of institutional agendas; (2) reformative, or attempts to change governmental policies and procedures so they reflect an appreciation of an earlier era; and (3) conservatory, predicated on the preservation of values, institutions, or goals which appear threatened in major environmental changes.

Quests are like sagas, in that the time frame is long term. But they differ from sagas in that the pattern of action is not

Figure 8. Rubin's Typology of Public Sector Strategies.

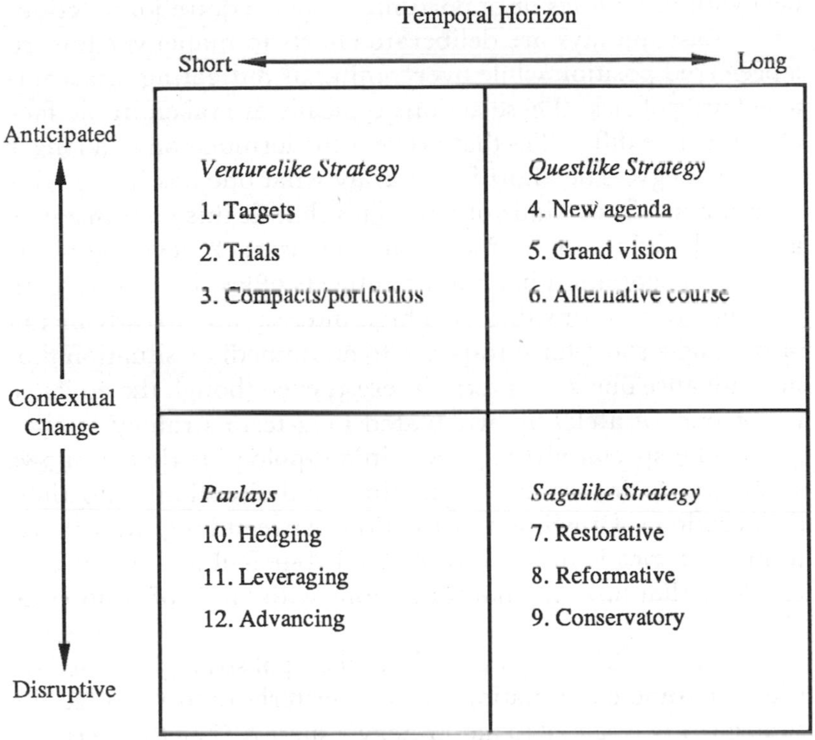

Temporal Horizon

Short ←————————————————————→ Long

Anticipated	*Venturelike Strategy* 1. Targets 2. Trials 3. Compacts/portfolios	*Questlike Strategy* 4. New agenda 5. Grand vision 6. Alternative course
Contextual Change	*Parlays* 10. Hedging 11. Leveraging 12. Advancing	*Sagalike Strategy* 7. Restorative 8. Reformative 9. Conservatory
Disruptive		

Source: Rubin, 1988.

aimed at the restoration, appreciation, or preservation of a venerable past, but at the creation of a new and different future. Again Rubin identifies three questlike strategies: (1) the new agenda of long-term goals or objectives often associated with newly elected or appointed officials; (2) the grand vision for an organization, city, region, or state; and (3) the alternative course of action, formulated as a direct but long-term response to an anticipated conflict or crisis.

Ventures are similar to quests except that the time frame is short term. The associated strategies are: (1) targets that focus efforts to take advantage of a short-term opportunity or overcome a current strategic issue or threat; (2) trials, or short-term experiments designed to deal with issues; and (3) compacts, or short-term agreements among departments or organizations to deal with difficulties or opportunities that require joint action.

Last, parlays are deliberate efforts to maneuver toward a preferred position while overcoming or mitigating unacceptable levels of risk. These actions typically are taken in the face of immediate difficulties that prevent the formulation of a longer term strategy. The effort is to parlay what one has into a winning hand. Three kinds of strategies that fit this circumstance are: (1) hedging, or counterbalancing risks; (2) leveraging, or strategic negotiation in areas or subjects of less interest to gain leverage in areas or subjects of high interest; and (3) advancing or making a short-term response to an immediate situation that may advance one's long-term interest, even though the advance is not part of a clearly articulated long-term strategy.

The special virtue of Rubin's typology is that it allows strategists to incorporate both time and situations into their deliberations. Drawing a distinction between long- and short-term strategies is quite conventional, but Rubin's is the only typology that links temporal horizons with kinds of contextual change.

Nutt (1984) proposes eight archetypal strategies based on whether some combination of three criteria used to judge the strategies are essential to the strategy's success. The three criteria are quality, acceptance, or innovation. The virtue of a criteria-based approach is that some lines of strategy development can be ruled out, because they will not meet the criteria. In addition, the team gains a better idea of what kinds of planning methods might prove most useful (see also Nutt and Backoff, 1987).

Barry (1986) has catalogued a number of strategies commonly pursued by nonprofit organizations: (1) Large nonprofits often choose growth and a diversification of funding resources as a way of gaining control over their environments. The Amherst H. Wilder Foundation discussed earlier in this book has pursued this strategy. (2) Nonprofits may choose to team up with other nonprofits through mergers, consolidations, joint programming, joint ventures, or shared services. (3) Organizations may choose to "downsize" through a reduction in the scope or scale of services to fit financial or other constraints. (4) Nonprofits may choose to specialize or focus their activities so that they only do what they can do well within a particular market niche. (5) "Piggybacking" can be an effective strategy; income earned in one sphere of activity can offset declining revenue in other areas or subsidize particularly desirable activities. (6) Nonprofits can seek contracts for service from governments or other organizations, a practice particularly common in the health and social service fields. (7) Nonprofits can choose to upgrade and "professionalize" their staff capabilities. (8) Or nonprofits can take an opposite tack and "deprofessionalize," organizing services provided through mutual help, community-based social support systems, client-to-client methods, or volunteers. (9) Finally, a nonprofit can choose to go out of business if the organization is no longer viable or if its mission has been fulfilled.

Porter (1980) provides a final set of strategy concepts useful for service or product management. He introduces the notion that in competitive situations organizations can pursue three generic strategies. They can choose differentiation—the creation of something that is perceived in the marketplace to be unique. They can choose cost leadership—production of the lowest-cost products or services. Or they can choose to focus—to aim at a particular customer group, segment of the product or service line, or geographic market. Porter argues that these strategies are mutually exclusive; an organization cannot pursue more than one at the same time for the same product or service and still succeed against savvy competitors.

Service Management

Based on the work of Normann (1984) and Pfeiffer, Goodstein, and Nolan (1986), I have developed what I call the service hexagon (Figure 9) as a way of helping organizations figure out what product or service strategies they should pursue. The service hexagon is based on the idea that for a product or service to be effective, to pass the "market test," there must be a linkage or correspondence among six elements: *who* wants the product or service (customer, payer, client, or user groups—the target market), *what* they want (the specific product or service), *where* they want it (location), *when* they want it (timing of delivery), *how* they want it (methods of delivery or sale and technologies used), and *why* they want it (functions fulfilled, purposes served, reasons for use).

Furthermore, the hexagon must be organized around an effective service management system (an integrated set of activities, methods, and technologies), a service philosophy, a service-oriented culture, and an appropriate image for the service delivery organization. In the case of products or services provided or produced (to use Kolderie's distinction) by a government or nonprofit organization, it is particularly important to remember that payers and users may be different groups. Different strategies may be needed to deal with each group.

Figure 9. The Service Hexagon.

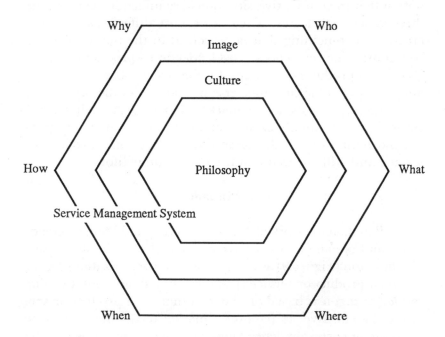

Portfolio Approaches

The adaptability of portfolio approaches to strategic purposes was discussed in Chapter Two and Resource C. A portfolio approach allows planners to measure strategies against dimensions deemed to be of strategic importance. The Philadelphia Investment Portfolio (see Chapter Two) is an example of how the portfolio idea can be used to evaluate strategies. The portfolio matrix is presented in Figure 10. The portfolio itself consists of fifty-six investment options (investments of public and private time and resources) arranged according to how well they facilitate achievement of the strategic objectives of the Philadelphia area (their "attractiveness") and the degree to which they take advantage of ongoing trends (their "position"). Each of the two dimensions consists of a set of economic, political, and social criteria. An individual organization or coalition would choose to pursue an option because the option fit with its particular strategic objectives, but the creators of the portfolio also can be assured that the city as a whole would benefit from the organization's desire to invest. The creators of the portfolio also can actively solicit investors to pursue options that are of the greatest strategic value as measured by their attractiveness and position.

San Luis Obispo, California, presents another example of the portfolio approach to evaluating strategic options (Sorkin, Ferris, and Hudak, 1984, p. 9). The decision matrix (or portfolio) presented in Figure 11 was prepared as part of the city's strategic planning effort. The matrix was used to evaluate the fiscal effects of the strategies against their ease of implementation. According to the matrix, housing expansion is a poor strategic choice, because fiscal benefits are low and implementation difficulties are high. On the other hand, tourist expansion may be a fairly good strategy, because fiscal benefits are fairly high and implementation difficulties may not be too hard to overcome. Unfortunately for the city, no strategies fall into the lower right-hand corner, in which fiscal benefits are high and implementation difficulties are low.

Figure 10. *Philadelphia Investment Portfolio Proposed Portfolio Assessment Matrix.*

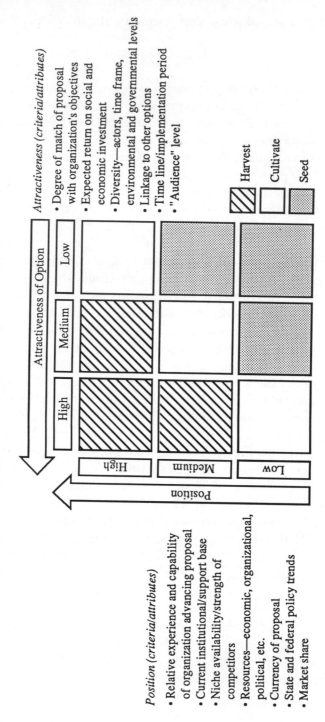

Source: Sorkin, Ferris, and Hudak, 1984.

Figure 11. Decision Matrix for Development Strategies, San Luis Obispo.

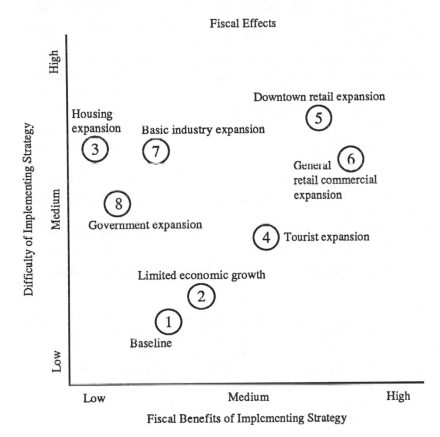

Fiscal Effects

Source: Sorkin, Ferris, and Hudak, 1984, p. 9.

Implementation Approaches

A number of authors have offered advice on formulating strategies with implementation in mind. This section will discuss the ideas of Nutt and Backoff (1987) and Mazmanian and Sabatier (1983).

Nutt and Backoff, drawing on the work of Freeman (1984), argue that different strategies will be needed for different organizational stakeholders depending on the importance of the stakeholders and their position with respect to any given course of action. Nutt and Backoff propose using the two-by-two matrix reproduced in slightly modified form in Figure 12. One dimension represents the stakeholder's importance to the organization, particularly in relation to the proposed course of action. The other dimension indicates whether the stakeholder supports or opposes the proposed course of action. For a given proposed course of action the strategic planning team would locate stakeholders on the matrix in order to determine whether a winning coalition is possible; the likely size of the opposition coalition; and neutral or ''swing'' stakeholders who might be targeted for special lobbying and influence efforts. Nutt and Backoff go on to propose a set of tactics to deal with the different categories of stakeholders (p. 51).

Potentially antagonistic stakeholders are those who would oppose the proposed course of action, but who are very important to the organization. Possible tactics to deal with this group include:

1. Identify potential coalitions by determining neutral actors in the problematic and low priority categories who are closely aligned or related to the antagonistic stakeholders.
2. Take steps to block formation of coalitions among antagonistic and neutral stakeholders.
3. Prevent antagonistic stakeholders from undermining support of supporters.
4. Determine which antagonistic supporters must be surprised (kept in the dark) to delay or prevent the mobilization of their opposition.
5. Anticipate the nature of antagonists' opposition and develop counterarguments in advance.
6. Engage selected antagonists in negotiations to determine and perhaps adopt changes in the proposed course of action that would change antagonists into neutrals or even supporters.

Potential supporters are stakeholders who are very important to the organization and who support the proposed course

Figure 12. Interpreting the Stakeholder.

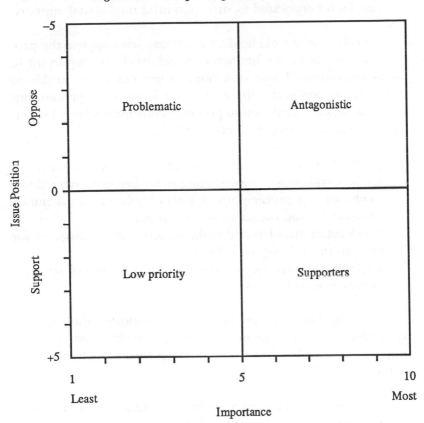

Source: Adapted from Nutt and Backoff, 1987, p. 52.

of action. They would be managed quite differently. Potential tactics to use with them include:

1. Provide information to reinforce beliefs.
2. Coopt by involving key supporters in some or all of the strategic planning team's deliberations.
3. Ask supportive stakeholders to sell the strategy to those who are neutral.
4. Some potential supporters who are at present neutral can

be invited to react to proposed strategies so that changes can be incorporated to turn potential into actual support.

Problematic stakeholders are those who oppose the proposed course of action but who are relatively unimportant to the organization. These stakeholders present fewer problems than antagonists and supporters, but important precautions should be taken nonetheless to prevent problematics from becoming antagonists. Possible tactics include:

1. Prepare defensive tactics to be used if a coalition of problematic stakeholders with antagonists becomes possible or likely, or if a problematic appears likely to take a public position in opposition to the strategy.
2. Moderately problematic stakeholders can be targeted for education or lobbying efforts.
3. Redefine the strategy to assuage the concerns of strongly negative stakeholders.

Finally there are low priority stakeholders who are relatively unimportant to the organization, but who do support the proposed course of action. Possible tactics for use with this group include:

1. Use low-cost education with those stakeholders who almost fall into the high importance category.
2. Find ways to promote involvement of low priority stakeholders with supporters to expand the size of the coalition in support of the proposed strategy.

Obviously many more tactics might be developed to use with each group of stakeholders. The main importance of Nutt and Backoff's scheme, however, is that it prompts strategists to think of the implementation (indeed, the formulation) of any strategy in stakeholder terms.

Mazmanian and Sabatier (1983, pp. 41–42) also provide valuable advice on how to implement strategies, particularly statutes or other policy decisions. Their model was outlined in

Resource C. They argue that six conditions are sufficient for effective implementation of a policy decision that represents a substantial departure from the status quo. Achievement of the goals of the policy will occur if:

1. The enabling legislation or other legal directive outlines clear and consistent policy objectives or criteria for resolving goal conflicts.
2. The legislation incorporates a sound theory of what is needed for achievement of the policy objective and gives implementing officials sufficient jurisdiction over target groups and other factors likely to affect achievement of the goals.
3. The legislation structures the implementation process to favor successful implementation, such as supportive and capable agencies, supportive decision rules, and adequate resources.
4. Key officials possess the necessary managerial and political skills and are committed to achievement of the goals.
5. A coalition of key supporters (including important legislators or chief executives) actively support the implementation process, and the courts are either supportive or neutral.
6. New priorities or conflicting policies do not emerge, and underlying social conditions do not change, to weaken the policy's political support or underlying causal theory.

Sample Strategies for Managing a Strategic Issue: A Suburban City Example

Suburban City used the five-part process for developing strategies to respond to strategic issues outlined in Chapter Eight. The strategies Suburban City designed to deal with one of its strategic issues are presented in this section. The strategic planning team collapsed parts four and five of the process into a single question.

The strategic issue was: Given the city's favorable location in the metropolitan area, what should the city do to enhance and improve its vehicular and pedestrian movements throughout its hierarchy of transportation facilities?

The strategies developed to respond to this issue are embodied in the answers to the following four questions:

I. What are the practical alternatives, dreams, or visions we might pursue to address this strategic issue?
    A. Gain local control of transportation facilities by
        (1) Requiring all public agencies to pay for improvements in their own rights-of-way.

       (2) Monitoring traffic signal timing to identify problems, change timing as needed.

       (3) Completing renovation of "X" Boulevard.

       (4) Changing the state aid laws to allow more flexibility on use of state aid funds.

       (5) Keeping control of key rights-of-way.

  B. Nucleate high-intensity development by

       (1) Reducing intensity of future development.

       (2) Encouraging high-density housing adjacent to office parks.

  C. Stimulate alternatives to the personal automobile by

       (1) Identifying internal trips to better utilize public transportation.

       (2) Operating intra-city bus system.

       (3) Developing park and ride sites.

       (4) Developing light rail transit.

  D. Establish a pedestrian district.

  E. Allow long-range planning to prevail by

       (1) Bridging barriers and maximizing connections among all projects.

       (2) Following through on design and final plan approval process for all projects.

  F. Complete existing facilities by

       (1) Constructing Interstate segment.

       (2) Building sidewalks along all collector streets and thoroughfares.

       (3) Completing construction of "Y" Avenue.

  G. Improve the delineation and identification of facilities such as street furnishings and lighting.

  H. Eliminate transportation/parking conflicts by

       (1) Eliminating parking requirements in downtown area.

       (2) Prohibiting all on-street parking.

II. What are the barriers to the realization of these alternatives, dreams, or visions?

  A. Insufficient funding due to

       (1) High cost of infrastructure.

       (2) Decreasing federal and state funds.

  B. Jurisdictional conflicts with other government units.

    C.   Public opposition to transportation projects in the form of
       (1)   Resistance to increased traffic.
       (2)   Resistance to public transportation.
    D.   Resistance to change occurs because
       (1)   Consensus on alternatives is not present.
       (2)   Alternatives are contrary to past practice.
    E.   Lack of perceived need for transportation project because
       (1)   Problems are not severe enough to require a solution.
       (2)   Light rail transit is too costly and has not been demanded by the public.
    F.   Political considerations affecting
       (1)   Tax base growth.
       (2)   Implementation of the comprehensive plan.

III.   What are the major proposals we might pursue either to achieve the practical alternatives, dreams, or visions directly or to overcome the barriers to their realization?
    A.   Enforce city codes and the comprehensive plan:
       (1)   Examine city codes for needed change.
    B.   Identify and promote benefits for proposed transportation projects through:
       (1)   Benefit/cost analysis.
    C.   Identify and develop alternate funding sources:
       (1)   City income tax for funding.
       (2)   Utilize alternative funding methods to construct facilities.
       (3)   Use tax increment financing where appropriate.
       (4)   Determine how much money is available now and the amount spent in past.
    D.   Develop short/long-range transportation policy:
       (1)   Interconnect all arterial/collector traffic signals.
       (2)   Emphasize development of long-range capital improvement projects.
       (3)   Focus on setting design and timetable for improvements (and then reject projects which do not fit).
    E.   Lobby for changes in legislation to

        (1)   Provide local control of federal, state, and county transportation.

        (2)   Appropriate more state funding for transportation purposes.

        (3)   Obtain approval for the development of light rail transit in the southwest corridor.

   F.   Develop public education programs on transportation to

        (1)   Show how a fragmented approach does not yield the best results.

        (2)   Promote car pooling to relieve traffic volume.

   G.   Enhance council and staff development on transportation issues:

        (1)   City staff and officials need hands-on experience with transit.

        (2)   Develop staff transportation planning skills.

   H.   Achieve greater representation on transportation issues:

        (1)   Establish citizen task force on transportation that would be advisory to the planning commission and council.

        (2)   Increase staff and council involvement in metro transportation activities.

        (3)   Lobby county to build light rail transit in southwest corridor.

IV.   What are the major actions and action steps that must be taken in the next six to twelve months to implement the proposals and who is responsible for the action?

   A.   Develop public education.

        (1)   Develop cable TV programs on

            (a)   light rail transit

            (b)   sidewalks

            (c)   public transportation

            (d)   alternative modes of transportation

        (2)   Identify public speakers and promote transportation as a public topic.

        (3)   Hold an intensive study session with council on transportation needs.

(1) Develop other public education/information tools:
  (a) citizen task force
  (b) cable programs
  (c) public relations programs
B. Increase funding for transportation:
  (1) Lobby for state funds and work with state department of transportation staff.
  (2) Analyze public and private funding sources and assess the probability of obtaining such funding.
  (3) Identify long-range funding strategies.
  (4) Hire a consultant to develop alternative financing methods for the city.
  (5) Gather annual expenditure data by road, type, and location.
C. Improve intergovernmental relations in transportation area:
  (1) Involve staff/elected officials in regional government's activities.
  (2) Identify/promote city representatives to transportation boards/commissions.
  (3) Reschedule the capital improvement plan with respect to other agencies.
  (4) Pursue more active coordination with other agencies.
  (5) Hire lobbyist for transportation issues.
D. Provide staff opportunities for development on transportation and transit issues:
  (1) Encourage staff members to attend transportation planning seminars.
E. Develop short-term transportation plan:
  (1) Recommend to council three- to five-year transportation plan that includes policies on
    (a) thoroughfares
    (b) light rail transit
    (c) signals
    (d) sidewalks and trails
    (e) financing options

   (2) Coordinate development of a short-term trans-
     portation plan with comprehensive plan.
 F. Develop long-range transportation plan:
   (1) Write a twenty-year capital improvement pro-
     gram based on the comprehensive plan.
   (2) Develop long-range cost projections.
 G. Develop a legislative program on transportation
   issues:
   (1) Set a special study session with council and
     legislative representatives to discuss transpor-
     tation needs and issues.
 H. Study code/comprehensive plan enforcement:
   (1) Permit shared use of parking facilities.
 I. Create incentives for changing transportation habits:
   (1) Develop reward system for car pooling.

Advanced Concepts for Establishing an Effective Organizational Vision for the Future

Several concepts appear useful to organizations interested in constructing a vision of success for themselves. One of them was discussed in Resource D: Bryson's service hexagon. This concept can help organizations that deliver related bundles of services envision what success would look like for them.

This section will discuss two additional concepts that can help organizations envision success. More broadly applicable than Bryson's service concept, these relate to both single- and multi-functional organizations and governments. The two concepts are key success indicators and excellence criteria or characteristics, as developed by Peters and Waterman in their book *In Search of Excellence* (1982).

The idea of key success indicators has been articulated by Peter Drucker (1973, pp. 552, 572–591), and related specifically to planning by several authors, including Jenster (1987) (although he calls these indicators "critical success factors"). These indicators are the ones against which an organization must demonstrate at least adequate performance if it is to survive and prosper. They are likely to be a distillation of the criteria used by key stakeholders to judge organizational performance. The indicators can be expected to be different for different organizations. For a private for-profit organization key indicators might include profit rate, return on investment, and market share.

Key success indicators for a government or nonprofit organization are likely to be more numerous and perhaps inherently more ambiguous than those of a private for-profit organization. Nonetheless, it is important to be clear about the indicators if performance against them is to be measured, appreciated, and rewarded. Key success indicators for Nursing Service, for example, include:

1. Public health nursing caseloads successfully completed, those still open, length of time from first enrollment until completion of the case, and cost per case.
2. Gaps in public health nursing services in the community.
3. Overlaps in public health nursing services in the community.
4. Coordination of the services of Nursing Service with other nursing services in Urban County.
5. Coordination of the services of Nursing Service with the health care system of Urban County.
6. Job satisfaction of Nursing Service employees.
7. Draw on the county property tax levy.

Two approaches to the development of key success indicators have been discussed in earlier chapters. One is the stakeholder analysis discussed in Chapter Five on mission and mandates. The stakeholder analysis asks organizational members to specify the organization's key stakeholders and the criteria that they use to judge organizational performance. By scrutinizing the list of stakeholder criteria, planners can develop a parsimonious list of success indicators. The other approach is to use the snow card technique to develop a set of key success indicators. The question put before strategic planning team members would be simply, "What are the key success indicators for our organization?"

Peters and Waterman developed eight interrelated criteria that seem to characterize successfully managed "excellent" companies. Their research was not particularly scientific, but the criteria do make sense as ideals for many public and nonprofit organizations. The criteria probably need some modification to be applied to general-purpose governments, however, and those modifications will be discussed later. Here are the eight criteria as they were formulated for businesses:

1. A bias for action. Companies that meet this criterion quickly identify problems, find answers, and implement them. Their motto is "Do it, fix it, try it."

2. Close to the customer. Excellent organizations spend a great deal of time and effort listening closely to what their customers want and then strive to meet those needs in a way that emphasizes quality, reliability, and service.

3. Autonomy and entrepreneurship. Excellent companies promote innovation and risk taking. The motto here comes from the 3M Corporation: "Never kill a good idea."

4. Productivity through people. People are viewed by the excellent companies as a valuable resource—indeed, their most valuable resource.

5. Hands-on, value driven. Excellent companies all have a clearly articulated philosophy and set of key values and their executives and employees behave in accord with them. People are deeply involved; they *live* the business.

6. Stick to the knitting. The excellent companies do not move far from the businesses that they know how to run well. They have core businesses that *remain* the core; they do not pursue ideas or acquisitions at odds with those businesses.

7. Simple form, lean staff. Structural forms are kept simple and corporate staffs are kept relatively small.

8. Simultaneous loose-tight properties. Excellent companies have some core values to which they cleave almost fanatically, but at the same time they promote decentralization and autonomy in decision making and action as long as they are in accord with the core values.

Table 3. "Excellence" Criteria Comparison.

Local government excellence criteria	Peters and Waterman criteria	Criteria differences	Public sector special conditions making "excellence" attainment difficult
1. Action orientation	A bias for action	None	Laws making it difficult for local government to act quickly Low inclination to take risks Limited resources
2. Closeness to citizens	Close to the customer	Customer becomes citizen	Multiplicity of public sector "publics" Captive consumers
3. Autonomy and entrepreneurship	Autonomy and entrepreneurship	None	Reluctance by local government to "market" or take risks
4. Employee orientation	Productivity through people	None	People-oriented programs sometimes perceived as a waste of tax-payers' money
5. Values	Hands-on, value driven	None	Traditional values that are hard to change
6. Mission, goals, and competence	Stick to the knitting	Expansion to include mission and goals	Difficulty of determining mission and goals Difficulty of measuring results
7. Structure	Simple form, lean staff	Combination of "simple form" and loose-tight properties	Some local governments with complex structures written into basic law
8. Political relationships	Simultaneous loose-tight properties	New local government criterion	Frequent changes in key actors Perceptions that roles of policy-makers and administrators are different and/or conflicting

Source: Sipel, 1984, p. 4. Reprinted by permission from "Putting *In Search of Excellence* to Work in Local Government," an article by George A. Sipel, as it appeared in the April 1984 issue of *Public Management Magazine.* © 1987, The International City Management Association, Washington, D.C.

It is easy to see how these criteria might apply to many single-function public authorities and to many nonprofit organizations. For example, the Amherst H. Wilder Foundation, discussed earlier, probably is characterized by these eight criteria (Bryson, King, Roering, and Van de Ven, 1986).

As noted above, however, adaptations or modifications of some criteria probably are necessary before they can be applied to general-purpose governments. Sipel (1984) recommends specific changes to apply the criteria to local government; they are listed in Table 3. As with Peters and Waterman's list, little research has been done on the criteria either individually or as a set. Nonetheless, since the criteria appeal to common sense, they are worth a second look by key decision makers.

Actually, the suggested changes are remarkably few. Whether the criteria apply at the state and federal levels is an open question. It would appear, however, that they at least would apply to major departments, even if they might be impossible to apply practically across the whole of a government.

References

Ackoff, R. *Redesigning the Future.* New York: Wiley, 1974.

Ackoff, R. *Creating the Corporate Future.* New York: Wiley, 1981.

Addams, J. *Twenty Years at Hull House.* New York: New American Library, 1981.

Allan, J. H. "A Case Study of the Ramsey County Nursing Service Strategic Planning Process. Plan B Paper." Minneapolis: School of Public Health, University of Minnesota, 1985.

Alexander, E. R. "After Rationality, What? A Review of Responses to Paradigm Breakdown." *Journal of the American Planning Association,* 1984, *50,* 62–69.

Allison, G. T. *Essence of Decision.* Boston: Little, Brown, 1971.

Amara, R., and Lipinski, A. *Business Planning for an Uncertain Future.* Elmsford, N.Y.: Pergamon Press, 1983.

Anderson, J. E. *Cases in Public Policymaking.* (2nd ed.) New York: Holt, Rinehart & Winston, 1979.

Andrews, K. *The Concept of Corporate Strategy.* Homewood, Ill.: Irwin, 1980.

Ansoff, I. *Corporate Strategy.* New York: McGraw-Hill, 1965.

Ansoff, I. "Managing Strategic Surprise by Response to Weak Signals." *California Management Review,* 1975, *18,* 21–33.

Ansoff, I. *Strategic Management.* New York: Wiley, 1979.

Ansoff, I. "Strategic Issue Management." *Strategic Management Journal,* 1980, *1* (2), 131–148.

Ansoff, I., Declerk, R., and Hayes, R. (eds.). *From Strategic Planning to Strategic Management.* New York: Wiley, 1976.

Armstrong, J. S. "The Value of Formal Planning for Strategic Decisions: Review of Empirical Research." *Strategic Management Journal,* 1982, *3* (2), 197–211.

Bardach, E. *The Implementation Game.* Cambridge, Mass.: MIT Press, 1977.

Barry, B. W. *Strategic Planning Workbook for Nonprofit Organizations.* St. Paul, Minn.: Amherst H. Wilder Foundation, 1986.

Behn, R. D. "The Fundamentals of Cutback Management." In R. J. Zeckhauser and D. Leebaert (eds.), *What Role for Government?* Durham, N.C.: Duke Press Policy Studies, 1983.

Bhambri, A. *Johnson and Johnson* (A). Cambridge, Mass.: Harvard Business School, Case 9-384-053, 1985.

Black, A. "The Comprehensive Plan." In W. I. Goodman and E. C. Freund (eds.), *Principles and Practice of Urban Planning.* Washington, D.C.: International City Management Association, 1968.

Bloom, C. "Strategic Planning in the Public Sector." *Journal of Planning Literature,* 1986, *1* (2), 253–259.

Boal, K. B., and Bryson, J. M. "Representation, Testing and Policy Implications of Planning Processes." *Strategic Management Journal,* 1987a, *8,* 211–231.

Boal, K. B., and Bryson, J. M. "Charismatic Leadership: A Phenomenological and Structural Approach." In J. G. Hunt, B. R. Balinga, H. P. Dachler, and C. A. Schriescheim (eds.), *Emerging Leadership Vistas.* Elmsford, N.Y.: Pergamon Press, 1987b.

Bolan, R. S. "Community Decision Behavior: The Culture of Planning." *Journal of the American Institute of Planners,* 1969, *35,* 301–310.

Bolan, R. S. "Generalist with a Specialty—Still Valid? Educating the Planner: An Expert on Experts." *Planning 1971: Selected Papers from the ASPO National Conference.* Chicago: American Society of Planning Officials, 1971.

Boschken, H. L. "Turbulent Transition and Organizational

Change: Relating Policy Outcomes to Strategic Administrative Capacities." *Policy Studies Review,* 1988, *7* (3), forthcoming.

Bourgeois, L. J., III. "Strategy and Environment: A Conceptual Integration." *Academy of Management Review,* 1980, *5,* 25–39.

Bracker, J. "The Historical Development of the Strategic Management Concept." *Academy of Management Review,* 1980, *5* (2), 219–224.

Bresser, R. K., and Bishop, R. C. "Dysfunctional Effects of Formal Planning: Two Theoretical Explanations." *Academy of Management Review,* 1983, *8,* 588–599.

Brickman, P. "Is It Real?" In J. H. Harvey, W. Ickes, and R. F. Kidd (eds.), *New Directions in Attributional Research.* Vol. 2. Hilldale, N.J.: Lawrence Erlbaum, 1978.

Bryson, J. M. "A Perspective on Planning and Crises in the Public Sector." *Strategic Management Journal,* 1981, *2,* 181–196.

Bryson, J. M. "Representing and Testing Procedural Planning Methods." In I. Masser (ed.), *Evaluating Urban Planning Efforts.* Aldershot, England: Gower Publishing, 1983.

Bryson, J. M. "The Policy Process and Organizational Form." *Policy Studies Journal,* 1984, *12,* 445–463.

Bryson, J. M., and Boal, K. B. "Strategic Management in a Metropolitan Area: The Implementation of Minnesota's Metropolitan Land Planning Act of 1976." In K. Cheung (ed.), *Academy of Management Proceedings 1983,* 1983.

Bryson, J. M., Boal, K. B., Poole, S., and Terrell, C. "A Contingent Planning Model for Programs and Projects." *Project Management Quarterly,* 1979, *10* (1), 19–29.

Bryson, J. M., and Cullen, J. W. "A Contingent Approach to Strategy and Tactics in Formative and Summative Evaluations." *Evaluation and Program Planning,* 1984, *7,* 267–290.

Bryson, J. M., and Delbecq, A. L. "A Contingent Approach to Strategy and Tactics in Project Planning." *Journal of the American Planning Association,* 1979, *45,* 167–179.

Bryson, J. M., and Einsweiler, R. C. "Editors' Introduction to the Strategic Planning Symposium." *Journal of the American Planning Association,* 1987, *53,* 6–8.

Bryson, J. M., and Einsweiler, R. C. (eds.). *Shared Power: What Is It? How Does It Work? How Can We Make It Work Better?* Lanham, Md.: University Press of America, 1988a.

Bryson, J. M., and Einsweiler, R. C. (eds.). *Strategic Planning— Threats and Opportunities for Planners.* Chicago and Washington: The Planners Press of the American Planning Association, 1988b.

Bryson, J. M., Freeman, R. E., and Roering, W. D. "Strategic Planning in the Public Sector: Approaches and Directions." In B. Checkoway (ed.), *Strategic Perspectives on Planning Practice.* Lexington, Mass.: Lexington Books, 1986.

Bryson, J. M., King, P. J., Roering, W. D., and Van de Ven, A. H. "Strategic Management at the Amherst H. Wilder Foundation." *Journal of Management Case Studies,* 1986, *2,* 118–138.

Bryson, J. M., and Roering, W. D. "Applying Private Sector Strategic Planning to the Public Sector." *Journal of the American Planning Association,* 1987, *53,* 9–22.

Bryson, J. M., Van de Ven, A. H., and Roering, W. D. "Strategic Planning and the Revitalization of the Public Service." In R. Denhardt and E. Jennings (eds.), *Toward a New Public Service.* Columbia, Mo.: Extension Publications, University of Missouri, 1987.

Burns, J. M. *Leadership.* New York: Harper & Row, 1978.

Carver, J. "Consulting with Boards of Human Service Agencies: Leverage for Organizational Effectiveness." *Consultation,* 1984, *3,* 27–34.

Carver, J. "Nonprofit Boards of Directors." Workshop presented under the auspices of the Amherst H. Wilder Foundation, St. Paul, Minn., May 15, 1986.

Center for Philadelphia Studies. *Philadelphia Investment Portfolio.* Philadelphia: University of Pennsylvania, 1982a.

Center for Philadelphia Studies. *A Philadelphia Prospectus.* Philadelphia: University of Pennsylvania, 1982b.

Chandler, A. *Strategy and Structure.* Cambridge, Mass.: MIT Press, 1962.

Charan, R. "How to Strengthen Your Strategic Review Process." *The Journal of Business Strategy,* 1982, *2,* 50–60.

Checkoway, B. (ed.). *Strategic Perspectives on Planning Practice.* Lexington, Mass.: Lexington Books, 1986.

Child, J. "Organizational Structure, Environment and Performance: The Role of Strategic Choice." *Sociology,* 1972, *6,* 1-22.

Christensen, K. S. "Coping with Uncertainty in Planning." *Journal of the American Planning Association,* 1985, *51* (1), 63-73.

Christensen, R., Andrews, K., Bower, J., Hammermesh, R., and Porter, M. *Business Policy: Text and Cases.* Homewood, Ill.: Irwin, 1983.

Cleveland, H. *The Future Executive.* New York: Harper & Row, 1973.

Cleveland, H. "The Future of Public Administration." An address to the American Society of Public Administration's National Conference, Honolulu, Hawaii, 1982.

Cleveland, H. *The Knowledge Executive.* New York: Harper & Row, 1985.

Cobb, R. W., and Elder, C. D. *Participants in American Politics: The Dynamics of Agenda Building.* Newton, Mass.: Allyn & Bacon, 1972.

Cohen, M. D., March, J. G., and Olsen, J. P. "A Garbage Can Model of Organizational Choice." *Administrative Science Quarterly,* 1972, *17,* 1-25.

Coplin, W. D., and O'Leary, M. K. *Everyman's Prince: A Guide to Understanding Your Political Problems.* Boston: PWS Publishers, 1976.

Cyert, R. M., and March, J. G. *A Behavioral Theory of the Firm.* Englewood Cliffs, N.J.: Prentice-Hall, 1963.

Dahl, R. A. *Modern Political Analysis.* Englewood Cliffs, N.J.: Prentice-Hall, 1984.

Dalton, G. W. "Influence and Organizational Change." In G. Dalton, P. Lawrence, and L. Greiner (eds.), *Organization Change and Development.* Homewood, Ill.: Irwin, 1970.

Dalton, G. W., and Thompson, P. H. *Novations—Strategies for Career Management.* Glenview, Ill.: Scott, Foresman, 1986.

Dayton Hudson Corporation. "Statement of Philosophy." Minneapolis, Minn.: Office of Corporate Communications, 1982.

Deal, T. E., and Kennedy, A. A. *Corporate Cultures: The Rites and Rituals of Corporate Life.* Reading, Mass.: Addison-Wesley, 1982.

Delbecq, A. L. "Negotiating Mandates Which Increase the Acceptance of Evaluation Findings Concerning Demonstration Findings in Human Services." A paper presented at the Annual Conference of the Academy of Management, Orlando, Fla., 1977.

Delbecq, A. L., and Filley, A. "Program and Project Management in a Matrix Organization." Monograph no. 9. Madison: Graduate School of Business, University of Wisconsin, 1974.

Delbecq, A. L., Van de Ven, A. H., and Gustafson, D. *Group Techniques for Program Planning.* Glenview, Ill.: Scott, Foresman, 1975.

Drucker, P. *Management—Tasks, Responsibilities, Practices.* New York: Harper & Row, 1973.

Duncan, R. B. "The Ambidextrous Organization: Designing Dual Structures for Innovation." In R. H. Killman, L. R. Pondy, and D. P. Slevin (eds.), *The Management of Organizational Design.* Vol. 1. New York: North, Holland, 1976.

Eadie, D. C. "Putting a Powerful Tool to Practical Use: The Application of Strategic Planning in the Public Sector." *Public Administration Review,* 1983, *43,* 447–452.

Eadie, D. C. "Strategic Issue Management: Improving the Council-Manager Relationship." *ICMA MIS Report,* 1986, *18* (6), 2–12.

Eadie, D. C., and Steinbacher, R. "Strategic Agenda Management: A Marriage of Organizational Development and Strategic Planning." *Public Administration Review,* 1985, *45,* 424–430.

Eckhert, P., Haines, K., Delmont, T., and Pflaum, A. "Strategic Planning in Hennepin County, Minnesota: An Issues Management Approach." In J. M. Bryson and R. C. Einsweiler (eds.), *Strategic Planning—Threats and Opportunities for Planners.* Chicago and Washington: The Planners Press of the American Planning Association, 1988.

Einsweiler, R. C. "What the Top People Are Saying About Central City Planning." *Planning,* 1980, *46* (Oct.), 15–18.

Emery, F., and Trist, E. "The Causal Texture of Organizational Environments." *Human Relations,* 1965, *18* (Feb.), 21–31.

Evan, W. "The Organizational Set: Toward a Theory of Inter-Organizational Design." In J. Thompson (ed.), *Approaches to Organizational Design*. Pittsburgh: University of Pittsburgh Press, 1966.

Feldman, M. S., and March, J. G. "Information in Organizations as Signal and Symbol." *Administrative Science Quarterly*, 1981, *26*, 171–186.

Filley, A. *Interpersonal Conflict Resolution*. Glenview, Ill.: Scott, Foresman, 1975.

Fisher, R., and Ury, W. *Getting to Yes: Negotiating Agreement Without Giving In*. New York: Penguin Books, 1981.

Fisher, W. R. "Narration as a Human Communication Paradigm: The Case of Public Moral Argument." *Communication Monographs*, 1984, *51*, 1–22.

Flynn, N. "Performance Measurement in Public Sector Services." *Policy and Politics*, 1986, 14(3), 389–404.

Folger, J. P., and Poole, M. S. *Working Through Conflict*. Glenview, Ill.: Scott, Foresman, 1984.

Fredrickson, J. G. "The Recovery of Civism in Public Administration." *Public Administration Review*, 1982, *42*, 501–508.

Fredrickson, J. W. "The Comprehensiveness of Strategic Decision Processes." *Academy of Management Journal*, 1984, *27* (2), 445–466.

Fredrickson, J. W., and Mitchell, R. R. "Strategic Decision Processes: Comprehensiveness and Performance in an Industry with an Unstable Environment." *Academy of Management Journal*, 1984, *27* (2), 399–423.

Freedman, N., and Van Ham, K. "Strategic Planning in Philips." In B. Taylor and D. Hussey, *The Realities of Planning*. Oxford, England: Pergamon Press, 1982.

Freeman, R. E. *Strategic Management: A Stakeholder Approach*. Boston: Pitman, 1984.

Freeman, R. E., and Lorange, P. "Theory Building in Strategic Management." In R. Lamb and P. Srivastava (eds.), *Latest Advances in Strategic Management*. Vol. 3. Greenwich, Conn.: JAI Press, 1985.

Galloway, T. D. "Comment on 'Comparison of Current Planning Theories: Counterparts and Contradictions,' by B. M.

Hudson." *Journal of the American Planning Association,* 1979, *45* (4), 399–402.

Giddens, A. *Central Problems in Social Theory.* London: Macmillan, 1979.

Glendening, P. N., and Reeves, M. M. *Pragmatic Federalism.* Pacific Palisades, Calif.: Palisades Publishers, 1977.

Greenblat, C. and Duke, R. *Gaming-Simulation: Rationale, Design, and Applications.* New York: Wiley, 1975.

Greenblat, C. S. and Duke, R. D. *Principles and Practices of Gaming Simulation.* Beverly Hills, Calif.: Sage, 1981.

Guibert, J. de. *The Jesuits: Their Spiritual Doctrine and Practice; A Historical Study.* (W. J. Young, trans. G. E. Gauss, ed.) Chicago: Institute of Jesuit Sources, 1964.

Hall, P. *Great Planning Disasters.* Berkeley and Los Angeles: University of California Press, 1980.

Hambrick, D. C. "Environmental Scanning and Organizational Strategy." *Strategic Management Journal,* 1982, *3* (2), 159–174.

Harrigan, K. "Barriers to Entry and Competitive Strategies." *Strategic Management Journal,* 1981, *2,* 395–412.

Henderson, B. *Henderson on Corporate Strategy.* Cambridge, Mass.: Abt Books, 1979.

Hennepin County, Minn. *Strategic Planning Manual.* Minneapolis: Office of Planning and Development, Hennepin County, 1983.

Hennepin County, Minn. *Strategic Planning. Phase I, Executive Report.* Minneapolis: Office of Planning and Development, Hennepin County, 1984.

Hickson, D. J., Butler, R. J., Cray, D., Mallory, G. R., and Wilson, D. C. *Top Decisions—Strategic Decision Making in Organizations.* Oxford, England: Basil Blackwell, 1986.

Hofer, C. "Towards a Contingency Theory of Business Strategy." *Academy of Management Journal,* 1975, *18,* 748–810.

Hofer, C., and Schendel, D. *Strategy Formulation: Analytical Concepts.* St. Paul, Minn.: West Publishing, 1978.

Hostager, T. J., and Bryson, J. M. "Poetics and Strategic Management." Discussion paper no. 59. Minneapolis: University of Minnesota, Strategic Management Research Center, 1986.

Howe, E. "Role Choices of Urban Planners." *Journal of the American Planning Association,* 1980, *46,* 398–409.

Howe, E., and Kaufman, J. "The Ethics of Contemporary American Planners." *Journal of the American Planning Association,* 1979, *45,* 243–255.

Humphrey, H. H. *The Education of a Public Man: My Life and Politics.* New York: Doubleday, 1976.

Jenster, P. "Using Critical Success Factors in Planning." *Long Range Planning,* 1987, *20* (4), 102–110.

Johnson, D. W., and Johnson, F. P. *Joining Together—Group Theory and Group Skills.* (3rd ed.) Englewood Cliffs, N.J.: Prentice-Hall, 1987.

Kahn, R. L., and others. *Organizational Stress: Studies in Role Conflict and Ambiguity.* New York: Wiley, 1964.

Kahn, S. *Organizing.* New York: McGraw-Hill, 1982.

Kanter, R. M. *Commitment and Community: Communes and Utopias in Sociological Perspective.* Cambridge, Mass. Harvard University Press, 1972.

Kanter, R. M. *The Changemasters.* New York: Simon & Schuster, 1983.

Kaufman, H. *Are Government Organizations Immortal?* Washington, D.C.: Brookings Institute, 1976.

Kaufman, J. L. "The Planner as Interventionist in Public Policy Issues." In R. Burchell and G. Sternlieb (eds.), *Planning Theory in the 1980's.* New Brunswick, N.J.: Center for Urban Policy Research, 1979.

Kaufman, J. L., and Jacobs, H. M. "A Public Planning Perspective on Strategic Planning." *Journal of the American Planning Association,* 1987, *53* (1), 21–31.

Kerr, S., and Jermier, J. "Substitutes for Leadership: Their Meaning and Measurement." *Organizational Behavior and Human Performance,* 1978, *22,* 375–403.

Kettering Foundation, Charles F. "Negotiated Investment Strategy." Dayton, Ohio: Charles F. Kettering Foundation, 1982.

King, J., and Johnson, D. A. "The Oak Ridge, Tennessee Experience." In J. M. Bryson and R. C. Einsweiler (eds.), *Strategic Planning—Threats and Opportunities for Planners.* Chicago and Washington: The Planners Press of the American Planning Association, 1988.

King, W. "The Importance of Strategic Issues." *The Journal of Business Strategy*, 1981, *1*, 74–76.

King, W. R. "Using Strategic Issue Analysis." *Long Range Planning*, 1982, *15* (4), 45–49.

Klay, W. E. "The Future of Strategic Management." A paper presented at the annual conference of the Academy of Management, New Orleans, La., August 10, 1987.

Klumpp, S. "Strategic Planning Booklet for the City of St. Louis Park." St. Louis Park, Minn., 1986.

Kolderie, T. *Many Providers, Many Producers—A New View of the Public Service Industry.* Minneapolis: Hubert H. Humphrey Institute of Public Affairs, University of Minnesota, 1982.

Kolderie, T. "Two Different Concepts of Privatization." *Public Administration Review*, 1986, *46*, 285–291.

Kotler, P. *Marketing Management.* Englewood Cliffs, N.J.: Prentice-Hall, 1976.

Kouzes, J. M., and Posner, B. Z. *The Leadership Challenge: How to Get Extraordinary Things Done in Organizations.* San Francisco: Jossey-Bass, 1987.

Kraemer, K. *Policy Analysis in Local Government.* Washington: International City Management Association, 1973.

Langer, E. J. "Rethinking the Role of Thought in Social Interaction." In J. H. Harvey, W. Ickes, and R. F. Kidd (eds.), *New Directions in Attribution Research.* Vol. 2. Hillsdale, N.J.: Lawrence Erlbaum, 1978.

Lawrence, P. R., and Lorsch, J. W. *Organization and Environment.* Homewood, Ill.: Irwin, 1967.

Leifer, R., and Delbecq, A. L. "Organizational/Environmental Interchange: A Model of Boundary Spanning Activity." *Academy of Management Review*, 1978, *3*, 40–50.

Lenz, R. "Environment, Strategy, Organization Structure and Performance." *Strategic Management Journal*, 1980, *1*, 209–226.

Levine, C. "More on Cutback Management: Hard Questions for Hard Times." *Public Administration Review*, 1979, *39* (March/April), 179–183.

Levitt, T. "Marketing Myopia." *Harvard Business Review*, 1960, *38* (4), 45–56.

Lewis, E. *Public Entrepreneurship: Toward a Theory of Bureaucratic Political Power.* Bloomington: Indiana University Press, 1980.

Lindblom, C. E. "The Science of Muddling Through." *Public Administration Review,* 1959, *19* (Spring), 79–88.

Lindblom, C. *Politics and Markets.* New York: Free Press, 1977.

Linneman, R. E., and Klein, H. E. "The Use of Multiple Scenarios by U.S. Industrial Companies: A Comparison Study, 1977–1981." *Long Range Planning,* 1983, *16* (6), 94–101.

Locke, E. A., Shaw, K. N., Saari, L. M., and Latham, G. P. "Goal Setting and Task Performance: 1969–1980." *Psychological Bulletin,* 1981, *90,* 125–152.

Lodahl, T. M., and Mitchell, S. M. "Drift in the Development of Innovative Organizations." In J. Kimberly and R. H. Miles and Associates, *The Organizational Life Cycle: Issues in the Creation, Transformation, and Decline of Organizations.* San Francisco: Jossey-Bass, 1980.

Long, N. "The Local Community as an Ecology of Games." *American Journal of Sociology,* 1958, *64* (Nov.), 251–261.

Lorange, P. "Formal Planning Systems: Their Role in Strategy Formulation and Implementation." In D. Schendel and C. Hofer (eds.), *A New View of Business Policy and Planning.* Boston: Little, Brown, 1979.

Lorange, P. *Corporate Planning: An Executive Viewpoint.* Englewood Cliffs, N.J.: Prentice-Hall, 1980.

Lorange, P. "Strategic Control." In R. Lamb (ed.), *Competitive Strategic Management.* Englewood Cliffs, N.J.: Prentice-Hall, 1984.

Lorange, P., Morton, M. F. S., and Ghoshal, S. *Strategic Control.* St. Paul, Minn.: West Publishing, 1986.

Lorange, P., and Vancil, R. F. *Strategic Planning Systems.* Englewood Cliffs, N.J.: Prentice-Hall, 1977.

Lowi, T. J. "Distribution, Regulation, Redistribution: The Functions of Government." In R. B. Ripley (ed.), *Public Policies and Their Politics—Techniques of Government Control.* New York: Norton, 1966.

Luke, J. "Managing Interconnectedness: The Challenge of Shared Power." In J. M. Bryson and R. C. Einsweiler (eds.), *Shared Power: What Is It? How Does It Work? How Can We Make*

It Work Better? Lanham, Md.: University Press of America, 1988.

Luttwak, E. *The Grand Strategy of the Roman Empire.* Baltimore: Johns Hopkins University Press, 1977.

McGowan, R. P., and Stevens, J. M. "Local Government's Initiatives in a Climate of Uncertainty." *Public Administration Review,* 1983, *43* (2), 127–136.

MacMillan, I. *Strategy Formulation: Political Concepts.* St. Paul, Minn.: West Publishing, 1978.

MacMillan, I. "Competitive Strategies for Not-For-Profit Agencies." *Advances in Strategic Management,* 1983, *1,* 61–82.

Maidique, M. A. "Entrepreneurs, Champions and Technological Innovation." *Sloan Management Review,* 1980, *21* (Winter), 58–76.

Mandelbaum, S. J. "Temporal Conventions and Planning Discourse." *Environment and Planning B: Planning and Design,* 1984, *11,* 5–13.

Mangham, I., and Overington, M. *Organization as Theatre: A Social Psychology of Dramatic Appearances.* New York: Wiley, 1987.

Manz, C. C. "Self-Leadership: Toward an Expanded Theory of Self-Influence Processes in Organizations." *Academy of Management Review,* 1986, *11,* 585–600.

Manz, C. C., and Sims, H. P., Jr. "Self-Management as a Substitute for Leadership: A Social Learning Theory Perspective." *Academy of Management Review,* 1980, *5,* 361–367.

March, J. G., and Olsen, J. P. *Ambiguity and Choice in Organizations.* (2nd ed.) Bergen: Universitetsforlaget, 1979.

March, J. G., and Simon, H. A. *Organizations.* New York: Wiley, 1958.

Mason, R., and Mitroff, I. *Challenging Strategic Planning Assumptions.* New York: Wiley, 1982.

May, J. V., and Wildavsky, A. B. *The Policy Cycle.* Beverly Hills, Calif.: Sage, 1978.

May, R. *Love and Will.* New York: Norton, 1969.

Mazmanian, D. A., and Sabatier, P. A. *Implementation and Public Policy.* Glenview, Ill.: Scott, Foresman, 1983.

Miles, R. E., and Snow, C. *Organizational Strategy, Structure, and Process.* New York: McGraw-Hill, 1978.

Miller, G. A. "The Magical Number Seven Plus or Minus Two: Some Limits to Our Capacity for Processing Information." *The Psychological Bulletin,* 1956, *63,* 81–97.

Milward, H. B. "Current Institutional Arrangements That Create or Require Shared Power." In J. M. Bryson and R. C. Einsweiler (eds.), *Shared Power: What Is It? How Does It Work? How Can We Make It Work Better?* Lanham, Md.: University Press of America, 1988.

Milward, H. B., and Wamsley, G. L. *Policy Networks—Key Concept at a Critical Juncture.* Blacksburg: Center for Public Administration and Policy, Virginia Polytechnic Institute and State University, 1982.

Mintzberg, H. *The Nature of Managerial Work.* New York: Harper & Row, 1973.

Mintzberg, H., and Waters, J. A. "Of Strategies, Deliberate and Emergent." *Strategic Management Journal,* 1985, *6* (3), 257–272.

Mitroff, I. "Systemic Problem Solving." In M. McCall and M. Lombardo (eds.), *Leadership: Where Else Can We Go?* Durham, N.C.: Duke University Press, 1978.

Montanari, J. R., and Bracker, J. S. "The Strategic Management Process." *Strategic Management Journal,* 1986, *7* (3), 251–265.

Moore, T. "Why Allow Planners to Do What They Do?" *Journal of the American Planning Association,* 1978, *44,* 387–398.

Nelson, B. J. *Making an Issue of Child Abuse.* Chicago: University of Chicago Press, 1984.

Normann, R. *Service Management—Strategy and Leadership in Service Businesses.* New York: Wiley, 1984.

Nutt, P. C. "A Strategic Planning Network for Non-Profit Organizations." *Strategic Management Journal,* 1984, *5,* 57–75.

Nutt, P. C., and Backoff, R. W. "A Strategic Management Process for Public and Third-Sector Organizations." *Journal of the American Planning Association,* 1987, *53,* 44–57.

Nystrom, P. C., and Starbuck, W. H. "Theoretical Observations on Applied Behavioral Science." *Journal of Applied Behavioral Science,* 1984, *20,* 277–287.

Oates, S. B. *Let the Trumpet Sound: The Life of Martin Luther King, Jr.* New York: Harper & Row, 1982.

Olsen, J. B., and Eadie, D. C. *The Game Plan: Governance with Foresight.* Washington: Council of State Planning Agencies, 1982.

O'Toole, J. *Vanguard Management.* New York: Doubleday, 1985.

Ouchi, W. *Theory Z: How Many American Businesses Can Meet the Japanese Challenge.* Reading, Mass.: Addison-Wesley, 1981.

Oxford University Press. *Oxford Reference Dictionary.* New York: Oxford University Press, 1986.

Peek, T. R., Duren, E. L., and Wells, L. C. *Minnesota K–12 Education: The Current Debate, The Present Conditions.* Minneapolis: University of Minnesota, Center for Urban and Regional Affairs, 1985.

Pelz, D. C., and Andrews, F. M. *Scientists in Organizations: Productive Climates for Research and Development.* New York: Wiley, 1966.

Peters, T. "Symbols, Patterns and Settings: An Optimistic Case for Getting Things Done." *Organizational Dynamics,* 1978, *7* (Autumn), 3–23.

Peters, T. J., and Waterman, R. H., Jr. *In Search of Excellence: Lessons from America's Best-Run Companies.* New York: Harper & Row, 1982.

Pettigrew, A. M. "Strategy Formulation as a Political Process." *International Studies in Management and Organization,* 1977, *7* (2), 78–87.

Pfeffer, J. *Power in Organizations.* Boston: Pitman, 1981.

Pfeffer, J., and Moore, W. "Power in University Budgeting: A Replication and Extension." *Administrative Science Quarterly,* 1980, *25,* 637–653.

Pfeffer, J., and Salancik, G. R. *The External Control of Organizations: A Resource Dependence Perspective.* New York: Harper & Row, 1978.

Pfeiffer, J. W., Goodstein, L. D., and Nolan, T. M. *Applied Strategic Planning: A How to Do It Guide.* San Diego, Calif.: University Associates, 1986.

Pflaum, A., and Delmont, T. "External Scanning, A Tool for Planners." *Journal of the American Planning Association,* 1987, *53* (1), 56–67.

Pinchot, G., III. *Entrepreneuring.* New York: Harper & Row, 1985.

Porter, M. *Competitive Strategy.* New York: Free Press, 1980.

Porter, M. *Competitive Advantage.* New York: Free Press, 1985.

Pressman, J., and Wildavsky, A. *Implementation.* Berkeley and Los Angeles: University of California Press, 1973.

Public Management. A Special Issue Devoted to Excellence in Public Management, 1984, *66*, 73–96.

Quinn, J. B. *Strategies for Change: Logical Incrementalism.* Homewood, Ill.: Irwin, 1980.

Rider, R. W. "Making Strategic Planning Work in Local Government." *Long Range Planning,* 1983, *16* (3), 73–81.

Ring, P. S. "Strategic Issues: What Are They and from Where Do They Come?" In J. M. Bryson and R. C. Einsweiler (eds.), *Strategic Planning—Threats and Opportunities for Planners.* Chicago and Washington: The Planners Press of the American Planning Association, 1988.

Ring, P. S., and Perry, J. L. "Strategic Management in Public and Private Organizations: Implications of Distinctive Contexts and Constraints." *Academy of Management Review,* 1985, *10*, 276–286.

Robinson, R. V., and Eadie, D. C. "Building the Senior Management Team Through Team Issue Management." *ICMA MIS Report,* 1986, *18* (12), 1–11.

Rubin, M. S. "Sagas, Ventures, Quests, and Parlays: A Typology of Strategies in the Public Sector." In J. M. Bryson and R. C. Einsweiler (eds.), *Strategic Planning—Threats and Opportunities for Planners.* Chicago and Washington: The Planners Press of the American Planning Association, 1988.

Rue, L. W., and Holland, P. G. *Strategic Management: Concepts and Experiences.* New York: McGraw-Hill, 1986.

Salancik, G. R. "Commitment and the Control of Organizational Behavior and Belief." In B. M. Staw and G. R. Salancik (eds.), *New Directions in Organizational Behavior.* Chicago: St. Clair Press, 1977.

Savas, E. S. *Privatizing the Public Sector.* Chatham, N.J.: Chatham House, 1982.

Schein, E. H. *Organizational Culture and Leadership: A Dynamic View.* San Francisco: Jossey-Bass, 1985.

Schelling, T. C. *Micromotives and Macrobehavior.* New York: Norton, 1978.

Schendel, D., and Hofer, C. (eds.). *A New View of Business Policy and Planning.* Boston: Little, Brown, 1979.

Schon, D. A. *Beyond the Stable State.* London: Temple Smith, 1971.

Schultze, C. "The Public Use of Private Interest." *Harpers,* 1977, *254* (May), 43–62.

Selznick, P. *Leadership in Administration.* Berkeley and Los Angeles: University of California Press, 1957.

Shaw, M. E. *Group Dynamics: The Psychology of Small Group Behavior.* New York: McGraw-Hill, 1971.

Sipel, G. W. "Putting *In Search of Excellence* to Work in Local Government." *Public Management,* 1984, *66* (4), 2–5.

Smart, C., and Vertinsky, I. "Designs for Crisis Decision Units." *Administrative Science Quarterly,* 1977, *22,* 640–657.

Sorkin, D. L., Ferris, N. B., and Hudak, J. *Strategies for Cities and Counties: A Strategic Planning Guide* and *Workbook.* Washington: Public Technology, 1984.

Starbuck, W. H., Greve, A., and Hedberg, B. L. T. "Responding to Crisis." *Journal of Business Administration,* 1978, *9,* 111–137.

Staw, B. M. "Knee-Deep in the Big Muddy: A Study of Escalating Commitment to a Chosen Course of Action." *Organizational Behavior and Human Performance,* 1976, *16,* 27–44.

Staw, B. M., and Ross, J. "Commitment to a Policy Decision: A Multi-Theoretical Perspective." *Administrative Science Quarterly,* 1978, *23,* 40–64.

Steinbreder, H. J. "Switching to Caplets." *Fortune,* Mar. 17, 1986, p. 8.

Steiner, G. A. *Strategic Planning—What Every Manager Must Know.* New York: Free Press, 1979.

Stuart, D. G. "Rational Urban Planning: Problems and Prospects." *Urban Affairs Quarterly,* 1969, *5* (December), 151–182.

Susskind, L. E., and Ozawa, C. "Mediated Negotiation in the Public Sector: The Planner as Mediator." *Journal of Planning Education and Research,* 1984, *4* (1), 5–15.

Taylor, B. "Strategic Planning—Which Style Do You Need?" *Long Range Planning,* 1984, *17,* 51–62.

Terry, R. W. "The Negative Impact on White Values." In

B. P. Bowser and R. G. Hunt (eds.), *Impacts of Racism on White Americans*. Beverly Hills, Calif.: Sage, 1981.

Thompson, J. D. *Organizations in Action*. New York: McGraw-Hill, 1967.

Tita, M. A., and Allio, R. J. "3M's Strategy System—Planning in an Innovative Organization." *Planning Review*, 1984 (September), *12* (5), 10–15.

Tokunaga, H. T., and Staw, B. M. "Organizational Commitment: A Review and Critique of Current Theory and Research." Presented at the national meeting of the American Psychological Association, Anaheim, Calif., Aug. 1983.

Tomazinis, A. R. "The Logic and Rationale of Strategic Planning." Paper presented at the 27th annual conference of the Association of Collegiate Schools of Planning, Atlanta, Oct. 1985.

Tuchman, B. *The March of Folly: From Troy to Vietnam*. New York: Knopf, 1984.

Van de Ven, A. H. "A Framework for Organization Assessment." *Academy of Management Review*, 1976a, *1* (1), 64–78.

Van de Ven, A. H. "On the Nature, Formation, and Maintenance of Relations Among Organizations." *Academy of Management Review*, 1976b, *1* (4), 24–36.

Van de Ven, A. H. "Central Problems in the Management of Innovation." *Management Science*, 1985, *32* (5), 590–607.

Van De Ven, A. H., and Hudson, R. "Managing Attention to Strategic Choices." In J. Pennings (ed.), *Strategic Decision Making in Complex Organizations*. San Francisco: Jossey-Bass, 1985.

Van Meter, D. S., and Van Horn, C. "The Policy Implementation Process: A Conceptual Framework." *Administration and Society*, 1975, *6*, 445–488.

Vickers, G. *The Art of Judgment*. London: Chapman and Hall, 1965.

Watzlawick, P., Weakland, J., and Fisch, R. *Change: Principles of Problem Formation and Problem Resolution*. New York: Norton, 1974.

Wechsler, B., and Backoff, R. "Dynamics of Strategy Formulation in Public Agencies." *Journal of the American Planning Association*, 1987, *53*, 34–43.

Weick, K. *The Social Psychology of Organizing.* Reading, Mass.: Addison-Wesley, 1979.

Weick, K. "Small Wins: Redefining the Scale of Social Problems." *American Psychologist,* 1984, *39* (1), 40–50.

Wetherbe, J. C. *Systems Analysis and Design: Traditional, Structured, and Advanced Concepts and Techniques.* (2nd ed.) St. Paul, Minn.: West Publishing, 1984.

Wildavsky, A. *The Politics of the Budgetary Process.* Boston: Little, Brown, 1979a.

Wildavsky, A. *Speaking Truth to Power.* Boston: Little, Brown, 1979b.

Wilensky, H. L. *Organizational Intelligence.* New York: Basic Books, 1967.

Wilson, J. Q. "Innovation in Organizations: Notes Toward a Theory." In J. D. Thompson (ed.), *Approaches to Organizational Design.* Pittsburgh: University of Pittsburgh Press, 1967.

Wind, Y., and Mahajan, V. "Designing Product and Business Portfolios." *Harvard Business Review,* 1981, *59,* 155–165.

Wright, D. S. *Understanding Intergovernmental Relations.* Boston: Duxbury Press, 1978.

Zaltman, G., Duncan, R., and Holbek, J. *Innovations and Organizations.* New York: Wiley-Interscience, 1973.

Zaltman, G., Florio, D., and Sikorski, L. *Dynamic Educational Change.* New York: Free Press, 1977.

Index

Index